THE CASTLE KITCHEN

THE
CASTLE
KITCHEN

*Recipes and Reminiscences from
Brodick Castle to Bangalore*

LADY FIONA HANNON

MAINSTREAM
PUBLISHING

EDINBURGH AND LONDON

To Catherine and Veronica
who asked for this

Copyright © Lady Fiona Hannon, 1994

All rights reserved

The moral right of the author has been asserted

First published in Great Britain in 1994 by
MAINSTREAM PUBLISHING COMPANY (EDINBURGH) LTD
7 Albany Street
Edinburgh EH1 3UG

ISBN 1 85158 655 5

A catalogue record for this book is available from the British Library

Typeset in Syntax and Baskerville by Litho Link Ltd, Welshpool, Powys, Wales
Printed in Great Britain by Butler & Tanner Ltd, Frome

ACKNOWLEDGMENTS

With grateful thanks to my husband, Peter, for his months of help in typing and editing; to Bill Cameron Johnson, my illustrator; to Lady Dunpark and Professor John Phillips, vice-principal of Glasgow Caledonian University, for their particular encouragement; and to Bob Worsfold, lecturer and culinary expert at the university, for his detailed care in going over my recipes.

CONTENTS

REMINISCENCES

INTRODUCTION

Cooking began for me in the kitchen of Brodick Castle, my grandmother, Molly, the Duchess of Montrose's home, on the Isle of Arran. Since then traditional Scottish dishes have always been part of my life though my travels have taken me to many other lands where I made a point of collecting recipes.

This book was written in the first place for my two daughters, each of whom is now setting up her own home and who wanted to know how to cook the dishes with which they have grown up; and for grandchildren who in the future may be interested in stories of another age.

My first cooking lesson was when I was about ten years old, and my brother and I had been out on the Arran hills all day with my father who was home on leave from the navy. We were tired and hungry. My father took me into the Castle kitchen and said that he would teach me to make an omelette. He added that anything a man decided to do he could do better than a woman. That was why all great chefs were men! This incensed my youthful feminism and I argued hotly.

The kitchen at Brodick is still a focus for visitors to the Castle now that it is in the care of the National Trust. Its 20-foot-high ceiling and open stairway leading down into it take one back into another age. At one end there is a clock high on the wall, and at the other, the big coal-fired range. That high ceiling must have been a boon for any cook when it was hot, but spare a thought for all the carrying up and down those stairs before one even got to the long passage to the dining-room.

I have loved good food all my life, perhaps first encouraged by what my grandmother served. I am grateful to my aunt, Lady Jean Fforde, who passed on to me many of the recipes with which I grew up. They range from fish and game – we were self-supporting in these – to chocolate puddings and cheeses. I record them here, together with others from different parts of the world where I have found myself cooking.

When we stayed with my grandparents at Brodick our recreations were shooting and fishing. I remember going out grouse-shooting with the guns and the agonising ache in my legs as we beat up the birds. After a while we children would be trailing behind until the grown-ups were forced to stop and wait for us. Then on they would go. No rest for us till the blessed relief of lunch on the hill. No food ever tasted so good as that, however damp and wet we were.

So it would be grouse for dinner with, perhaps, lobster the next day if we had been out with the lobster pots. You would be lucky not to get your fingers tweaked by their claws as the lobsters were all over the bottom of the boat. Then mackerel eaten fresh from the sea after a day's fishing, or herrings done in oatmeal, followed by venison if the stalking season was open. If all else failed there was always rabbit, though it was not my favourite. Then there was lovely creamy milk, fresh from my grandmother's cows, and home-made butter. Out on a picnic one day we had some milk left over. I was told that if I shook the bottle long enough I would get butter. This kept me happily occupied all the way home. Sure enough there were some flakes of butter which we made into a pat which I had for tea.

During the war we lived at Auchmar, my grandparents' second home, overlooking Loch Lomond. My mother was working for the Girls Training Corps and as general secretary for Scotland's Garden Scheme which paid for the district nurses in the days before the National Health Service. She also helped at Auchmar to look after five military doctors who worked at Buchanan Castle hospital, four landgirls, a governess and a staff of four.

Buchanan Castle had been the seat of the Dukes of Montrose until the war. When my grandfather inherited it it had forty bedrooms and one bathroom by the back door for the men coming in from shooting. It was impossible to maintain, so they built Auchmar, incorporating a farmhouse on the estate, and tried without success to turn the Castle into a hotel. Then it was requisitioned as a military hospital for wartime, after which the roof was taken off to save taxes as nobody would buy it.

My second cooking lesson came from my grandmother, the Duchess – Seannie, as my brother and I called her, being an anglicised form of *Seannabha*, 'grandmother' in Gaelic. She took me into the Auchmar kitchen to make the recipe for pudding that day, a light treacle sponge, and a great favourite of my grandfather.

One of the staff at Auchmar was Wee Isa, who had never been in the countryside before. She had been sent to us from Glasgow because of shellshock from the bombing. Her excitement knew no bounds when she saw a 'kangaroo' in the field outside the house. We rushed to the window to view this phenomenon only to be disappointed with the sight of a large hare. Then there was Big Isa, whose hand could be large and rather heavy if annoyed. They were the housekeepers and gave me my first lessons in bedmaking. Next was Kitty, the parlourmaid, and Miss Sneddon, the cook. She refused to be called Mrs, as was the tradition, for she was young and wished to marry. If one managed to be up early enough one would be able to enter the usually forbidden preserve of the kitchen and prick the sausages we ate for Sunday breakfast, or cut out the scones.

We had rationing like everyone else. With so many in the house it was quickly felt that some were eating more than their fair share. So little dishes were bought for each one, with different-coloured tops, into which at the beginning of the week were placed our 2 oz of butter and 2 oz of jam. My brother would divide his out to make sure it lasted, while my philosophy was to have a really good feed and then do without for the rest of the week.

Our first Christmas of the war there was consternation – what to eat? Nothing to serve for all those doctors! Snow came early and then, what a blessing, we saw the geese coming in on their migration. They always stopped by the lochside on their way south. My mother and the doctors found some skis, dressed themselves in white sheets and hoods, and set off at dusk with their shotguns, to our great excitement. We had our Christmas feast!

There was little we children did not know of what went on around us. One day we came on men digging a great cave in the side of the steep riverbank. We were quickly shooed away but soon found out that it was planned as the first hideout for an underground guerrilla force which would take to the hills in the event of invasion. My mother prepared boxes of first-aid equipment and sacks of potatoes for each man. Those stocks were to figure later, unofficially, in my own plans for escape from our hated governess. Fortunately, these never came to fruition as she departed first!

SOUPS

Soups have always figured largely in our family meals. My mother said that if you served everybody a good soup it saved expense as they did not need so much meat for the main course. Our soups were homemade. Nowadays, for a light meal, I often simply serve a rich soup, sometimes with croutons, followed by bread, cheese or pâté, and fresh fruit. With some of the recipes I have given large quantities as I find it useful to freeze the extra. If the recipe includes cream or milk, this should be added when the soup is re-heated.

The soups which follow are traditionally Scottish.

BARLEY BROTH

For 8

2 oz / 50 g fresh or dried peas
1½ lb / 700 g neck of mutton
4 pints / 2½ litres water
2 oz / 50 g barley
salt and pepper
1 onion
1 leek, white part
8 oz / 225 g diced swede or turnip
8 oz / 225 g diced carrot
½ small white heart cabbage
1 tblsp / 15 ml parsley

Wash the dried peas and soak overnight in cold water.

Wipe and trim the meat. Put it in the broth pot with the cold water, the dried peas, the barley and salt. Bring to the boil and skim. Simmer for 45 minutes.

Slice the onion and leek. Add to the soup with the diced turnip and carrot. Simmer slowly for 45 minutes. Add the shredded cabbage and simmer for another 30 minutes.

Before serving, add chopped parsley and adjust the seasoning to taste.

BAWD BREE (Scots Hare Soup)

For 12

1 hare
2 onions
1 thick slice turnip or swede
1 stick celery
pot posy (1 sprig each of parsley, thyme and bay leaf)

Prepare the hare the day before. Remove the lungs and insides, being careful not to break them. Hold the hare over a basin to catch all the blood, which contains much of the hare's flavour. Wipe carefully with a damp cloth to remove any small hairs. Remove the best part of the flesh from the head, shoulders and rump. Place the remainder in a deep

13

¼ tsp / 1ml mace
6 peppercorns
salt
2 oz / 50 g bacon fat or dripping
2 tblsp / 30 ml oatmeal
2 tblsp / 30 ml mushroom
  ketchup
cayenne pepper
1 or 2 glasses of port wine

dish and cover with cold water overnight.

Next day, strain the red water from soaking the hare into the broth pot and bring slowly to the boil. Add the roughly cut up vegetables, and pot posy tied up in a muslin bag, mace and peppercorns. Add salt. Simmer for 2 to 3 hours.

When the soup is simmering, flatten the pieces of hare you have removed. Season, dredge in flour and fry in the bacon fat. Parboil the hare's liver and pound it in a mortar or chop it in a food processor along with some of the fried hare. Add it to the soup along with the lightly toasted oatmeal. Simmer for at least half an hour.

Strain the blood into a small bowl adding a little cold water mixed with flour. Add a teacup of hot soup and turn it all into the broth pot. Keep it just below boiling for 10 minutes, being careful not to curdle it.

Withdraw from the heat and add the mushroom ketchup, cayenne pepper and adjust the salt. Port wine enriches the flavour. Rowan jelly can be added to the pot to sweeten.

This is traditionally eaten with a dish of mealy (floury) potatoes. It certainly makes a full meal.

For 4

1 plump fowl
salt
a slice of ham
1 onion, chopped
1 stick celery, chopped
pot posy (2 sprigs parsley, sprig
  of thyme, blade of mace)
2 pints / 1.2 litres water
¼ pint / 150 ml chicken stock
2 or 3 egg yolks
2 tsp / 10 ml cream
2 tsp / 10 ml chopped parsley

FEATHER FOWLIE

Joint the fowl (into 8 pieces) and soak in water with 2 tsp / 10 ml salt for half an hour. Wash the pieces well and put into the stew pan with the slice of ham, the onion, celery, herbs and water. Cover and bring to boil, simmering gently for 1½ hours. Strain and remove all grease.

Return the soup to the rinsed pan and add the stock. Heat for 15 minutes. Add some minced white meat of the fowl. Remove from the heat and, just before serving, whisk in the strained egg yolks mixed with warm cream. Add parsley and serve.

The remainder of the fowl may be served with egg, bread or parsley sauce, and curled, grilled rashers of bacon. Or it can be made into patties.

For 6

1 lb / 450 g crab meat, tinned,
  fresh or frozen
2 oz / 50 g long-grain rice

PARTAN BREE
(a Scottish form of Crab Chowder)

If fresh, cook the crab in boiling water for about 30 minutes. Cook the rice in the milk. Reserve a quarter of the crab meat. Stir the remainder into the rice and liquidise for 1 minute or

1 pint / 600 ml milk
1 pint / 600 ml chicken stock
½ tsp / 3 ml anchovy essence
salt
freshly ground black pepper
¼ pint / 150 ml double cream
chopped parsley

pass through a sieve.

Pour into a clean saucepan and gradually stir in the stock over a low heat. Bring to the boil. Add the anchovy essence. Stir in the rest of the crab meat, season with salt and pepper, and heat through.

Stir in the cream just before serving in warmed bowls – do not allow to boil – and decorate with chopped parsley.

LENTIL SOUP

For 12

8 oz / 225 g carrot
8 oz / 225 g onions
8 oz / 225 g turnip (swede)
1 oz / 25 g butter
3 pints / 1.8 litres ham or
    vegetable stock or water
8 oz / 225 g red lentils
1 tsp / 2 ml black pepper
salt to taste
2 tblsp / 30 ml cornflour
    (optional)
1 pint / 600 ml milk (optional)

Dice the vegetables finely and sweat them in the butter in a saucepan with the lid on until they are soft and tender – about 10 minutes. Add the stock or water with the lentils and simmer for about 1 hour. Season to taste. Ham stock will be salty.

If you want a smooth purée, the soup may be sieved or liquidised. Rinse out the pan, return the soup to it and bring back to the boil. If you like it thickened, mix the cornflour and milk and stir them in, bringing the soup back to the boil.

Serve with croutons or fairy toast (see below).

FAIRY TOAST
Buy a thin sliced loaf of white bread. Toast the slices lightly. Cut the crusts off. Split the slices laterally.

Dip each split slice in milk and place on a tray in a warm oven to dry out.

RED POTTAGE

For 12

1 lb / 450 g haricot beans
1 large beetroot
2 onions
4 sticks celery
6 tomatoes
2 oz / 50 g butter or dripping
3 qrts / 4 litres stock or water
salt and pepper

Wash and soak the beans overnight. Wash the beetroot but do not break the skin. Slice the onions and cut up the celery. Skin, de-seed and cut up the tomatoes.

In a saucepan fry the onions and celery gently in the butter until soft. Add the stock, the drained beans, the tomatoes and the whole beetroot. Season to taste. Bring to the boil, skim if necessary, and simmer for 3 to 4 hours.

Remove the beetroot, skin it and chop or grate it finely. Return it to the pot. The soup may now be eaten. If you like a smooth soup, liquidise or rub it through a sieve. Check for seasoning, reheat and serve.

Note: Lentils may be substituted for beans and parsnips for celery.

For 4

1 × 11 oz/300 g can of
   condensed cream of chicken
   soup
½ pint / 250 ml milk
1 avocado
salt and pepper
2 oz / 50 g grated hard cheese,
   such as cheddar
1 tblsp / 15ml chopped parsley

For 8

dripping to brown the meat
1 calf's foot
3 lb / 1½ kg shin or beef bone
   with some meat on it
2 onions, peeled and quartered
1 thick slice turnip (swede)
2 carrots, diced
3 quarts / 3½ litres water
a pot posy (parsley, bay leaf,
   sage, thyme, tied in muslin or
   cloth bag)
salt and pepper
2 egg whites and their shells to
   clarify the stock
2 tblsp / 30 ml sherry

AVOCADO SOUP

Pour the soup into a fairly large saucepan. Gradually stir in the milk and bring just to boiling point.

Dice the avocado flesh, add to the saucepan and adjust the seasoning. Stir well and top with grated cheese to serve. *Do not boil* or it turns bitter – as I learnt to my cost having prepared it as a treat for a dinner party only for it to be inedible.

BEEF CONSOMMÉ (Hot or Iced)

This takes two days to make from scratch. Begin by making a good beef stock. First melt the dripping into a deep pan. Add the calf's foot and the bones and brown them all over. Add the chopped vegetables. Put the lid on, turn the heat down to simmer and allow the vegetables to sweat without colouring for 10 minutes.

Add the water, herbs, pepper and salt. Bring to the boil and skim off the scum. Cover the pan and leave the stock to simmer gently for 3 hours. You must only just simmer it or the stock will be cloudy and reduce too much. Strain off the stock and leave to chill. Any fat will harden on the surface and may be lifted off next day.

Put the stock into a large enamel or stainless-steel saucepan. Take the two egg whites and their shells. Whisk them to a froth. Add them to the stock and continue whisking while bringing it to the boil. Stop whisking and allow it to boil up to the top of the pan. Remove it from the heat and allow the stock to settle. Return to the heat and again boil up. Repeat once more without breaking the crust.

Now take a clean, scalded cloth, stretch it over a bowl and pour the stock into it. Tie up the ends of the cloth and fix to a hook over the bowl, allowing the stock to drain through. On no account squeeze the cloth or push the stock through or your consommé will be cloudy. If the liquid is still cloudy after the first straining, repeat a second or even a third time.

Taste for seasoning. Add the sherry. The soup may be served cold as a jellied consommé. Present a slice of lemon per person.

A clear Beef Consommé is a good basis for many soups.

CONSOMMÉ JULIENNE

In this, vegetables such as carrots, turnips and onions are cut into matchstick – julienne – pieces and boiled until soft in the consommé. This may then be flavoured with sherry or lemon juice.

CHICKEN STOCK

If roasting a chicken I always boil up the carcass afterwards in a pressure cooker for half an hour at 15 lbs / 6 kg pressure.

If you have no pressure cooker, boil for 2 hours in enough water to cover the chicken, with a carrot and onion added for flavour.

Strain the stock, discarding the bones, and set it aside to cool, putting it in the fridge overnight. The fat may then be lifted off.

HAM STOCK

I simply freeze the water in which I have boiled the ham or bacon joint.

This is particularly good when making lentil, dried pea or bean soup.

WHITE STOCK

a knuckle of veal
1 chicken carcass
2 pints / 1.2 litres water
salt
a strip of lemon rind
a stick of celery, cut up
1 small onion, sliced
juice of 1 lemon
4 cloves
1 tsp / 5 ml white peppercorns

Bring the veal knuckle and chicken carcass to the boil in the water, with salt and the lemon rind added. Skim if necessary.

After 1 hour add the roughly chopped vegetables, lemon juice, cloves and peppercorns. Cover again and simmer for 2 more hours. Strain and cool as before.

VEGETABLE STOCK

8 oz / 225 g each of chopped
onions, carrots and ½ head
celery
1 clove garlic, chopped
1 oz / 25 g butter
4 pints / 2.4 litres boiling water
bouquet garni
1 tsp / 5 ml marmite
1 tblsp / 15 ml peppercorns
8 oz / 125 g tomatoes
outer leaves of a lettuce
salt

Gently fry the onions, garlic and carrots in the butter in a covered saucepan until soft. Add the water, celery, bouquet garni, marmite, peppercorns and the tomatoes, skinned and de-seeded. Bring to the boil, covered. Simmer for 30 minutes.

Add the roughly chopped lettuce leaves and salt. Cook for 10 more minutes. Strain through a sieve and use the liquid, discarding the vegetables.

To give a rich brown colour, add onion skins to the bouquet.

BORTSCH (A Russian speciality)

For 6

2 raw beetroots
2 pints / 1.2 litres of the clarified
consommé
2 tblsp / 30 ml sherry
¼ pint / 125 ml sour cream

I make Bortsch when I have a glut of beetroot. Begin by making a good Beef Consommé as described above.

Peel and grate the beetroots into 1 pint / 600 ml cold water. Bring the stock to the boil and add it to the beetroot and water. Add the sherry, re-heat it and check the seasoning.

As you serve the soup, swirl a spoonful of sour cream into each plate.

MUSHROOM SOUP

For 8

8 oz / 225 g onions, chopped
1 oz / 50 g butter
1 lb / 450 g mushrooms
1 tblsp / 15 ml lemon juice
2 pints / 1.2 litres chicken or
vegetable stock
½ pint / 300 ml white wine
salt and pepper
½ pint / 300 ml whipping or
single cream or ½ pint /
300 ml milk plus 1 tblsp /
15 ml cornflour

Fry the chopped onions gently in the butter until soft. Slice the mushrooms. Add them to the onions with the lemon juice and stock. Cover the saucepan, bring to the boil and simmer for 15 minutes. Add the wine and bring back to the boil.

Just before serving, add the cream. Do not boil after the cream is added. If you are using milk, mix it with the cornflour, stir it into the soup and bring it back to the boil before serving.

For 8

1 lb / 450 g parsnips, peeled and
     sliced
1 large onion, chopped
2 cloves garlic, finely chopped
1 oz / 25 g butter
2 tblsp / 30 ml curry powder
3 pints / 1.8 litres good stock
1 big apple, peeled, quartered
salt and pepper
4 fl oz / 125 ml cream, whipped
2 tblsp / 30 ml chopped parsley

CURRIED PARSNIP SOUP

Fry the parsnips, onion and garlic gently in the butter in a covered saucepan until soft. Add the curry powder, turning this for a moment or two. Then add the stock and the apple. Cover and bring to the boil. Simmer for 40 minutes.

Purée in a liquidiser or through a moulin-légume. Return it to the cleaned saucepan and bring back to the boil. Season to taste.

Just before serving, whip the cream and put a dollop on each plateful of soup with a sprinkle of chopped parsley.

For 4 to 6

4 potatoes
2 onions
1 lb / 450 g cabbage
1 red pepper, de-seeded and
     sliced
6 carrots
3 stalks celery
4 tomatoes, skinned
1 oz / 25 g butter
3 tblsp / 45 ml cooking oil
2 pints / 1.2 litres stock or water
1 clove of garlic, crushed
1 tsp / 5 ml marmite
1 tblsp / 15 ml tomato purée
salt and fresh ground black
     pepper to taste
4 oz / 125 g macaroni
grated parmesan cheese for
     topping

WINTER VEGETABLE SOUP

Dice the vegetables. Heat the butter and oil in a large saucepan. Add the vegetables and toss for about 15 minutes until soft but not brown.

Add the stock, garlic, marmite, tomato purée and seasoning and simmer, covered, for 1 hour. Add the macaroni and cook for a further 20 minutes.

Serve in a heated tureen, sprinkled with cheese.

For 4

CREAM OF PEA SOUP

I have made this with peapods since a French friend who came to stay with us, Evelyne Seydoux, was horrified that I threw them out. To prepare the pods you will need a moulin-légume, a strainer with a paddle in it, which Evelyne gave me, saying that no French cook would be without one. This recipe does not lend itself to using a food processor unless it has a coarse sieve able to separate the membrane.

2 lb / 900 g fresh peas
2 pints / 1.2 litres water
½ oz / 12 g butter
½ onion, finely diced
salt and pepper
2 or 3 sprigs of mint
1 tblsp / 15 ml sugar
1 tblsp / 15 ml cornflour, mixed
  with a little milk
¼ pint / 125 ml whipping cream

Wash and shell the peas, using them as a separate vegetable. Put the pods in a large pan and cover with the water. Simmer for 30 minutes.

Take the moulin-légume and, bit by bit, push the pods through the liquid, discarding the tough membrane. You now have a pea purée.

Melt the butter in a deep pot and gently fry the onion until soft, but not coloured. Add the pea purée and bring to the boil. Season to taste. Take the leaves off the mint and chop them with a little sugar. When the soup is boiling, stir in the cornflour mixed in milk and bring the soup back to the boil. Stir in the chopped sugared mint and the cream. Season. Heat but do not boil again. Serve at once.

CRECY SOUP

For 4

8 oz / 225 g each of finely diced
  carrots and onions
1 oz / 25g butter
2 pints / 1.2 litres bouillon,
  chicken or white stock
1 tblsp / 15 ml flour in 2 fl oz /
  50 ml water
2 fl oz / 50 ml whipping cream
1 egg yolk

Sauté the onions and carrots together in the butter in a covered saucepan until tender. Add the bouillon or stock and boil for 30 minutes.

Make a thin paste of the flour and water and whisk it into the boiling soup, pouring it through a sieve. Re-heat the soup. Mix together the cream and egg yolk and stir in just before serving. Do not boil again.

EINLAUF SOUP

For 4

1¾ pints / 1 litre chicken bouillon
1 tblsp / 15 ml flour
2 fl oz / 50 ml milk
a pinch of salt
1 tblsp / 15 ml chopped parlsey
1 egg

Bring the bouillon to the boil. Beat together the flour, egg, milk and salt. Add the chopped parsley and stir the mixture into the bouillon, just off the boil. Keep stirring or it will curdle. Serve at once.

FRENCH ONION SOUP

For 8

6 medium onions, finely sliced
butter or margarine
2 pints / 1.2 litres beef stock
salt and pepper
4 slices of toast, halved
2 oz / 50 g parmesan cheese

Slowly sauté the onions in butter till lightly browned, stirring to cook evenly. Add the beef stock and bring to the boil, simmering for 15 minutes. Season.

Serve each plate of soup with a piece of toast covered with grated cheese.

GREEK EGG AND LEMON SOUP

For 8 to 12

3¼ pints / 2 litres chicken stock
4 oz / 125 g rice or semolina
8 egg yolks
1 tblsp / 15 ml cornflour
½ pint / 300 ml milk
the juice of 1 large lemon
1 tblsp / 15 ml melted butter
1 tblsp / 15 ml chopped parsley

Bring the stock to the boil. Add the rice or semolina and cook until tender – about 20 minutes.

Mix the egg yolks with the cornflour and milk. Whisk slowly into the stock. When the mixture has thickened, stir in the lemon juice and slowly add the butter and chopped parsley. Do not allow to boil again.

TOMATO SOUP WITH ORANGE

For 8

8 oz / 225 g each of onion,
  carrot, turnip (swede)
2 cloves garlic
2 oz / 50 g butter
6 oz / 175 g tomato purée
3 pints / 1.8 litres chicken or
  vegetable stock
2 bay leaves
¼ tsp / 1 ml pepper
salt to taste
1 tblsp / 15 ml sugar
½ tsp / 3 ml tabasco sauce
  (optional)
1 tblsp / 15 ml cornflour, mixed
  with a little water
1 pint / 600 ml orange juice
4 fl oz / 125 ml sour cream
grated rind of 1 orange

Chop the onions, carrots, turnip and garlic finely. Fry them gently in the butter in a deep, covered saucepan until soft but not coloured – about 15 minutes. Stir in the tomato purée before adding the stock and bay leaves. Simmer for half an hour.

Remove the bay leaves and purée the soup in a liquidiser or moulin-légume. Season to taste with salt, pepper, sugar and, if wished, the tabasco sauce. Bring back to the boil. Whisk in the cornflour mixed in cold water. Boil again. Just before serving add the orange juice and re-heat. Do not boil.

Serve cream topped with grated rind on each helping.

CREAM OF SWEETCORN SOUP

For 4

1 small onion, finely chopped
1 oz / 25 g margarine
1 × 17 oz / 485 g tin of creamed
  sweetcorn
½ pint / 300 ml each of milk
  and chicken stock
salt, pepper and sugar
2 tblsp / 30 ml flour

In a saucepan fry the onion gently in the margarine until transparent. Add the sweetcorn, milk and chicken stock. Bring to the boil. Season well with salt, pepper and sugar. Thicken by whisking the flour into cold water and pour into the boiling soup, stirring well.

A QUICK CREAM SOUP

For 6

1 tin condensed cream of
  mushroom soup
1 tin condensed cream of
  chicken soup
2 tinfuls of milk, or milk and
  chicken stock
2 tsp / 10 ml curry powder
3 tblsp / 45 ml toasted coconut
4 fl oz / 125 ml whipped cream

This is good for an unexpected party.

Mix the soups in a saucepan with the milk (and stock) and curry powder. Bring to the boil.

Serve garnished with whipped cream topped with the coconut.

CRÈME VICHYSSOISE — GLACÉ

For 8

4 leeks (white part only)
1 medium onion
5 medium potatoes
2 oz / 50 g butter
2 pints / 1.2 litres chicken broth
1 pint / 600 ml milk
1 pint / 600 ml light cream
1 pint / 600 ml heavy cream
chives, finely chopped

Finely slice the leeks and onions. Cube the potatoes and gently sauté the vegetables in the butter in a deep, heavy-bottomed pan. Do not allow to brown.

Add the broth and boil the vegetables till tender. Pass this through a fine sieve or liquidise. Add the milk and light cream. Bring back to the boil. Cool overnight and chill.

Just before serving, whip the double cream a little, add most of it, and serve the soup with a spoonful of the remaining whipped cream on top, sprinkled with the chopped chives.

ICED CUCUMBER SOUP

For 8

1 large cucumber
1 spring onion or shallot, sliced
small bunch of mint
2 pints / 1.2 litres chicken stock
½ pint / 300 ml yoghurt
salt and pepper
¼ pint / 150 ml light cream

I made this soup for my mother's 80th birthday.

Peel the cucumber. Cut it in half lengthways and scoop out the seeds. Dice the flesh finely and put it in a saucepan with the spring onion and a small bunch of mint, tied with a string. (Keep some of the mint leaves in reserve.) Add the stock and bring to the boil. Cover the pan and let it cook gently for about 15 minutes.

Remove the bunch of mint and set the soup aside to cool before chilling it. It may be liquidised if a smooth soup is wanted.

When ready to serve, add the yoghurt, check the seasoning, and then add the cream. Serve in individual plates or cups with a tiny sprig of mint on top.

GAZPACHO

For 6 to 8

1½ lb / 750 g ripe tomatoes
4 slices white bread
1 clove garlic
2 small onions
1 green pepper
half a cucumber
½ pint / 250 ml tomato juice
2 tsp / 10 ml tarragon vinegar
2 tsp / 10 ml olive oil
salt and pepper
butter

A very popular soup in South Africa.

Reserve two tomatoes. Peel, de-seed and chop the remainder. Put in a big bowl. Remove the crusts from 2 slices of bread and soak them in cold water for 5 minutes. Squeeze out the water and add the bread to the bowl of tomatoes. Peel the garlic, chop it finely or press it and add it to the bowl.

Peel and chop the onions. Set aside half and add the rest to the bowl. De-seed the green pepper, dice it finely and add half to the bowl, reserving half. Peel the cucumber. Remove the seeds and dice the flesh, adding half to the bowl.

Lastly, add the tomato juice, vinegar and oil. Liquidise the soup. Check the seasoning. Chill it well and chill the reserved

23

halves of the diced vegetables, each in separate bowls.

Take the remaining 2 slices of bread, dice them and fry them gently in a little butter till crisp and dry.

Serve the soup from a tureen with the reserved tomato, onion, green pepper, cucumber and croutons in separate small bowls for people to help themselves.

The soup is very good with yoghurt added – about ½ pint / 250 ml.

ENTRÉES

The quantities in this section are for small helpings of entrée, served before the main dish. They can be expanded to provide a light meal.

MEAT PÂTÉ

This recipe is from my great-aunt, Easter Pugh. Her nephew, Dr Griffith Pugh, was the doctor on Sir John Hunt's expedition when Mount Everest was climbed for the first time.

There is a story told of him crossing the street in London. He did not see an approaching car and, about to be knocked down, could only put his hand on the bonnet and vault over it. My aunt said with a laugh, 'He's mad, quite mad; but his reactions are so quick!'

For 6

8 oz / 225 g lean beef mince
1 × 14 oz / 392 g tin condensed chicken soup
3 eggs
2 tsp / 10 ml parmesan cheese
1 tblsp / 15 ml curry powder
1 tsp / 5 ml cumin powder
4 rashers of fatty bacon
lettuce leaves and olives to decorate

Put the mince in a bowl with the undiluted soup. Beat the eggs separately and add them. Stir in the cheese and the curry and cumin powder. Mix well with a fork.

Butter a soufflé dish or baking tin. Cut the rinds off the bacon rashers and lay the rashers to cover the base of the soufflé dish. Pile the mixture on top and smooth it. Cover with a butter paper and then tinfoil.

Stand the dish in a baking tin, with water halfway up the sides, and bake in the oven at 350°F / 180°C / gas 4 for 1¼ to 1½ hours. A skewer, when inserted, should come out clean when it is ready.

Take out the soufflé dish, place a saucer with a weight on it over the pâté and leave until cold.

Turn it out, decorate it with lettuce leaves and olives, and serve with brown bread and butter.

CHICKEN LIVER PÂTÉ

For 6

8 oz / 225 g chicken livers
2 oz / 50 g butter

Cook the chicken livers in half the butter and set aside.

Add the chopped onion and garlic to the frying pan and

1 medium onion, chopped
1 clove garlic, crushed
2 sprigs each of thyme and
    parsley
1 bay leaf
½ tsp / 2 ml salt
¼ tsp / 1 ml fresh black pepper
1 tblsp / 15 ml brandy

For 6

8 oz / 225 g chicken livers
2 medium tomatoes, skinned,
    de-seeded and the juice
    removed
2 tblsp / 30 ml olive oil
1 tblsp / 15 ml tarragon vinegar
    or to taste
salt and pepper
3 or 4 lettuce leaves, blanched
    for 1 minute in boiling water,
    drained and chopped

For 6 to 8

½ lb / 225 g turbot or halibut
6 oz / 175 g butter
½ lb / 225 g fresh white
    breadcrumbs
sprig of parsley, chopped
salt
pinch of cayenne pepper
½ tsp / 2 ml ground mace
1 beaten egg yolk mixed with
    milk (to make 4 fl oz / 125 ml)
½ lb / 225 g smoked haddock

cook gently until transparent. Add the parsley, thyme, bay leaf and salt and pepper to taste. Allow to cool.

Add the chicken livers and put the mixture in the food processor. Chop with the metal blade, adding the remaining butter and brandy.

Pack firmly into a terrine and chill for 6 hours or overnight with a weight on top.

Serve the pâté with butter and fairy toast (see Index).

HAMILTON SALAD

This is a recipe from my Hamilton great-grandmother.

Lightly fry the chicken livers (not to be done too much). Pound the livers up with the prepared tomatoes and pass them through a fine sieve or mix them in a food processor. Add oil, vinegar, salt and pepper to taste, and then mix in the prepared lettuce leaves.

Place in the fridge for 2 hours before serving. Present on a bed of lettuce, with slices of brown bread and butter.

FISH PÂTÉ

Clean and chop the turbot, making sure all the bones and skin are removed. Mix with 4 oz / 125 g of the butter. Add the breadcrumbs and the parsley. Season well with salt, pepper and mace. Bind together with the egg yolk and milk.

Skin and bone the haddock and cut it into thin strips. Layer the turbot mixture and the haddock into a terrine. Put the remaining butter in dabs on top.

Cover the dish with a butter paper and place on a roasting tin with cold water in it to come halfway up the dish. Bake in the oven at 350°F / 180°C / gas 4 for 1 hour or until done. Test with a skewer. If it comes out clean, the pâté is ready.

Take the terrine out and let the pâté cool in it with a weight on top before serving.

For 4

12 large open mushrooms
1 oz / 25 g butter

Stuffing
2 oz / 50 g butter
1 onion, chopped
½ tsp / 3 ml each of sage,
    thyme, chopped parsley
8 oz / 225 g soft breadcrumbs
1 egg
1 oz / 25 g grated cheese
sliced tomato to serve

STUFFED MUSHROOMS

Put the mushrooms on a grill pan, open side up. Use the 1 oz / 25 g of butter to put dabs into each mushroom. Grill for 5 minutes.

Meanwhile melt the remaining butter and fry the chopped onion until transparent. Add the sage, thyme and parsley. Mix it all in with the breadcrumbs. Beat up the egg and mix it in.

Pile the stuffing into the mushroom cups, sprinkle cheese on top and put them under a medium grill for about 15 minutes before serving. Or they can be heated in a moderate oven.

Serve with sliced tomato.

For 6 to 8

1 onion, chopped
2 oz / 50 g butter
1 tsp / 5 ml each of thyme and
    chopped parsley
8 oz / 225 g mushrooms
8 tblsp / 120 ml each of chicken
    stock and white wine
4 fl oz / 125 ml cream

MUSHROOM RAMEQUIN

Fry the onion gently in the butter until transparent. Add the herbs. Divide this between the ramequins (small ovenproof cups). Slice the mushrooms and similarly divide them among the ramequins. Add the wine and stock. Bake in the oven at 350°F / 180°C / gas 4 for 15 minutes.

Remove from the oven and divide the cream between the ramequins. Return to the oven for 5 minutes to heat before serving. Serve with triangles of toast and butter.

GLOBE ARTICHOKES

1 big or 2 small artichokes per
    person
butter and a little lemon juice,
    per person

Cook the artichokes in boiling, salted water for about half an hour until a fork pierces them easily.

Drain them and serve warm on a plate. Each person has an egg-cup half-filled with melted butter mixed with ½ tsp / 2 ml of lemon juice.

To eat: each leaf is pulled off in your fingers, the soft bit at the bottom dipped in the egg-cup of butter and pulled off with your teeth. The rest of the leaf is discarded.

When you come to the hairy bit – the choke – in the centre, cut it off the artichoke heart and discard it. The heart, a speciality, is cut up and eaten with the remaining butter.

Now that I grow artichokes in the garden I find them easy to serve. When there is a glut of them I blanch them for 5 minutes in boiling water, plunge them into cold water, turn them upside down to drain, freezing them for cooking later.

For 4

1 lb / 450 g asparagus
butter and lemon sauce, as for
  the artichokes above.

FRESH ASPARAGUS

Pare or lightly peel the asparagus stalks, unless they are very young and tender. Then tie them in a bundle and steam in a covered pan with the heads above some salted water until soft – 10 to 15 minutes.

Serve hot with the lemon and butter as above, or a hollandaise sauce (see Index). The asparagus is eaten with your fingers, dipping the tops in the melted butter. Discard the woody end.

Provide finger-bowls and napkins for your guests. I have been at parties as a young girl where I did not know how to cope!

AVOCADO PEAR

There are many ways of serving this delicious fruit. The following can all be served with brown bread and butter.
(1.) Cut the fruit in half just before serving, so that the flesh does not brown. Sprinkle with lemon juice and serve 1 half per person with salt and freshly ground pepper.
(2.) Serve avocado with Carlton salad dressing (see Index) with a small tin of shredded crab or shrimps mixed in.
(3.) Scoop out the flesh, cut it into cubes, mix with cubed pineapple and pile it back into the shell. Serve with a vinaigrette dressing.

For 4

4 oz / 125 g shortcrust pastry
  (see Index)
egg white
4 canned artichoke hearts
6 oz / 175 g cream cheese
1 egg
2 tblsp / 30 ml chopped chives
3 drops of tabasco sauce
6 drops of Worcester sauce
salt and pepper

CHEESE TARTS

Roll out the pastry to fill 8 cups in your patty pan and cut out the necessary shapes with a fluted cutter. Press the pastry shapes into the cups. Brush the pastry cups with a little egg white.

Put half an artichoke heart into each cup. Beat the cream cheese with the egg, chives and the sauces. Season to taste. Cover the artichoke hearts with this mixture. Bake at 425°F / 220°C / gas 7 for 10 minutes until puffed and golden.

Note: Mushrooms could be substituted for the artichokes, but they should be cooked first.

CHEESE SOUFFLÉ IN TOMATO

For 8

8 large tomatoes
8 fl oz / 225 ml cream
2 oz / 50 g butter
4 tblsp / 60 ml flour
5 fl oz / 150 ml grated cheese
2 eggs, separated
salt
cayenne pepper
8 slices of bread, cut into rounds
   and lightly toasted

Cut the tops off the tomatoes. With a teaspoon scoop out the seeds, being careful not to pierce the skin. Push this tomato pulp through a sieve. Measure the quantity you have and make it up to ½ pint / 300 ml with the cream.

Melt the butter in a saucepan. Stir in the flour. Add the tomato mixture. Bring to the boil and take it off the heat. Stir in the cheese until melted. Beat in the 2 egg yolks. Season to taste with the salt and cayenne.

In a separate bowl beat the egg whites until stiff, and fold them into the cooked mixture.

Fill the tomato cases three-quarters full with the soufflé mixture. Stand each tomato on a lightly browned piece of toast. Place them in the hot oven (425°F / 215°C / gas 7) for 10 minutes until the soufflé is risen and brown on top.

Serve at once. Have people seated at the table and bring in the tomatoes on individual plates, direct from the oven otherwise the soufflé will sink.

COURGETTES AU GRATIN

For 8

1 lb / 450 g courgettes, sliced
   about 1/2" / 1cm thick
2 eggs
8 fl oz / 250 ml whipping cream
4 tblsp / 60 ml each of grated
   cheddar and parmesan cheese
salt and freshly ground black
   pepper
butter

Just cover the courgettes with boiling salted water and cook until they are soft and the water almost evaporated.

Meanwhile, mix the eggs, cream and most of the grated cheeses, keeping 2 tblsp / 30 ml for later use. Season.

When the courgettes are cooked put them into a gratin dish or individual ramequins. Pour the cream, egg and cheese mixture over them, and sprinkle the reserved cheese over the top. Dot with shavings of butter.

Bake in the oven at 400°F / 200°C / gas 6 for 10 minutes or till just set. Then brown them under a hot grill and serve at once.

POOR MAN'S ASPARAGUS

For 4

8 oz / 225 g spinach stalks
½ pint / 300 ml Béchamel sauce
   (see Index)
4 fl oz / 125 ml whipping cream
4 oz / 125 g grated cheese
4 slices of toast

I experimented with this one day when I had fresh spinach stalks left. We liked it so much that I have included it here.

Cut the leaves off long-stalked spinach beet or perpetual spinach and save them for another occasion.

Cut the stalks into 1 inch / 2.5 cm pieces. Boil them in a little salted water for about 10 minutes, until tender. Drain them and place in 4 buttered ramequin dishes.

Make the Béchamel sauce, using for liquid the water in which the spinach stalks have cooked, with extra cream or milk to make it up to ½ pint / 300 ml.

Ladle this sauce over the stalks in each dish and cover thickly with grated cheese. Grill until hot and bubbly and serve with the toast.

MOUSSE DE FROMAGE FROID

For 8

My mother, as a young bride in 1930, had never done any cooking, so she took a 6-week course at the Cordon Bleu Institute in London. This was one of her star recipes.

½ pint / 300 ml milk
1 slice of onion
a bouquet of herbs
1½ oz / 40 g butter
1½ oz / 40 g flour
1 tsp / 5 ml each of English and
    French mustard
cayenne and paprika
salt
1 tblsp / 15 ml gelatine soaked
    in 2 tblsp / 30 ml cold water
3 eggs, separated
1 oz / 25 g each of Gruyère and
    parmesan cheese
4 tblsp / 60 ml whipping cream
slices of cucumber and tomato
    for decoration

Simmer the milk with the onion slice and bouquet of herbs.

In another pan melt the butter. Stir in the flour, the mustards and a dash each of cayenne and paprika. Strain the hot milk onto this roux while stirring. Bring it back to the boil and season with salt.

Take the pan off the heat and stir the softened gelatine into the sauce until dissolved. Beat in the egg yolks, followed by the cheese. Make sure the cheese melts fully. If it has not, put the pan over hot water until it does. Do not boil it again.

Pour all this into a basin and allow to cool but not set. Whip the egg whites stiffly and fold them in. Then whip the cream and fold it in.

Have a mould ready. Dip it in cold water and then pour the cheese mousse into the wet mould. Leave it in the fridge for at least 6 hours or overnight.

Invert the mould onto a dish and decorate around the edge with slices of cucumber and tomato.

Serve with fairy toast (see Index), fresh rolls or brown bread and butter.

OEUFS FROIDS À LA RUSSE

For 8

4 tomatoes, sliced
1 cup each of cooked peas, baby
    carrots and asparagus pieces
½ cup cooked cubed beetroot
4 hard-boiled eggs
2 pickled gherkins
4 tinned anchovies

Arrange the vegetables in sections or strips on a separate plate for each guest.

Halve the hard-boiled eggs and set one half on top of the vegetables on each plate.

Beat the cream until thick. Mix together in a cup all the other dressing ingredients before folding them into the cream.

Put the dressing over each half egg. Chop the gherkins

Dressing
4 fl oz / 125 ml whipping cream
½ tsp / 3 ml French mustard
2 tblsp / 30 ml tomato ketchup
1 tsp / 5 ml sugar
pinch of pepper and paprika
½ tsp / 2 ml salt
1 tblsp / 15 ml each of lemon
   juice and vinegar

and sprinkle over the top. Cut the anchovies lengthways and lay 1 slice over the dressing on each half egg.

STUFFED EGGS

For 4

4 hard-boiled eggs
2 tblsp / 30 ml mayonnaise
2 tblsp / 30 ml sour cream
seasoning
1 small bunch of chives
1 tblsp / 15 ml curry powder
   (optional)

I find it best to put the eggs on to boil in a pan of cold water to which a teaspoon of salt has been added. Bring to the boil and boil for 5 minutes. Run cold water over the eggs and leave in cold water. This should avoid that dark ring around the yolk that sometimes appears.

Peel the eggs and cut them in half lengthways. Take out the yolks and mash them in a bowl with the mayonnaise, sour cream and seasoning. Chop the chives finely and add them. Season to taste. Add the curry powder if desired.

Pile the mixture back into the hollows of the eggs and serve with lettuce and toast.

BOUCHÉES

For 8

These are little puff pastry cases in which you can use various fillings of your choice.

Buy ready-made puff pastry (or make your own – see Index). Roll it out ½" / 1 cm thick. Take 2 fluted cutters, one smaller than the other. First cut out 16 rounds with the bigger cutter. Place these on a wet baking sheet and cut halfway through with the smaller cutter. Be careful not to cut all the way through.

Brush each cut-out with a light egg wash made of 1 egg beaten up with 2 tblsp / 30 ml milk. Place in the hot oven – 425°F / 210°C / gas 7 – for about 10 minutes until puffed and golden.

Take them out of the oven. Cut out the little 'hats' made by the inside cut. Scoop out any soft pastry inside. Leave until cold and fill with the filling of your choice.

Fillings

(1.) Camembert cheese. Remove the rind and cut in squares. Fill this into the pastry case.

(2.) Cooked chicken and ham cut into cubes and mixed with a Béchamel sauce, flavoured with lemon juice.

(3.) Fry mushrooms until soft. Chop them and put in a Béchamel sauce, flavoured with lemon juice.

(4.) Fry bacon and chop it up. Grate cheese and mix the two together with a skinned, chopped tomato.

(5.) Mash sardines with lemon juice and cream cheese.

When you have filled the cases, replace the 'hats' and, just before serving, return them to a hot oven 425°F / 210°C / gas 7 for 5 to 8 minutes so that the fillings are heated through.

POIRES AU ROQUEFORT

For 8

lettuce
4 tblsp / 60 ml hot milk
4 oz / 125 g each of Roquefort
    and cream cheese
8 pears halves, tinned or cooked
watercress
paprika

Arrange some lettuce on 8 plates.

Mash together 2 tblsp / 30 ml of the hot milk with the Roquefort. Do the same with the cream cheese.

If using fresh pears, poach them in a light syrup made with 4 oz / 125 g granulated white sugar to 1 pint / 600 ml water. Fill the hollow of each pear with the Roquefort cheese and then cover it with the cream cheese. Dust with paprika and decorate with lettuce and watercress.

Note: This may be made with tinned or fresh peach halves instead of with pears. The juice may be kept for separate use, e.g. fruit salad.

SALADS

CUCUMBER SALAD

1 large cucumber
2½ fl oz / 45 ml each of water
   and vinegar (or ½ vinegar and
   lemon juice)
freshly ground black pepper
pinch of sugar and salt

Wash and dry the cucumber. Cut it into extra-fine slices. Mix the water and vinegar. Add the seasoning.

Lay the cucumber on a plate and pour the dressing over it, leaving it to marinade for 1 to 1½ hours before serving.

As an alternative cucumber salad, grate half a cucumber (including the skin) into a carton of yoghurt. Season to taste and serve. This is particularly good as an accompaniment to curries.

GREEK SALAD

quartered tomatoes
chopped black olives
sliced radishes
sprigs of uncooked cauliflower
green peppers
celery
Feta cheese

This is simply a mixture of uncooked vegetables together with diced cheese. You can vary quantities according to taste.

Toss all the ingredients together and pour over them a strong French dressing made with garlic and olive oil. Do not add sugar to the dressing if you want to be authentic.

WILTED LETTUCE SALAD

For 8

1 head iceberg lettuce
8 rashers of streaky bacon
Dressing
4 oz / 125 g butter
8 fl oz / 225 ml sour cream
6 tblsp / 90 ml vinegar
2 tblsp / 30 ml soft brown sugar
1 tsp / 5 ml salt
¼ tsp / 1 ml each of dry
   mustard and paprika
3 eggs

Fry the bacon until crisp and crumble it. Melt the butter gently. Add the cream, vinegar, sugar, salt, mustard and paprika. Beat the eggs together and add to the pan over a low heat, stirring constantly until thick. It will look a little curdled but this is fine.

Put the washed lettuce in a salad bowl and pour the hot dressing over it without turning the lettuce. Sprinkle the crumbled bacon over the top.

COLESLAW

For 8

¼ of a large white cabbage
1 red apple
¼ of an onion, grated
2 tsp / 10 ml caraway seeds

Dressing
2 tblsp / 30 ml vinegar
1 tblsp / 15 ml lemon juice
1 tsp / 5 ml salt
¼ tsp / 1 ml fresh black pepper
2 tsp / 10 ml sugar
4 tblsp / 60 ml olive oil
4 fl oz / 125 ml sour cream
4 fl oz / 125 ml yoghurt

Mix together the vinegar, lemon juice, salt, pepper and sugar. Whisk in the olive oil and then the sour cream and yoghurt.

Shred the cabbage finely. Cut the apple, removing the core but keeping the skin. Slice the apple into the cabbage. Add the grated onion and toss everything with the dressing.

Serve with caraway seeds sprinkled over the top.

Note: If pressed for time you can use mayonnaise mixed with yoghurt for the dressing.

POTATO SALAD

For 8

1 lb / 450 g potatoes boiled in their skins
1 onion, chopped
½ pint / 300 ml well-flavoured stock
chives
Dressing
4 tblsp / 60 ml lemon juice
6 fl oz / 175 ml unsweetened evaporated milk
1 tsp / 5 ml each of mustard and salt
¼ tsp / 1 ml pepper
2 tsp / 10 ml sugar

Peel the skins off the hot potatoes and cut up the potatoes.

Blanch the chopped onion by pouring boiling water through it. Add the onion to the potato and pour the hot stock over this. Leave until cold, when the potatoes will have absorbed most of the stock. Drain off any excess stock.

Mix together all the ingredients for the dressing and toss the cooled potato and most of the chopped chives in it.

To serve, sprinkle the remaining chives on top.

CARROT SALAD

For 6

2 sharp-tasting apples
½ lb / 225 g raw carrots
1 orange
1 tblsp / 15 ml lemon juice
4 oz / 125 g raisins
1 tsp / 5 ml each of salt and sugar
¼ tsp / 1 ml pepper

Grate the unpeeled apples and peeled carrots together. Grate the orange rind finely and sprinkle 1 tsp / 5 ml of it on the carrots. Squeeze the orange and add the juice, together with the lemon juice and raisins.

Season with the salt and sugar. Add pepper to taste.

For about 8

SOUSBOONTJIES
(South African Bean Salad)

1 lb / 450 g red kidney beans
2 onions, sliced
4 tomatoes, skinned and
   chopped up
1 lemon
¼ pint / 150 ml evaporated milk

Soak the beans overnight in cold water. Next day put them in fresh water and cook until tender – about 1 hour – and then drain.

Add the sliced onions and tomatoes. Season with salt and allow to cool. Add the juice of the lemon and the evaporated milk.

For about 8

BEETROOT JELLIED SALAD

4 fl oz / 125 ml boiling water
1 packet (1 tblsp / 15 ml)
   gelatine, soaked in 2 tblsp /
   30ml cold water
2 fl oz / 60 ml cider vinegar
4 fl oz / 125 ml golden syrup
8 oz / 225 g fresh cooked
   beetroot, diced
4 oz / 125 g celery, diced

Pour the boiling water over the soaked gelatine and stir until dissolved, standing the cup in hot water if necessary. Add the vinegar and syrup and make it up to ½ pint / 300 ml with cold water. Put this aside until it begins to set, then fold in the diced beetroot and celery.

Pour the mixture into a wetted mould and leave for 6 hours or overnight.

Turn out as in the following recipe.

Serve on a bed of shredded lettuce.

For 8 or more

CUCUMBER JELLIED SALAD

¼ pint / 150 ml double cream
6 fl oz / 170 ml yoghurt
4 tblsp / 60 ml mayonnaise
2 tsp / 10 ml lemon juice
1 large unskinned cucumber,
   grated
1½ packets (1½ tblsp / 22 ml)
   gelatine
2 tblsp / 30 ml cold water
4 fl oz / 125 ml double strength
   chicken stock (1 stock cube)
salt and pepper to taste

Mix together the cream, yoghurt, mayonnaise and lemon juice. Add the grated cucumber.

Soak the gelatine in the cold water in a cup. Stand this cup in a basin of freshly boiled water until the gelatine has dissolved. Add this to the cold chicken stock and then combine it with the cucumber mixture. Season to taste.

Pour into a wetted mould and leave for at least 6 hours or overnight before turning out. To help release the jelly, dip the mould for 30 seconds in hot water. If it does not release, repeat this before inverting onto a plate.

Decorate with watercress and tomato around the edges.

For about 8

1 × 14 oz / 400 g tin of
    tomatoes
2 tblsp / 30 ml tomato purée
1 tblsp / 15 ml lemon juice
1 tsp / 5 ml Worcester sauce
4 tblsp / 60 ml orange juice
1 packet (1 tblsp / 15 ml)
    gelatine, soaked in 2 tblsp /
    30 ml cold water
2 tblsp / 30 ml boiling water
1 tblsp / 15 ml sugar
salt and pepper to taste

TOMATO JELLIED SALAD

Purée the tomatoes in a food processor or pass through a sieve. Add the tomato purée, lemon juice, Worcester sauce and orange juice.

Dissolve the soaked gelatine in the boiling water and add it to the tomato mixture together with the sugar and seasoning. Make the total up to 1 pint / 600 ml with extra water or orange juice, to taste. Pour it into a wetted mould and leave for 6 hours or overnight.

Turn out as for the cucumber salad and decorate with fresh lettuce.

All these jellied salads are very attractive made in a ring mould. This is very easy to make by standing a jam-jar full of water in a basin and pouring the salad mixture around the jam-jar.

For about 8

1 packet (1 tblsp / 15 ml)
    gelatine soaked in 2 tblsp /
    30 ml cold water
2 fl oz / 60 ml boiling water
6 fl oz / 170 ml of the grapefruit
    juice
1 tblsp / 15 ml lemon juice
sugar, salt and pepper
4 fl oz / 125 ml grapefruit
    segments, tinned in their own
    juice, and drained
8 oz / 225 g peeled cucumber,
    diced

GRAPEFRUIT JELLIED SALAD

Pour the boiling water over the soaked gelatine and stir until dissolved. Pour the grapefruit juice into this and add the lemon juice, with sugar, salt and pepper to taste.

Leave until cold. Just before it sets, add the grapefruit segments and cucumber. If you put them in earlier they will sink to the bottom. Put aside to set for at least 6 hours before turning out as in the other jellied recipes.

DRESSINGS FOR SALADS

AVOCADO SALAD DRESSING

2 tblsp / 30 ml sugar
5 tblsp / 75 ml tomato ketchup
1 tsp / 5 ml each of salt and
  paprika
4 tblsp / 60 ml vinegar
2 tsp / 10 ml Worcester sauce
8 fl oz / 225 ml olive oil

Mix together everything apart from the oil. Beat until smooth. Then beat in the oil.

SALAD DRESSING

2 tblsp / 30 ml vinegar (cider or
  brown)
1 tsp / 5 ml each of dry mustard
  and tarragon
½ tsp / 2-3 ml salt
pepper
1 tsp / 5 ml sugar (optional)
4 tblsp / 60 ml olive or salad oil
2 tblsp / 30 ml yoghurt or cream

Mix together the vinegar, mustard, tarragon, salt, pepper and sugar. Beat in the oil and yoghurt or cream.
  Serve over a tossed lettuce salad.

SOUR CREAM DRESSING

1 egg, slightly beaten
2 fl oz / 50 ml vinegar
2 tsp / 10 ml salt
1 tsp / 5 ml mustard
2 tsp / 10 ml sugar
pinch of pepper
8 fl oz / 225 ml sour cream

Combine the egg, vinegar and dry ingredients. Mix them thoroughly and add to the cream.
  Place the bowl over a pot of boiling water and cook, stirring until the dressing is thick. This is good served with potatoes.

SALAD DRESSING WITH EGGS

2 hard-boiled eggs
8 fl oz / 225 ml whipping cream
2 tblsp / 30 ml vinegar
sugar to taste
1 tsp / 5 ml dry mustard
salt and pepper

Take the yolks of the eggs and chop them finely. (Set aside the whites which may be chopped and used as decoration.)

Slowly add the cream to the yolks, being sure to mix in the yolks smoothly.

Add the vinegar and sugar, mustard, salt and pepper to taste.

VINAIGRETTE OR FRENCH DRESSING

1 clove garlic, crushed
1 tsp / 5 ml salt
¼ tsp / 1 ml pepper
a pinch of cayenne
2 fl oz / 50 ml cider or wine
   vinegar
2 tsp / 10 ml sugar (optional)
6 fl oz / 175 ml olive oil or salad
oil

Combine the garlic, salt, pepper and cayenne with the vinegar, adding the sugar if desired. Mix in the oil.

Use this dressing to flavour a tossed green salad with lettuce.

MAYONNAISE

2 egg yolks
1 tsp / 5 ml dry mustard
1 tsp / 5 ml salt
½ tsp / 2 ml white pepper
1 tsp / 5 ml icing-sugar
2 tblsp / 30 ml lemon juice
1 pint / 600 ml olive oil (or half
   olive and half salad oil)
3 tblsp / 45 ml vinegar (brown
   or cider)

Basically this is oil beaten into egg yolks, with vinegar and lemon juice, and then flavoured. The trick is to do it so that it does not curdle. To achieve this, the oil is beaten in ½ tsp / 3 ml at a time. If it does curdle, take another egg yolk and, ½ tsp / 2 ml at a time, very slowly beat the curdled mixture into it.

Break the 2 egg yolks into a bowl, saving the whites for other use. Add the mustard, salt, pepper and icing-sugar.

Beat in ½ tsp / 3 ml of the lemon juice. Then, drop by drop, beat in half the oil. (With a mixing machine, add the oil ½ tsp / 3 ml at a time.) It will be very thick.

Now start adding, ½ tsp / 3 ml at a time, the lemon/vinegar mixture, alternating with the remaining oil.

Put the mayonnaise into a jar with a lid and it will keep in the fridge for about 2 weeks.

Mayonnaise can be treated in different ways:

Mix it with tomato purée or ketchup and a couple of spoons of cream and you get a Sauce Aurore for use with shellfish.

GREEN MAYONNAISE

A handful of spinach leaves
1 tblsp / 15 ml chopped parsley
and chervil (or basil)
½ pint / 300 ml mayonnaise
3 tblsp whipped cream

Put the spinach, parsley and chervil (or basil) in a pan. Add 2 fl oz / 50 ml boiling water and boil till the leaves are just soft but still bright green – 3 minutes or so. Push them through a sieve or liquidise them and then add to the mayonnaise and whipped cream. Serve at once. This is an attractive sauce for cold salmon.

SAUCE TARTARE

¼ pint / 150 ml cream or
yoghurt
½ pint / 300 ml mayonnaise
1 tblsp / 15 ml capers
2 tsp / 10 ml pickled gherkins,
chopped
1 pickled onion, chopped
1 tblsp / 15 ml chopped parsley

Put the yoghurt and mayonnaise in a bowl. Mix into it the drained capers, gherkins, onion and parsley.

ROQUEFORT CHEESE DRESSING

4 tblsp / 60 ml mayonnaise
2 tblsp / 30 ml Roquefort,
crumbled
6 fl oz / 175 ml French dressing
½ tsp / 2 ml Worcester sauce

Mix the mayonnaise and the Roquefort. Very slowly mix in the French dressing and lastly add the Worcester sauce.

CARLTON SALAD DRESSING

8 fl oz / 225 ml mayonnaise
2 tblsp / 30 ml tomato purée
½ tblsp / 7 ml icing-sugar
½ tblsp / 7 ml lemon juice
½ tsp / 3 ml Worcester sauce

Combine all the ingredients in a bowl. This is often used to accompany shellfish.

CHINESE DRESSING

Used over fruit such as pears, peaches or bananas, eaten as a starter

4 fl oz / 125 ml redcurrant jelly (see Index)
10 fl oz / 275 ml mayonnaise
2 oz / 50 ml chopped almonds
4 fl oz / 125 ml whipped cream

Place the jelly in a pan over hot water until it melts. Then add it to the mayonnaise, together with the nuts. Add the whipped cream.

FISH

On one holiday Sunday at Brodick Castle church was over. My cousin Simon and I were looking for ways to amuse ourselves until lunch. Suddenly we had an idea, 'Come, let's go fishing!' We owned neither fishing rods nor hooks. The grown-ups kept those. Nothing daunted we set off, found some poles, string and, searching around the boathouse, a few hooks. Thus equipped we caught some small baby crabs to use as bait. I do not remember catching any fish but we had a wonderful time. Finally, getting hungry, we decided to return to the Castle, only to be met by an irate grandmother. Did we not know the time? 2.30! She had been shouting for us for an hour. And – awesome threat – she would see us in her Boudoir! There was no lunch for us that day as she gave us such a dressing-down as neither of us

has forgotten, ending with the plea, 'Can't you let the little fishes have a rest even on Sunday?'

We were very fond of her, but she could be an awe-inspiring person. During the war the island was packed with 8,000 commandos training on the moors and the beaches for the invasion of North Africa. Some got a bit out of hand, using their firearms on the local game. Twenty beasts were found wounded and the islanders were up in arms. A professor friend of ours here in Ireland, as a young man, spent his holidays in Arran and told us the story as it came to his ears. 'Today this could have developed into a major incident,' he said, 'but, at the time, your grandmother summoned the Brigadier. The interview ended, it is reported, with her words, "If you cannot control your men here in Arran, how do you expect to control them in North Africa?"'

End of incident!

SOME NOTES ON BUYING FISH

I learnt these when I joined the South African Women's Cultural Organisation in Cape Town.

FRESH FISH
The eyes should be moist, glistening and protruding. If they are sunken, red and cloudy the fish is not fresh. The gills should be bright red, not dull. The smell should be fresh, not strong. For fillets, the flesh should be firm, not soft and mushy.

FROZEN FISH
Run your finger along the box. If it is a tiny bit dusty or pink, it has defrosted at some time. Shake the box. The fish should move around loosely. It should be stored at a temperature of minus 18°C.

NUTRITION
White fish is lower in cholesterol and sodium than meat; is a source of Vitamin D; contains iron, though not as much as meat; has a low fat content.

Oily fish, such as tuna, mackerel, herring and yellowtail, are high in fish liver oils. When you catch them, break their necks straight away. This slows deterioration and it is important to eat them fresh. Oily fish are good fried, grilled or barbecued.

Do not overcook fish. The highest temperature should be 350°F / 180°C / gas 4. For fried fish do not have the oil too hot. To steam fish, put a good stock under them and place them on herbs.

In many places where I have been it has seemed to me that fish was presented in a very dull way, just grilled or fried. So I have made a point of experimenting with recipes from many countries as well as my own. I remembered so well the delicious fresh fish and seafood from our holidays on the Isle of Arran – those lobsters or crabs straight from the lobster pots, crawling around our bare, sandalled feet. Or the excitement of that first pull of the fish on the line.

I don't know why, but I never learnt to cast expertly with a rod. Perhaps I did not have enough patience, unlike my mother who, when she died at 83, still held the record for two salmon – 27 lb and 22 lb – caught on the River Aline in Argyllshire when she was a girl of 17.

GRAVLAX (Cured Salmon)

This recipe comes from Margaret Denny, married to my husband's uncle, Edward Denny, shipbuilder of Dumbarton on the Clyde.

She writes, 'This is a Swedish recipe. Before the days of freezers the salmon was wrapped in linen and thick brown paper and buried in the ground for a period of curing.'

a 2 lb / 900 g salmon
1 tblsp / 15 ml dark brown sugar
2 tsp / 10 ml whisky if wished
   (I always do)
2 tblsp / 30 ml coarse sea salt
fresh dill

Split the fish and remove the backbone. Lay half the fish in a shallow dish. Mix the other ingredients. Rub half into the fish, pressing well in. Lay a good bit of fresh dill on top – dried if fresh is unobtainable. Rub most of the remaining mixture into the other half of the fish and clap together. Sprinkle the rest of the mixture on top.

Cover the dish with clingfilm and weigh it down. Leave undisturbed in the fridge for 3 days. Then draw off the liquid, slice and use as smoked salmon.

It freezes very well and is most easily sliced when half frozen. It is softer and more succulent than smoked salmon. Sea trout is excellent if similarly treated, but big thick fish are indicated.

BACALHAU OF THE THOUSAND DEVILS (Portugal)

For 6

Soak 1 lb / 450 g Bacalhau (salt dried codfish) in water overnight. Or Finnan Haddock, unsoaked, may be used.
olive oil
4 large onions
3 cloves garlic, crushed
2 lb / 1 kg potatoes, boiled
6 eggs
seasoning
parsley

This is a Portuguese recipe for fish omelette.

Put a generous amount of olive oil in a wide, flat frying pan. Add thinly sliced onions and garlic and fry gently until soft, stirring occasionally.

Meanwhile boil the fish for about 10 minutes. Drain it. Remove all the skin and bones. Shred the fish. When the onions are soft, but not brown, add the shredded fish and mix together for a few moments. Then add the boiled and roughly chopped potatoes and mix again.

Just before serving add the beaten-up and seasoned eggs and stir the mixture until the eggs have set a little but remain fairly soft.

Add some chopped parsley and serve with a simple green salad.

CULLEN SKINK

For 4

1 lb / 450 g smoked haddock
¾ pint / 450 ml milk
1 medium onion, sliced
4 oz / 125 g mashed potato
1 tblsp / 15 ml butter
salt and pepper

Poach the haddock for 4 minutes in just enough milk to cover it. Turn the fish and remove the skin. Add the sliced onion and simmer for a further 10 minutes. Take the fish out and remove the bones. Return the fish to the pan. Bring to the boil and add enough mashed potato to give a creamy consistency. Add the butter in small pieces and beat in. Season to taste.

Serve in a dish with triangles of dry toast or crispy fried bread. Decorate with chopped parsley. *Cullen* means 'haddock' and *skink* means 'essence' in Gaelic.

DEVONSHIRE FISH WITH MUSHROOMS

For 4

1 lb / 450 g cod fillet
salt and pepper
3 large tomatoes, skinned and chopped
4 oz / 125 g mushrooms, sliced
½ pint / 300 ml cider or clear apple juice
butter
1 lb / 450 g mashed potato *or* serve with plain, boiled rice

This was one of our favourite family dishes when we were in South Africa where our daughters spent much of their first 14 years.

Skin the cod, if not already done, and cut into slices suitable to serve. Place the cod in a buttered fireproof dish. Season. Add the skinned, chopped tomatoes and the mushrooms. Pour the cider over so that it almost covers and dot with shavings of butter. Cover with greaseproof paper and a lid and place in a moderate oven 350°F / 180°C/ gas 4 for about 30 minutes, until the fish is cooked.

Sauce
¾ oz / 20 g butter or margarine
2 tblsp / 30 ml plain flour
4 oz / 125g grated cheese
1 skinned, sliced tomato for
   decoration

For the sauce, strain the liquid from the cooked fish into a saucepan and bring to the boil. Make a beurre manié – flour and butter worked together. Gradually beat this into the boiling stock. Be sure to whisk it constantly. When the sauce has thickened and cooked, season it to taste and pour over the fish in the casserole.

Mashed potato may now be piped around the edge of the dish, grated cheese sprinkled on top and the casserole returned to brown in the oven, now heated to 400°F / 200°C / gas 6 for about 10 minutes.

For 4

HAKE FILLETS IN MUSTARD AND CREAM SAUCE

1 ½ lb / 750 g hake fillets
ready-made mild mustard
4 fl oz / 125 ml fresh cream
salt and pepper
parsley and tomato to garnish

Lay the fish skin-side down in an ovenproof dish with a lid. Spread some mustard lightly over the fillets. Beat the cream lightly and spread over the fish. Season to taste.

Bake in the oven at 350°F / 180°C / gas 4 for 25 minutes. For the last 5 minutes of cooking remove the lid to enable the dish to brown. Garnish it with parsley and slices of tomato.

For 4

FISH PAPRIKA

½ lb / 225 g sliced onions
2 oz / 50 g butter / margarine
1 ½ lb / 700 g fresh hake or
   bream
1 tblsp / 15 ml lemon juice
8 fl oz / 400 ml fresh cream *or*
   4 fl oz / 125 ml sour cream
2 tsp / 10 ml paprika
salt and pepper

My father farmed in Rhodesia, now Zimbabwe, for about 50 years. His cook, Kenyas, prepared this dish one day when the family and I were visiting.

Fry the onions in the butter until they become transparent. Place them on the bottom of an ovenproof dish and add the fillets and lemon juice. Cover with greaseproof paper and the lid and place in the oven heated to 350°F / 180°C / gas 4 for 30 minutes or till done.

Skin the fish, removing the bones. Pour over the cream mixed with the paprika, salt and pepper and return to the oven to bake for 15 minutes more, with the lid off, to brown.

Serve it from the dish with rice and fresh green beans.

For 4

a generous 1 lb / 500 g smoked
   haddock
¾ pint / ½ litre milk

Sauce
1 ½ oz / 30 ml butter
2 tblsp / 30 ml flour
1 hard-boiled egg
1 tblsp / 15 ml chopped parsley

FINNAN HADDOCK

To cook this traditional Scottish dish, place the haddock in a buttered casserole with a lid. Almost cover with the milk. Put a buttered paper over the fish and then the lid. Cook in a moderate oven (350°F / 180°C / gas 4) for about half an hour. Take it out and keep warm.

Melt the butter, mix in the flour and pour the milk from the fish slowly over this roux, stirring constantly till it boils. Season to taste, add the chopped egg and pour over the fish.

Decorate with the parsley and serve with a sliced tomato salad.

Boiled potatoes and spring greens or broccoli go well with this dish.

FISHER'S HERRING

This is a dish which Chrissie would have lived on. She was a Gaelic-speaking girl from the Island of Lewis whom my mother engaged to look after my brother and me, when she left us, with my grandparents on the Isle of Arran, to return to my father in Rhodesia.

Life at Brodick Castle cannot have been easy for Chrissie. She was only 17 when she left the croft in the Western Hebrides where she had grown up to come to join us. Her mother was a widow and had taken in washing to bring up the family. Chrissie had never seen a train before. Now, suddenly, she was in a castle.

She had a room in the tower which would shake in the winter storms. She once told me she was saved by the melodeon which her brother sent her. When her work was done and my brother and I were asleep, she would take it up to her room and sing the old songs and others she herself composed and set to music. Now her son Donald is a popular Gaelic singer. Many of his songs come from his mother.

When the war came Chrissie was called up. We were very sad to see her go for we loved her. After the war Chrissie went home, married and became the local schoolteacher – and a very good one, I am sure – for 18 years. She was, however, compulsorily retired by the local council just two years before she qualified for her pension because of new legislation that every teacher must have formal qualifications. Now her two boys have left home and she lives with her husband, who has become blind, on a small croft. She herself has had cancer but, hopefully, this has been treated and she is able to manage.

Growing up, Chrissie's staple food was oatmeal porridge, fresh herring, potatoes and such vegetables as they could grow on the croft. Fisher's Herring is typical all over Scotland.

1 or 2 herrings per person
salt and pepper
coarse oatmal
fat or dripping for frying

Split the herrings and clean them. Remove the head and tail and de-scale them. Wash and pat them dry. Season with salt and pepper if wished (I don't). Dip in the coarse oatmeal, pressing it well in.

Heat some dripping in a frying pan and fry the fish well, skin-side last. Serve with either boiled potatoes or brown bread and butter and tomato salad.

KIPPERED HERRINGS

We often had these for breakfast. And in Scotland and Ireland for high tea, served with brown bread and butter, scones and jam, fruit cake or apple pie and, of course, tea.

Taking at least one kipper per person, they can be grilled

with a pat of butter on top, or poached in a covered pan with a little water and a butter paper placed over them.

KIPPER PASTE

8 oz / 225 g kipper, boned and
    skinned
4 oz / 125 g butter
1 tblsp / 15 ml lemon juice
fresh ground black pepper to taste

Any leftovers from the kippered herrings can be used in this dish.

Pound the kippers, being sure all the bones and skin have been removed. Pound in the other ingredients, well mixed. Pack into a small dish and decorate with parsley.

Serve as a savoury with fairy toast (see Index).

STRÖMING (Little Herring)

For 8

2 lb / 1 kg small herrings
4 oz / 125 g caviar (black or red
    according to choice)
8 fl oz / 250 ml light cream
2 tblsp / 30 ml tomato ketchup

I spent a winter in Sweden and was introduced to some of their marvellous fish dishes.

Cut off the head and open and clean the fish. If you cannot get small ones then fillet ordinary-sized herring, removing the backbone, but leaving on the skin.

Roll the herring round a dash of caviar and place in a casserole greased with butter. Continue till the dish is full of the rolls. If any caviar remains, add it together with the cream mixed with the tomato ketchup.

Cover the dish and bake in the oven at 350°F / 180°C / gas 4 for about 45 minutes.

RAIE À L'ORANGE

For 4

1 lb / 500 g skate (raie), cod,
    hake or monkfish
¼ pint / 150 ml red wine
juice of ½ lemon
bouquet of herbs (parsley, bay
    leaf, thyme)
1 tblsp / 15 ml butter

Sauce
2 oz / 50g butter
2 shallots, finely chopped
1 clove garlic, crushed
1 tblsp / 15 ml each of flour,
    tomato paste and sherry
1 tomato, skinned and de-
    seeded
2 oz / 50 g mushrooms, sliced

This was my mother's party recipe. Skin the fish and remove the bones. Then cut it into portions and place in a well-buttered casserole. Pour over the wine and lemon juice. Add water (if needed) to cover the fish, with the herb bouquet and the remaining butter. Place in a moderate oven (350°F / 180°F / gas 4) for 20 to 30 minutes till done. Strain off the stock and keep the fish warm.

To make the sauce, melt three-quarters of the butter. Add the shallots and the garlic and fry gently until transparent and soft, but not brown. Add the flour and cook well. Then add the roughly chopped tomatoes, tomato paste and the mushrooms. Season to taste with salt and pepper.

Pour over the stock from the cooked fish and stir over the heat till boiling. Simmer for 15 minutes. Add the sherry, the olives if used, and the orange rind. Simmer another 5 minutes. Take off the heat and add the remaining butter, bit by bit.

2 oz / 50 g black olives, stoned
    (optional)
finely shredded rind of 1 orange,
    blanched and strained

Arrange the fish on a big serving dish (or ashet, as it is known in Scotland). Pour the sauce over the fish.

To decorate, cut the skin, including all the pith, off the oranges and cut the sections free of the membrane. Arrange these down one side of the dish and place fried croutons down the other. The croutons are made from 2 slices of white bread with the crusts removed, diced and fried gently till crisp.

Serve with boiled new potatoes and a green vegetable.

Now comes a whole section on salmon. Today this is, perhaps, a luxury, but in the old days it was commonplace. There is the story of the Scot who went to London with his manservant. They were dining together. He said he would have the roast beef, but 'Let Donald have the salmon'.

My grandparents had the netting rights on Loch Lomond together with the Colquhouns of Luss on the opposite shore, so we lived on salmon. Sometimes we were allowed to go out with the men and help catch the great, silvery fish.

(a 5 lb salmon should
serve 12)

POACHED SALMON OR SALMON TROUT

Scale and clean the fish without too much washing or handling. Keep the head, tail and skin on. To de-scale run the back of a knife up the fish from tail to head under running water. To clean the fish, slice the stomach open from the gills to the vent. Lay back the flap thus formed. Have a piece of newspaper open and drop the innards onto this. Wash off any remaining blood.

Ideally, you should have a big oval fish kettle with a fitted strainer and lid to simmer on top of the stove. Failing this you can use a roasting pan with a rack in the oven. Place the fish on the rack and cover with a buttered paper. Pour boiling court bouillon (see over) in the pan to just cover the fish and cover with a lid or with tin foil. Bring to boil, skim it clear, then let it simmer at 8 minutes to the lb.

To serve hot, lift the fish strainer and rest it across the top of the pan, covering the fish with a damp folded cloth, being sure the skin does not stick to it. Do not leave the fish in the water as it will become soft. Put the fish onto a heated platter, covered with a folded napkin. Serve with hollandaise sauce (see Index) or with melted butter and slices of lemon.

To serve the fish cold, simmer it for 4 minutes to the lb. Then take the pan off the heat, cover it with a tight lid and leave the fish in the liquid overnight or until cold. Lift out the strainer and skin the fish, leaving on the head and tail. Clarify the liquid with egg white and shells (as in fish aspic, see Index) and boil until reduced by half. Pour a little over the fish. Garnish with finely sliced cucumber, lemon and hard-boiled egg. Pour over the remaining glaze and chill it.

For the Matric Dance at my daughter Catherine's school in Cape Town, when the parents did the catering, I made this dish not with salmon but with the local kingklip, a beautiful fish. It was a focal point of the table.

COURT BOUILLON

2 pints / 1.2 litres water
6 black peppercorns
4 sprigs parsley
1 bay leaf
½ lemon, sliced
1 sprig fennel, if possible
1 wine-glass of white wine

Bring all the ingredients for the bouillon to the boil. This is used for poaching salmon or other fish.

For 4

GRILLED SALMON CUTLETS

4 fl oz / 125 ml wine vinegar
2 shallots, sliced
1 small blade of mace
2 cloves
salt
4 salmon steaks
olive oil

Bring the vinegar, shallots and seasonings to the boil. Leave until cold. Pour over the cutlets in an earthenware dish. Add as much olive oil as will stand on top and marinade the cutlets for at least 30 minutes.

Drain the cutlets and grill for 15-20 minutes, turning once.

Serve with a pat of lemon parsley or anchovy butter on top of each cutlet and a big bunch of parsley on the side of the ashet.

LEMON PARSLEY BUTTER

4 oz / 125 g butter
1 lemon, squeezed
2 tsp / 10 ml chopped parsley

Cream the butter, gradually beating in the lemon juice and chopped parsley. Shape into a long roll and chill, wrapped in waxed paper.

To serve, unwrap the butter, cut it into pats and place on the steaks as you bring them to the table.

ANCHOVY BUTTER

2 oz / 125 g unsalted butter
anchovy paste
cayenne pepper

Cream the butter, add anchovy paste and cayenne pepper to taste. Continue as for lemon parsley butter.

FERA NORMANDE (Salmon-Trout)

For 6

juice of 1 lemon
1 ½ pints / 900 ml water
4 oz / 125 g button mushrooms
2 ½ lb / 1 kg salmon-trout
4 shallots or spring onions, finely
 sliced
1 bay leaf
salt and pepper
2 hard-boiled eggs
2 tblsp / 30 ml chopped parsley
Sauce
1 ½ oz / 40 g butter
4 tblsp / 60 ml flour
¾ pint / 400 ml juice from the
 fish
4 fl oz / 125 ml light cream
the cooked mushrooms

Mix the lemon juice with water. Place in a pan and cook the mushrooms in this until done. Strain them off.

Place the whole salmon-trout on a rack in a fish kettle. Add the strained juice from cooking the mushrooms, the shallots, bay leaf and seasoning.

Cover the kettle and poach the fish gently until done – about 30 minutes. Strain off the juice and keep the fish warm, but do not allow it to dry out.

To make the sauce, melt the butter and stir in the flour. Then gradually stir in the juice from the fish. Bring to the boil, stirring constantly. Remove from the heat and add the cream and the cooked mushrooms.

To serve, skin the fish and place on a platter. Garnish with chopped hard-boiled egg placed alternately with stripes of chopped parsley. Put a big bunch of parsley at the head. Serve the sauce separately.

FILLET OF SOLE VÉRONIQUE

For 6

1 ½ oz / 30 g butter
2 shallots, finely sliced
6 fillets of sole
salt and pepper
2 fl oz / 50 ml each of dry white
 wine and water
1 egg yolk
½ lb / 250 g seedless white
 grapes
¼ pint / 150 ml whipped cream

Melt ½ oz / 10 g butter in a shallow pan and gently fry the shallots. Season the fish with salt and pepper and arrange on the shallots. Add the wine and water.

Cut wax paper to fit the pan. Butter one side and place it, butter-side down, on the fish. (I always keep the paper from the butter and use that.) Bring the contents of the pan to the boil and poach gently, barely bubbling, for 10 to 12 minutes.

Carefully remove the fish to a heatproof, heated serving dish.

Cook the liquid remaining in the pan until reduced to ¼ pint / 150 ml. Add the cream sauce (see over) mixed with the egg yolk and the remaining butter. Cook, while stirring, until the butter is just melted. *Do not boil*.

Having blanched the grapes in boiling water for 3 minutes, now place them around the fish. Fold the whipped cream into the sauce and pour over the fish. Brown quickly under a hot grill and serve immediately. It is lovely with rice and a green vegetable such as broccoli, peas or beans.

CREAM SAUCE FOR SOLE
VÉRONIQUE
2 oz / 50 g butter
3 tblsp / 45 ml flour
¼ pint / 150 ml cream and
  ½ pint / 300 ml milk, heated
  together

Melt the butter, add the flour and whisk in the cream and milk all together. Continue stirring until it comes to the boil and is thickened and smooth. Season with salt, pepper and nutmeg to taste. Use as needed.

TROUT

My mother was a very keen fisherwoman, trained by her father. She was not allowed onto the water until she could throw a cast onto a handkerchief on the lawn.

The best way to eat trout is the same evening as you have caught them. Build a fire of heather and wood – making sure it is safe. While the fire is burning down to embers, gut and clean your fish. When the fire is ready, grill the fish on a rack over the red-hot embers and eat straight away.

Failing that, the following is a recipe for cooking at home: clean and de-scale one trout per person. Make 3 slits in the skin on each side. Dip in oatmeal and fry in bacon fat until crisp and tender, turning when half-done. Serve with lemon wedges.

For 4

4 oz / 125 g filleted fish
lemon juice
1 oz / 25 g soft white bread
  crumbs
¼ pint / 150 ml milk
1 oz / 25 g butter
2 eggs, separated
2 tblsp / 30 ml whipping cream

FISH SOUFFLÉ

This may be made with leftover fish, in which case omit the first part of the cooking instructions.

Cook the fish with a little water and lemon juice in the oven at 350°F / 180°C / gas 4 for about 10 minutes.

Put the crumbs, milk and butter in a pan, stirring until thick. Remove from the heat and add the egg yolks, well beaten with the cream. Flake the fish and add it (being sure the bones are removed). Season to taste, adding more lemon juice if you wish. Beat the egg whites till stiff and fold them in.

Grease a pudding basin well. Add the fish mixture. Tie a butter paper and a cloth over it. Place in a pan filled halfway up the basin with boiling water. Cover it and steam gently for 30 minutes.

Turn the soufflé out of the pudding basin onto a heated serving dish. Have ready a parsley, curry, tomato or other flavoured sauce to pour over the soufflé, and serve.

For 4

1 ½ lb / 700 g skinned cod,
   hake or haddock
1 onion, sliced
1 oz / 25 g butter
1 tblsp / 15 ml (or more) curry
   powder
6 peppercorns
1 tsp / 5 ml salt
¼ pint / 150 ml cider vinegar
½ pint / 300 ml water

CURRIED PICKLED FISH

Gently fry the onion in the butter until transparent. Add the curry powder and fry a moment longer.

Cut the fish into long strips. Roll these up and place in a casserole with a lid. Sprinkle over them the fried onions and curry powder. Add the peppercorns and salt. Pour the combined water and vinegar over the fish.

Bake at 350°F / 180°C / gas 4 for half an hour. Take out of the oven and leave until cold. It is good served with home-made brown wheaten bread and butter, and sliced tomatoes.

FISH SALADS

FISH CREAM SALAD

For 8

2 lb / 1 kg cooked white fish
4 hard-boiled eggs
¼ pint / 150 ml shrimps
4 tsp / 20 ml chopped capers
4 tsp / 20 ml chopped gherkins
2 oz / 50 g chopped onions,
    fried until transparent
seasoning
½ pint / 300 ml mayonnaise
2 lb / 1 kg macedoine of
    vegetables, made up of freshly
    cooked or tinned diced
    carrots, beans, peas, onions
1 lb / 450 g sweetcorn

Bone, skin and flake the fish. Chop and add 2 eggs, half the shrimps, all the capers, gherkins, seasoning and fried onion.

Mix with enough mayonnaise to bind to a creamy consistency. Mound this in the centre of a platter. Drain the macedoine and corn and mix well with a little mayonnaise. Edge the dish with the macedoine. Decorate with the remaining egg and shrimps.

SALMON AND TUNA MOUSSE

For 8

For my daughter Catherine's 21st birthday at the Oxford University Union, I cooked and froze food for 120 people at home in Ireland. We then took the ferry and drove through the cool of a summer's night to the college freezer in Oxford. Having a terror of being left with too little, I had prepared 16 litres of mousse as part of the meal. Catherine's friends lived on this for the following days!

14 oz / 400 g each of pink
    salmon and tuna fish
1 tblsp / 15 ml lemon juice
2 tblsp / 30 ml onion juice,
    achieved by grating an onion
2 gherkins, chopped finely
4 fl oz / 125 ml tomato paste

Put the salmon and tuna in a bowl discarding the skin and bones. Add the lemon and onion juice and the chopped gherkins and the tomato paste. Pound the mixture to a paste or put it in the food processor. When it is well pounded, add the Béchamel sauce you have prepared.

Soak the gelatine in 2 fl oz / 50 ml of cold water. Add to it the half pint / 300 ml of hot fish aspic (see below) and

1 pint / 600 ml Béchamel sauce
(see Index)
2 tblsp / 30 ml gelatine
½ pint / 300 ml fish aspic (see
below for recipe)

dissolve. *Do not boil* the gelatine. Add it to the other ingredients and mix everything well.

Take a 2 pint / 1.2 litre mould. Rinse with cold water. Pack the mousse into it and leave it to set in the fridge overnight.

Next morning dip the mould into a basin of hot water for a minute, being careful not to get water into the mould, and turn out onto a platter. Patience is required as a vacuum will have formed. It can help to slip a knife down the inside.

Before serving the mousse, decorate with slices of tomato and cucumber, hard-boiled egg slices and stuffed olives. The egg slices can also be placed around the edge of the mousse.

Have a further cup of fish aspic ready and warmed till it is liquid. Gently spoon this over the decoration on the mousse, being careful not to disturb it. You may need to do this twice, returning it to the fridge in between so that it sets.

This can be served as a starter for a dinner party with fairy toast, or for a Sunday supper with brown bread and a fresh lettuce salad.

FISH ASPIC
1 small onion and 1 carrot,
peeled and sliced
½ a bay leaf
12 peppercorns
1 lb / 450 g fish bones, heads or
tails
1 sprig each of parsley and
thyme
1 pint / 600 ml each of dry
white wine and water
2 egg whites and their shells

Combine everything except the egg and shells in a saucepan. Bring to the boil and simmer for an hour. Skim as necessary to remove foam.

To clarify, take 2 egg whites and their shells, beat them to a froth, add them to the bouillon and bring to the boil 3 times, removing from the heat in between to prevent the contents foaming over. Do not stir or remove the froth. Line a sieve with a scalded cloth and pour the aspic through it. It should come out quite clear. Any excess can be frozen for future use.

For 8

MOUSSE OF CRAB MEAT AND FISH

My grandmother used to employ a fisherman at Brodick. We knew him as Boden. He would take us out fishing with a line tied to a square of wood, trailing four or six hooks. Boden was a philosopher. I remember him talking about the Middle East as I steered the boat while my brother and cousins fished. You had to keep on the right side of him. Once we took the boat without his permission. What a scolding we got! He would take us around the lobster pots which would also catch crabs. This is one recipe for them.

1 lb / 450 g of either pike, cod
   or hake fillet
6 oz / 175 g butter
2 eggs
2 egg yolks
pinch of nutmeg
½ tblsp / 10 ml each chopped
   chervil and parsley
½ pint / 300 ml whipped cream
2 tblsp / 30 ml brandy
5 oz / 150 g of crab meat,
   flaked

Make sure the fish is free of bones. Pound or work to a paste in a processor. Gradually feed in the butter, eggs and yolks, adding seasoning and herbs to taste. Fold in the whipped cream, the brandy and the crab meat. Turn into a buttered mould and poach for 35 minutes. Serve as an entrée with wholewheat bread and butter.

CRAB MEAT CHOWDER

For 4 to 6

2 oz / 50 g butter
4 large mushrooms, chopped
   finely
3 tsp / 15 ml onion, grated
2 tomatoes, peeled and seeded
12 oz / 350 g fresh or frozen
   crabmeat
8 fl oz / 225 ml double cream
2 tsp / 10 ml each of chopped
   parsley and finely sliced chives
2 tblsp / 30 ml lemon juice

Melt the butter in a large oven-to-table pot. Add the mushrooms and cook gently over moderate heat, stirring from time to time. Add the prepared onions and tomatoes and cook till soft – about 10 minutes. Add the crab meat and seasoning (salt and cayenne) to taste, stirring gently to keep the meat whole. Heat to boiling point. Take off the heat and stir in the cream, parsley, chives and lemon juice. Serve at once. Plain, hot boiled rice can accompany it for a main meal.

Note: The recipe may be made substituting white fish for crab.

BRODICK CASTLE SCALLOPS

For 4

1 medium carrot
1 medium onion
4 oz / 125 g butter
1 bay leaf
2 stalks parsley
a pinch of powdered thyme
1 leek, white part only, sliced
8 scallops
¼ pint / 150 ml white wine or
   lemon juice
2 tomatoes, skins and pips
   removed

Peel the carrot and the onion. Dice finely and place in a medium saucepan with half the butter. Add the herbs tied in a muslin bag. Stew gently with the lid on for 10 minutes, adding the leeks after 5 minutes, till the vegetables are cooked.

Add the white and red parts of the scallops. Replace the lid and stew gently till almost done. Add the wine and the tomatoes and cook for a further 10 minutes.

Remove the scallops from the pan and keep warm. Reduce the remaining leeks and vegetables in the pan to ½ pint / 300 ml. Remove from the heat and flake in the remaining butter to thicken the sauce slightly. *Do not boil*.

Taste for seasoning. Place the scallops on their shells, masked with sauce and sprinkled with fresh chopped parsley.

Note: For those who do not like or cannot eat scallops, this is delicious made with white fish.

For 6

1½ lb / 700 g cod or monkfish
a slice of onion
1 bay leaf
a slice of orange peel
6 oz / 300 g cooked or tinned
    crab meat, cut in large pieces
4 oz / 125 g butter
3 tblsp / 45 ml chopped onion
1 tblsp / 15 ml flour
8 oz / 450 g cooked shrimps
¼ pint / 125 ml scalded cream
½ dried chilli pepper, very finely
    sliced
¾ pint / 450 ml long-grain rice
1½ pints / 900 ml chicken stock
4 oz / 125 g peas, cooked
1 tinned pimento, chopped
1 orange
1 grapefruit

PESCADO CON FRUTAS (Argentina)

Steam the fish in a little boiling water with a slice of onion, a bay leaf and a slice of orange peel until soft – about 15 minutes.

Fry the crab meat and shrimp in half the butter with the finely chopped onion. Sprinkle flour over the seafood and stir in thoroughly, being sure there are no lumps. Add the hot cream and simmer slowly with the chilli pepper for 10 minutes. Flake the cod and stir in. Season to taste.

In a separate pan, fry the rice in the rest of the butter. Add the chicken stock and cook the rice gently until all the water has evaporated. Stir in the cooked peas and the chopped pimento.

Make a ring of rice around the edge of a large serving platter. Place the cooked fish mixture in the centre.

Having freed the segments of the orange and the grapefruit arrange the orange on top, surrounded by the grapefruit. To prepare the orange and grapefruit, take a small, sharp knife and slice off the skin and pith as if peeling an apple. Over a bowl (to catch the juice) slice to the centre in between each membrane to separate the segments in one piece. When you have removed the segments squeeze the membranes to get all the juice out.

For 4

1 lb / 450 g peeled shrimp, fresh
    or frozen
2 oz / 50 g butter

Sauce
1 pint / 600 ml milk
a strip of lemon peel
a slice of onion
2 oz / 50 g butter
4 tblsp / 60 ml flour
1 egg yolk
1 tblsp / 15 ml sherry or lemon
    juice

SHRIMP NEUBERG

Fry the shrimps gently in the butter with the lid on for about 15 minutes. Take them out and de-vein them if necessary by pulling out the dark line along the back.

For the sauce, heat the milk with the strip of lemon peel and the slice of onion. Melt the butter and, stirring in the flour, cook gently for a moment. Strain in the heated milk and bring to the boil.

Beat the egg yolk, adding a little of the hot sauce to it and then beat it into the remaining sauce. *Do not allow to boil or it will curdle.*

Add the sherry or lemon juice and then the cooked shrimp.

Serve with a ring of rice around the edge of the platter and the Shrimp Neuberg in the middle. Decorate with chopped parsley.

FISH LEFTOVERS

FISH PIE

For 4

4 oz / 125 g shell or other type
  pasta
½ lb / 250 g cooked fish (tinned
  tuna can be used)
4 hard-boiled eggs, quartered
8 oz / 225 g cooked peas

Sauce
2 oz / 50 g butter
2 oz / 50 g onion, chopped
1 pint / 600 ml milk
a strip of lemon rind
2 tblsp / 30 ml flour
4 oz / 125 g cream cheese
  makes it extra good
4 tblsp / 60 ml dried
  breadcrumbs
2 oz / 50 g cheese, grated

Put a large pan of water on to boil. When boiling, add a little oil (1 tblsp / 15 ml) to it with 1 tsp / 5 ml salt. Add the pasta and boil fast for 15 minutes. Strain.

Take a 2 pint / 1 litre casserole. Smear it with butter. Put in the pasta, the fish, hard-boiled eggs and cooked peas.

Make the sauce by melting the butter, adding the chopped onion and frying gently till soft. Meanwhile heat the milk with the strip of lemon rind. Add the flour to the butter and onion and cook for a few moments before straining in the hot milk. Whisk to remove any lumps and bring to the boil, stirring constantly. If you wish, stir in the cream cheese.

Pour the sauce over the fish etc in the casserole. Sprinkle the dried breadcrumbs and the grated cheese over the top.

Put the fish in the oven (heated to 350°F / 180°C / gas 4) for half an hour, until it is hot and bubbling and the top is brown.

You may vary this pie by substituting tinned tomatoes and their juice for the milk and adding a chopped pepper.

KEDGEREE

For 4

2 oz / 50 g butter
2 oz / 50 g onion, chopped
½ pint / 300 ml rice
1 pint / 600 ml water
½ lb / 250 g cooked fish
4 hard-boiled eggs, quartered

This is particularly good made with smoked haddock, herring, tuna or mackerel which have already been cooked.

Melt the butter in a saucepan. Add the chopped onion and fry gently till soft but not brown. Add the rice and stir it around. Next add the water and bring to the boil. Turn the heat down and simmer the rice until all the water has disappeared.

Meanwhile, flake the fish, removing any bones or skin. Add the fish and the hard-boiled eggs to the rice. Put the lid on and leave to steam gently for 10 minutes. When ready to serve, fork in the rice with the fish and eggs.

The kedgeree is improved with the addition of 2 tblsp / 30 ml cream to the cooked dish. Or crack a raw egg over the rice as you fork it in with the fish.

FISHCAKES

For 4

½ lb / 225 g cooked fish
1 lb / 450 g mashed potato
4 tblsp / 60 ml flour
salt and pepper
1 egg, mixed with 2 tblsp /
    30 ml milk
dried breadcrumbs

Flake the fish, removing any bones, and mix it into the potato.

Take 3 soup plates. In the first, put flour, seasoned with salt and pepper. In the second, put the egg mixed well with the milk. In the third put the breadcrumbs.

Form the fish and potato into flat cakes 1" / 3 cm thick, and dip each cake in the seasoned flour to cover it. Shake off excess and dip into the egg mixture, turning with a fork till well covered. Then dip in the breadcrumbs, turning with a separate fork, and set them on a board.

Heat some oil in a frying pan and fry the cakes on each side for about 10 minutes. Delicious served with tomato salad.

This recipe may be made with leftover mashed potato and any well-flavoured fish or tinned tuna.

POTATO AND FISH PANCAKES

For 4

1 lb / 450 g mashed potato
12 oz / 350 g cooked fish or
    tinned tuna
2 raw eggs

Mix everything together well. Heat some oil in a frying pan and drop spoonfuls of the batter into it. Cook on one side until brown, then turn and cook on the other. Serve with a green salad.

FISH FRITTERS

For 4

8 oz / 225 g fresh or smoked
    cooked fish – or use leftovers

Batter
4 oz / 125 g plain flour
pinch of salt
1 tblsp / 15 ml oil
¼ pint / 125 ml water
1 tblsp / 15 ml lemon juice
1 egg white, whisked

Sieve the flour and salt together. Make a hole in the flour and pour in the oil, lemon juice and water all at once. Beat the liquid, gradually incorporating the flour.

Leave to stand for 15 minutes, then add the whisked egg white and the flaked fish. In hot oil deep fry a spoonful / 10 ml at a time, until golden – about 3 minutes. Remove with a slotted spoon and drain on kitchen paper. Serve with parsley sauce and slices of lemon or with green mayonnaise.

GAME

THE LEGEND OF THE WHITE STAG

The island of Arran was a gift from King James IV to my grandmother's family, the Hamiltons, in 1503. James, third Marquess of Hamilton, was raised to the Dukedom in 1643.

Arran has many historical connections. King Robert the Bruce, having been defeated in Scotland, fled to Rathlin Island off the north coast of Ireland from where you can see the peak of Goatfell on Arran on a clear day. Hiding in a cave on Rathlin he watched the spider spin a long thread and try to cross on it to the wall. Six times it tried and failed. The king said to himself, 'If it tries the seventh time and wins I, who have lost six times myself, will go back again to free my country.'

The spider did succeed and so the king returned, coming

first to Arran. One part of Brodick Castle, my grandparents' home, is known as Bruce's Tower. From Arran he returned to the mainland and regained his country's freedom.

The island was a gift but, as I originally heard the story, the Hamiltons were unsure about the auguries so they called in the soothsayers to advise them whether to accept. The soothsayers consulted and said that the gift was good and that it would remain in the family until the day that a white deer was seen on the island.

My grandmother was the only child of the 12th Duke of Hamilton. She had no cousins of the male line for five generations. When her father died, she was seven years old, and the title and all the entailed estates passed to distant relatives. Arran, however, came to her. On her death the Castle and 10,000 acres were accepted by the Treasury in lieu of death duties, and passed to the National Trust.

At this time some visitors to the island from Glasgow were hiking across the moors and came down to one of the villages with the extraordinary story of the white stag which they had seen. They knew nothing of the legend but it had come true. White deer have been seen various times since on the death of other members of the family.

MARINADE FOR VENISON

This is my great-grandmother the Duchess of Hamilton's recipe. She was known to us as 'Tat'. If she came to the nursery door, or if anyone was seen at mealtimes with elbows on the table, she would call out, 'Rat-a-tat-tat.'

2 medium onions, finely sliced
a sprig each of thyme and parsley
a few peppercorns
½ pint / 300 ml each of best salad oil and port wine
¼ pint / 150 ml each of white wine vinegar and sherry
2 carrots, sliced
2 bay leaves
2 cloves

Mix all this together. Soak the venison in it in a china bowl for 2 or 3 days, turning twice a day. Do not use a metal bowl or it will taint the marinade. This marinade will tenderise the venison. To cook, lard the venison with fat bacon and roast in tinfoil.

ROAST VENISON EN CROÛTE

6 to 8 oz / 175 to 225 g venison
 per person
salt and pepper
4 oz / 125 g fat bacon

The pastry or croûte
1 lb / 450 g plain flour
2 tsp / 10 ml salt
8 oz / 225 g prepared suet,
 chopped

The haunch or leg is preferable. My aunt, Lady Jean Fforde, whose recipe this is, says that if the venison is hung properly it needs no marinade.

Season the meat with very little salt and some pepper. Lard it with the bacon. To do this, cut inch-deep gashes all over the joint and into each one push a slice of fat bacon.

To make the pastry, mix the flour, salt and suet. Add sufficient water for a firm dough. Roll it out ¼" / 1 cm thick and big enough to enclose the joint. Place the meat in the centre of the dough. Dampen the edges of the dough and bring them up to meet, sealing the joint inside. Cut 2 slashes in the dough to allow air to escape.

Place the roast en croûte in a roasting pan in the oven heated to 375°F / 190°C / Gas 5. Cook until done, allowing approx. 20 minutes per 1lb / 45 minutes per kg, plus 20 minutes extra.

Serve garnished with watercress, a rich gravy and rowan jelly. Break the crust open as you serve it and carve the meat thinly. Mashed potato is traditionally good with this dish.

VENISON HOT POT

For 6 to 8

2 lb / 1 kg potatoes, sliced
2 large onions, sliced
2 lb / 1 kg venison, cubed or
 sliced
2 sheep's kidneys, sliced
salt and pepper

This was originally made with beef, but, in wartime, my grandmother developed this recipe.

Take a deep, ovenproof dish. In it first place a layer of sliced potato, then a layer of sliced onion, then a layer of venison and kidney. Season with salt and pepper. Repeat the layers, finishing with a double layer of potato. Pour water into the dish, halfway up.

Cover the pot and place in a bain-marie – a pan of hot water – in the oven heated to 350°F / 180°C / gas 4 and cook for about 3 hours, topping up the water in the bain-marie when necessary.

For the last half-hour of cooking, remove the cover of the dish to brown the potatoes.

DOUGARIE COTTAGE PIE

Dougarie was the shooting-lodge to Brodick Castle, sited near the shore on the other side of the island. Its boathouse is full of cartoons, drawn on the walls, of my great-grandfather and his friends.

4 cloves garlic
2 large onions
8 oz / 225 g chopped
   mushrooms
2 lb / 1 kg minced game (can be
   leftovers)
1 lb / 450 g tinned tomatoes
tabasco sauce and other
   seasoning to taste
mashed potato

Fry the onions and garlic in a little fat till soft. Add the chopped mushrooms and cook. Then add the meat and cook it if it is fresh. Lastly add the tomatoes and tabasco sauce to taste. Place it all into a deep pie dish.

Have ready some mashed potato and cover the dish lightly with this. Bake the whole in an oven heated to 350°F / 180°C / gas 4 for about 1 hour, until crisp and well browned.

GAME PIE PÂTÉ

This recipe comes from Mrs Skirt, the housekeeper at Brodick Castle before the war.

Take some gamebirds, rooks or rabbits. Slice the meat from the breast and set aside. Strip the remainder from the legs and carcases. Pound it and put it through a sieve. Also pound the livers of the birds. Line the sides of a pie dish with thin slices of fat bacon. Put in a layer of bread, sage and onion stuffing (see Index). Then some slices of game and of hard-boiled egg. Truffles are an improvement if available. Repeat the layers until the dish is full. Cover the dish with a paste of flour and water. Bake for 2 hours in a moderate oven (350°F / 180°C / gas 4).

When cooked, remove the paste and put a saucer or plate with a weight on top till set and cold.

While the pie is cooking, put the bones of the birds on to simmer to make a good stock. Add aspic and fill the dish to cover the meat as well as decorate it when it has cooled.

My Aunt Jean writes, 'We used to have rooks in the spring at Buchanan Castle. We paddled an old boat on the Endrick River to the wood, a delight of dog mercury, wood sorrel and bluebells just coming out. There we lay in wait, shooting the squabs – the young rooks.'

HARE FILLETS WITH CHERRIES

Remove the fillets from a young hare – the nice pieces of meat along the backbone. Beat them flat and lard them with fat bacon, pushing portions of bacon into the meat. Cut each fillet into two or three pieces, according to size.

Prepare a compôte of cherries: stew fresh cherries with a little water. Have ready some mashed potato.

About 15 minutes before serving, heat some butter and oil in a frying pan over a quick heat and cook the prepared fillets on either side.

Dish the fillets on a border of mashed potato with a compôte of cherries in the centre.

Meanwhile, take the remaining bones of hare, brown them in a little fat, and then boil them up to make a good gravy. Strain off the gravy, thicken with a little cornflour stirred in, and serve in a sauceboat.

A GERMAN RECIPE FOR HARE

For 6

2 saddles of hare
1 bottle of white wine
carrots and onions, chopped up
mixed herbs
bay leaf
2 cloves
4 oz / 125 g fat bacon
salt and pepper
8 fl oz / 225 ml sour cream

Marinade the young hare in an earthenware dish with the wine, vegetables, herbs and cloves, basting as often as you remember for 2 days. Keep the marinade cool.

Lard the saddles with some fat bacon. Put the vegetables from the marinade on the bottom of the roasting tin. Place the saddles of hare on top of them. Pour the marinade juice on top, and season with salt and pepper.

Roast at 350°F / 180°C / gas 4 for about 1½ hours. When tender, remove the hare from the pan. Pour off the grease and strain off the vegetables, keeping the liquid. Place the hare in a casserole and add the liquid from the pan. Cover it all with sour cream. Re-heat in the oven and serve.

RAGOÛT OF HARE

For 4 to 6

4 joints of hare
3 oz / 75 g butter
4 oz / 125 g mushrooms, stalks and all; if button mushrooms, use whole
3 tblsp / 45 ml flour
4 fl oz / 125 ml port wine

Brown the joints of hare well in the butter. Take them out of the pan and set them aside in a casserole. Sauté the mushrooms in the butter and add them to the hare.

Stir the flour into the pan, scraping round the sides. Cook for a minute or two, adding more butter if needed. Add the port wine and 3 teacups of water. Let this cook and thicken. If too thick, add a little more water. Pour it over the hare,

salt and pepper
juice of 3 oranges

cover it and bring back to the boil. Place in the oven –
325°F / 170°C / gas 3 – for about 1½ hours, until tender.

Just before serving, add the juice from the 3 oranges and
simmer for 5 minutes. Sprinkle some chopped parsley over
the top, and serve.

If hare is unavailable, 1½ lb / 700 g of lamb or mutton can
be used instead.

For 6

2 rabbits
6 tomatoes, skinned, seeded and
    sliced
2 large onions, sliced and fried
    until soft
2 oz / 50 g gammon, cut into
    chunks
salt and pepper

RABBIT CASSEROLE

Cut the rabbit into joints and fry in a little oil to a nice, golden
colour. Place in a casserole.

Add the sliced tomatoes, fried onions and the gammon
pieces. Season the whole well. Add water to reach halfway
up the ingredients.

Cover the casserole, place in the oven at 350°F / 180°C /
gas 4 and cook for about 1½ hours until tender. Thicken the
juice with 2 tblsp / 30 ml flour mixed with water.

Serve hot with mashed potato, green vegetables and
tomato sauce.

GALANTINE OF RABBIT

1 lb / 450 g rabbit meat
onion
parsley
herbs
1 lb / 450 g bacon
2 eggs
salt and pepper
4 oz / 125 g breadcrumbs, dried
    and browned

Put the meat, onion, parsley, bacon and herbs twice through
the mincer. Add the eggs and seasoning. Tie tightly in a long
rolypoly shape in a damp pudding-cloth dusted with flour.
Simmer in water for 2 hours.

When cool, untie the cloth and roll the meat in the
browned breadcrumbs. Serve cold.

This recipe may also be made with chicken.

GAME BIRDS

Grouse and pheasant were the most usual game we had.
After shooting, they should be hung, head down, in a
draught in a fly-proof place for anything between one and
three weeks, depending on the weather and on whether you
like them 'high' (strongly flavoured) or not. The hanging is
to tenderise the meat. The birds are ready when the tail
feathers come out easily.

Pheasant and grouse are then plucked and drawn (cleaned out), the head and feet being removed. If there is down left on the birds after plucking, singe the skin with a lighted taper.

Young birds are best for roasting. Older ones can be braised as indicated. Game birds have very little fat of their own so need extra fat, such as bacon, in cooking.

BRAISED or ROAST PHEASANT

TO BRAISE A GROUSE or PHEASANT
oil and butter for frying
8 oz / 225 g baby onions
8 oz / 225 g ham or bacon, cut
    up and the rind removed
½ bottle of red wine
8 oz / 225 g mushrooms
½ a head of celery
salt and pepper
water to cover

THE TRIMMINGS
These are important additions to go with the birds:
game chips – very finely cut chips, deep fried until crisp
dried breadcrumbs, fried and crisp
rolls of bacon, fried or grilled
bread sauce – see Index
redcurrant or rowan jelly
a green vegetable such as peas, beans or broccoli

For braising, put the jointed birds in a deep, flame-proof casserole. Grouse may be divided in half, pheasants in quarters. Brown the joints quickly in a mixture of oil and butter and set them aside.

Add the whole baby onions and the ham or bacon, cover the casserole and let them sweat for about 10 minutes. Return the joints to the casserole, add half the wine, the mushrooms, celery, salt and pepper to taste, and water to cover, and simmer very slowly for about an hour until tender.

Strain off the gravy and reduce it over heat to 1 pint / 600 ml. Add the remaining wine, re-heat and return to the casserole to serve.

Pheasant may be roasted the same way as grouse, though, as it is a larger bird, cook for about 50 minutes at 375°F / 190°C / gas 5.

For 2 to 4, dependent on the size

a brace of grouse
2 oz / 50 g butter
6 rashers of bacon
2 slices of bread
flour
2 fl oz / 50 ml water
¼ pint / 150 ml red wine
1 tsp / 5 ml Worcester sauce

ROAST GROUSE

Pluck and draw (clean out) the birds. Truss them neatly, putting a knob of butter in the cavity and laying the bacon rashers over the breast. Place each on a croûte – a slice of bread, fried. Roast in the oven at 400°F / 200°C / gas 6 for about 30 minutes. Just before the end, remove the bacon from the breast, dredge with flour, baste with the juice in the pan and return to the oven for a further 10 minutes or so.

Serve the grouse on the croûte. Make gravy in the pan by adding the water, red wine and Worcester sauce. The gravy should not be thickened.

WILD DUCK

Water birds are not hung as their flesh tends to go off. Pluck and draw the duck, removing the head. The feet should be twisted underneath, though I prefer to remove them.

Scald the bird in boiling salted water for a minute or so. Set it in the roasting pan. Season with salt and pepper, dredge with flour and baste it generously with butter.

Roast for about 30 minutes at 350°F / 180°C / gas 4. They are often eaten somewhat under-done. Or cook for 1 hour if you like them well done. Serve on a platter.

GRAVY

Add ½ pint / 300 ml red wine to the roasting pan and de-glaze it by stirring it over a low heat. Mix 1 tblsp / 15 ml cornflour with a little water and pour it into the pan, stirring until thickened. Flavour to taste with Worcester sauce and Bovril or a beef stock cube. Serve the gravy separately.

Duck is usually served with an orange salad. Peel 2 oranges as you would an apple, removing all the pith. Cut them in fine slices, removing the pips, and pour a little vinaigrette dressing over them. Serve with watercress.

PORK

My husband and I worked for 14 years in South Africa when the children were growing up. We were very lucky to have a home overlooking one of the best beaches in the Cape Peninsula at Fish Hoek.

Veronica's life was the beach and the boys in the life-saving club. She learnt to swim by the time she was three and had absolutely no fear of the water – a somewhat risky thing.

I always insisted that, though they could go to the beach after nine o'clock church on Sunday morning, they must always be home for Sunday lunch. It surprised me to find how few families ever sat down together for a proper meal.

The girls could bring home with them any companions they wished and I made sure I always had a really good meal ready. In the winter months this was usually a roast with all the trimmings, while in the summer we often had a barbecue – or braaivleis, as it was known – with chops, boerewors (a South African sausage speciality) or chicken.

Other friends, black, white and brown, would often join us and lunch could last until six in the evening.

ROAST PORK WITH CRACKLING

Take a leg or loin of pork, with the skin still on. Score the skin with a sharp knife right through to the fat. Weigh the joint and place it in a roasting tin. Rub the pork all over with salt and pepper, and some dripping or oil. Place 3 or 4 carrots, cut in chunks, and 3 or 4 whole onions alongside it. Put in the oven at 450°F / 220°C / gas 8 for about 20 minutes.

Reduce the oven heat to 325°F / 170°C / gas 3 and continue cooking until done: 35 to 40 minutes per 1lb / 450 g. The roast should be basted with the juices about 3 times during cooking. If the vegetables are getting too brown, remove them with a slotted spoon.

Dish up together with the vegetables. Serve with apple sauce or fried apple slices.

GRAVY

3 tblsp / 45 ml flour
1 pint / 600 ml boiling stock or
    water
1 tblsp / 15 ml soya sauce
1 tblsp / 15 ml lemon juice
salt and pepper

Pour off the fat from the juices in the roasting pan. (The fat will look transparent.) Place the roasting pan on a gentle heat and thicken the juice with the flour, stirring it in. Have ready the boiling stock and whisk it into the roux (the flour and juices mixture). Bring it to the boil, stirring constantly and season with the soya sauce, lemon juice, salt and pepper. Perhaps add a stock cube if the flavour is thin.

Serve in a gravy boat.

Pork is better with mashed potato rather than roast as the meat is so rich. Serve with a good green vegetable such as broccoli.

For 4

4 good sized chops
2 tblsp / 30 ml margarine
1 onion, finely chopped
1 tsp / 5 ml each of dried sage,
    thyme and chopped parsley
3 slices of white bread, crumbed,
    with crusts removed
2 tblsp / 30 ml tomato ketchup
1 apple, peeled, cored and cut
    up

STUFFED PORK CHOPS

Melt the margarine in a frying pan. Fry the chops quickly on both sides and put in a casserole dish. Add the chopped onion and fry gently until transparent. Add the herbs and breadcrumbs with salt and pepper to taste. Take off the heat.

Place the stuffing ingredients on top of the chops in the casserole, with some tomato ketchup on top of each. Pour enough water into the casserole to cover the bottom. Add the prepared apple. Put on the lid and bake in a moderate oven (350°F / 180°C / gas 4) for 1 hour. Add more water if it looks like drying out.

Serve from the casserole.

For 4

1 lb / 450 g stewing pork, as
    lean as possible
2 large onions
½ lb / 225 g carrots
3 tblsps / 45 ml flour, seasoned
    with salt and pepper
2 tblsp / 30 ml vinegar
2 tblsp / 30 ml Worcester sauce
2 tblsp / 30 ml tomato ketchup
2 tblsp / 30 ml soft brown sugar

SAVOURY STEW

Slice the carrots and onions. Cut up the meat, trimming off the fat. Put the flour in a plastic bag with the meat and shake it. This covers the meat with minimum mess.

Place the meat and vegetables alternately in a casserole. Mix separately the Worcester sauce, tomato ketchup, brown sugar and any leftover flour. Pour this over the casserole together with boiling water to cover. Put the casserole into a moderate oven (350°F / 180°C / gas 4) until it comes to the boil – about half an hour. Reduce the heat to 300°F / 150°C / gas 2. Put the lid on the casserole and leave to simmer for 2 hours.

Serve with plain boiled rice.

BARBECUED SPARE RIBS

Have the butcher slice through the ribs so that each rib is about 6" / 15cm long. Allow about 5 ribs per person.

Brown the ribs in some hot oil in a frying pan and then place in a casserole. Pour over them a barbecue sauce (see Index).

Cover the casserole and place in a moderate oven (350°F / 180°C / gas 4). Bake for about 45 minutes, being careful the spare ribs do not dry out. Add a little water if necessary.

Note: The barbecue sauce may be served separately with lamb chops or steak.

PORK CHOPS WITH NOODLES

For 4

1 lb / 450 g frying pork
a little oil for frying
¼ cabbage, 1 large or 2 small leeks, all shredded finely
4 stalks of celery, diced
12 oz / 350 g fine noodles or fettucini
1 red pepper, de-seeded and chopped
parsley

Cut the pork into bite-sized chunks and fry them in oil in a saucepan until browned and set them aside. Fry all the vegetables in the same oil for 3 minutes. Return the meat to the top of the vegetables in the pan, put on the lid and cook on a gentle heat, being sure it does not burn, for 15 minutes or until the vegetables are cooked.

Meanwhile, put on a big pan of salted water and bring to the boil. Add a tablespoon of oil and boil the noodles until done – 8 to 15 minutes according to how fine they are. Strain them.

Take a casserole and layer the vegetable / meat mixture alternately with the noodles, ending with noodles. Sprinkle chopped parsley and red pepper on the top and serve.

LEFTOVER PORK MEAT BALLS

For 4

12 oz / 350 g cooked pork
6 tblsp / 90 ml unsweetened apple sauce
1 tsp / 5 ml sage, chopped
2 tsp / 10 ml parsley, chopped
4 tblsp / 60 ml beansprouts
2 spring onions, chopped
grated rind of half a lemon
2 tsp / 10 ml soya sauce
2 tsp / 10 ml tomato ketchup
pepper
4 oz / 125 g blanched, chopped almonds

Chop the pork very finely in a food processor. Add the apple sauce, herbs, chopped beansprouts, spring onions, lemon rind, soya sauce, ketchup and pepper. Form this mixture into balls, roll them in the almonds and fry them until brown.

To vary this recipe, omit the apple, adding about 3 tablespoons of finely diced preserved ginger instead.

Instead of nuts, the balls can be coated in batter made with 3 oz / 75 g self-raising flour, salt, pepper and half a cup water mixed together. Chill the balls, dip them in the batter and deep-fry in oil. Serve either hot or cold with rice and sweet and sour sauce.

For 4 to 6

2 oz / 50 g each of butter and
    flour
½ pint / 300 ml milk
12 oz / 350 g cooked pork
1 tsp / 5 ml each of finely
    chopped parsley, grated onion
    and lemon juice
a dash of Worcester sauce
salt and pepper
1 egg beaten with 1 tblsp / 15
    ml water
¾ cup of fine dried breadcrumbs

CROQUETTES

First make a white sauce, melting the butter and stirring in the flour. Cook for a moment and then whisk in the milk and continue stirring until it boils and thickens.

Mince the meat or chop it in a food processor. Add the parsley, lemon juice, onion and Worcester sauce. Season with salt and pepper and stir in the cooked white sauce.

Chill the mixture for at least half an hour. Shape into rolls in your hand. Have ready 3 dishes filled thus: (1) seasoned flour; (2) the egg and water mixed together; (3) the breadcrumbs. Coat the rolls first in the flour, then in the egg and finally in the breadcrumbs, transferring them from one dish to the next with a fork.

Deep-fry the rolls in hot oil until brown. Drain them on paper towels. Serve with slices of lemon and a bunch of parsley.

A mushroom and spinach sauce is good with these rolls (*see* Sauces).

I do not know if the day will ever come again when people cure their own bacon and ham. I remember going with my grandmother round the cottages on Arran and seeing their pig hanging and being cured for their winter's supply.

Here are two recipes, one from Brodick Castle for a whole pig, and the other from Buchanan Castle, my great grandfather's home, for smoked ham. I find that I cannot buy saltpetre in Northern Ireland without a licence!

THE PIG

7 lb / 3 kg curing salt (rough, not table salt)
4 lb / 1.8 kg brown sugar
G lb / 125 g Jamaica (pimento) pepper
G lb / 125 g white pepper
G lb / 125 g ground cloves
G lb / 125 g baking soda

Mix all the ingredients thoroughly in a basin. Rub this mixture into each side, placing them flat on top of each other in a wooden tub. Change and rub every day for 21 days, giving each side its turn at the bottom of the tub.

Remove the sides, hang them up and allow to drip for a day. Then roll tightly and tie, keeping the strings 2" / 5 cm apart. Put a hanging string in the small end of the pig, cover it with muslin and hang in a cool, dry place.

¼ lb / 125 g black pepper
1 oz / 25 g saltpetre (from the
    chemist)

The ribs may be cut and used for bacon and the leg joints for ham. If the cure is too salty, steep it in water before cooking.

SMOKED HAM

This is sufficient to cure up to a 55 lb / 20 kg side

½ lb / 225 g brown sugar
2 oz / 50 g black pepper
2 oz / 50 g saltpetre
1 lb / 450 g bay salt
½ tblsp / 8 ml rough salt

Mix all the ingredients together and rub the ham with them, letting it lie in the mixture. Turn and rub every day for a week. Now add 4 lb / 1.8 kg black treacle to the mixture, basting the ham all over with it. Turn and baste daily for 6 weeks.

Hang and drain it for a day.

To smoke it, use wild juniper in a chimney or as narrow a place as possible and let the juniper smoulder with the ham hanging above it for 24 to 48 hours.

Tie and wrap as in the previous recipe and hang in a dry, cool place away from flies. It will keep for 6 months.

BOILED HAM

For a 4 lb / 1.8 kg ham:

6 peppercorns
1 carrot
1 bay leaf
1 onion
1 stick of celery

Soak the ham for 12 hours in cold water before cooking.

Put the ham in a saucepan with the ingredients and fresh water to cover. Bring to the boil and simmer for about 2¾ hours (40 minutes to the lb, 90 minutes to the kg, cooking time). The ham is then skinned. You can serve it in different ways:

COLD HAM:
Let it cool in the water to keep moist. Drain it and roll in dried breadcrumbs.

ROAST HAM (1):
Put the skinned ham in a roasting pan. Pour in a bottle of stout and ½ lb / 225 g demerara sugar. Put in the oven at 325°F / 170°C / gas 3 for 1 hour and baste it often with the boiling stout and sugar. Serve hot.

ROAST HAM (2):
Slice through the fat on the ham making a diamond pattern.

Stick a whole clove in the centre of each diamond.

Make a paste with 4 oz / 125 g soft brown sugar, 1 tblsp / 15 ml dry mustard and 2 tblsp / 30 ml of honey. Rub this all over the surface of the ham, and roast for 30 minutes 325°F / 170°C / gas 3.

Serve with mashed potato, a green vegetable and raisin sauce (see Sauces). Instead of the raisin sauce you can use slices of fried pineapple. Another option is caper sauce (see Sauces).

I always keep the ham stock to make either lentil or dried pea soup.

COLCANNON

For 4

1 lb / 450 g sliced back bacon, cut in pieces
1 large onion, sliced
1 lb / 450 g potatoes, or more
¼ to ½ cabbage
pepper, freshly ground

For my version of this Scots dish, you need a large, deep pan with a lid. I use an electric frying pan. Fry the bacon in its own fat and set it aside. Then fry the onion gently and set that aside.

Peel and slice the potatoes. Layer them to cover the bottom of the pan. On top of them put the onion and bacon. Slice the cabbage finely and pile it on top. Sprinkle with pepper. I find the bacon provides enough salt.

Put the lid on the pan and cook gently on a low heat for about 45 minutes. The potatoes on the bottom should be nice and brown and the cabbage just cooked in its own steam. Serve from the pan.

DEVILS ON HORSEBACK

For 4

12 rashers of streaky bacon
12 stoned prunes
toothpicks or skewers

Cut the rind off the bacon and stretch it with a knife. Wrap it around the prunes, holding it in place with the skewers or toothpicks.

Have the oven heated to 425°F / 220°C / gas 7. Put the Devils in a tin and bake for about 20 minutes. Serve as a savoury or for a light supper, about 3 Devils per person.

If you wish, the prunes may be stuffed with a little liver pâté (see Index).

SKINKLADA

For 4

This ham recipe was given to my mother on a visit to Sweden. For their honeymoon my father took my mother on a walking tour up through Sweden and down through

Norway. Later she revisited some of the friends she had made. Alice Wallenberg was one of them. Her husband's cousin had been helping thousands of Jews to escape from the Nazis under his diplomatic cover. At the end of the war he disappeared, believed to have been abducted by the Russians, and was never found, though for many years there were rumours that he had been seen in Russia.

8 oz / 225 g fat, smoked ham
4 eggs
1 pint / 600 ml milk
2 tblsp / 30 ml flour

Cut the ham into small squares and fry in its own fat. Place this in a buttered pie dish with the fat from the frying.

Beat the eggs and mix in the flour and milk. Pour this mixture over the ham in the pie dish and put in a hot oven (425°F / 220°C / gas 7) for 20 minutes until puffed and golden.

For 4 to 6

TOAD IN THE HOLE

Make this the same way as Skinklada, using 1 lb / 450 g sausages in place of the ham. The sausages should be lightly fried before adding the batter.

For 4

RAGMUNKER (from Sweden)

1 onion
1 lb / 450 g potatoes
8 oz / 225 g bacon, finely chopped
4 oz / 125 g flour
1 egg
¼ pint / 150 ml milk
a little oil for frying

Slice the onion and fry until soft. Grate the raw potatoes and mix them in a bowl with the onion, bacon, flour, egg and milk. Leave it to swell for 1 hour.

Take a frying pan and heat a little oil in it. Drop the mixture from a spoon into the pan in dollops and fry as pancakes on both sides. Drain on a paper towel and serve hot.

VEAL

In 1949 I decided that I had had enough of school. My mother did not know it, but a stand-up row with my headmistress led to a parting of the ways. I had been to London for a dance and yet again was late back to school. My headmistress let fly. I said not a word, but determined that that was it. So there I was, at 17, not knowing what next.

I had been invited a couple of years before by Scottish friends to the Moral Re-armament international conference at Caux in Switzerland, which had been established as a centre for post-war reconciliation. I was fascinated to see there the first meetings between French and Germans and many others after all the horrors of the war, and the costly reconciliations which had such a part in laying the foundations for the new Europe.

Many of us who were young longed to make sure we never

KATE CROSS

had to experience such a war again, and I felt that perhaps Caux offered me an opportunity to do something worthwhile. When I arrived there I was invited by a remarkable Canadian, Kate Cross, to work with her and other volunteers in the kitchen.

Kate, with her marvellous head of flaring white hair, had an infectious enthusiasm for food and its imaginative presentation. Rumour had it that she was the inspiration for the wartime song,

'K – K – K – Katie, beautiful Katie,
I'll be waiting at the k – k – k – kitchen door!'

She intrigued me with the idea of cooking as an important and natural way to care for people. She believed that meals should create the atmosphere for people to talk freely and openly. She sometimes took me by surprise by telling how Christ used meals to bring healing – quite a new idea to me.

Soon I was preparing lunch or dinner for up to a thousand people at a time – heads of state, coal-miners, industrialists and housewives from 50 or more countries. It was the beginning of work which in the next 15 years before I married took me to Germany, Sweden, Britain, the United States, India and Africa, very often cooking, though sometimes as a change working backstage in theatre productions. The kitchen, however, always seemed to draw me back. Not everyone understood what I was up to, but I was certain that this was what I wanted to do. And, looking back on 40 years, I am more than ever glad I took that decision.

At Caux, whenever I had prepared a recipe which I liked, Kate would always say, 'Write it down. Write it down!' So I suppose that was the beginning of this book.

Veal is much more a continental than a British speciality. At Caux I was soon cooking Wiener Schnitzel by the hundred.

WEINER SCHNITZEL

For 4

1½ lb / 700 g veal steaks
4 tblsp / 60 ml flour, seasoned with salt, pepper and paprika
1 egg mixed with 2 tblsp / 30 ml milk
oz / 125 g dried breadcrumbs

Cut any fat or gristle from the meat. Pound the meat with either a meat mallet or a rolling-pin to tenderise it. Have 3 plates lined up, the first with the seasoned flour, the second with the egg mixed with milk, and the third with the breadcrumbs. Dip the steaks in the flour, then in the egg on both sides, and finally in the breadcrumbs. Heat a little oil in a frying pan and fry the

41 lemon, cut in quarters

steaks on both sides till brown. Drain them on a paper towel and serve at once with the quartered lemon. This dish is often served with red cabbage and mashed potato or noodles. Pork or turkey can be used if veal is not available.

For 4

4 slices of bacon, chopped finely
1½ lb / 700 g veal steak cut in thin slices
2 tblsp / 30 ml oil
2 tblsp / 30 ml onion, chopped
1 tsp / 5 ml paprika
salt and pepper
4 fl oz / 125 ml tomato ketchup
8 fl oz / 225 ml sour cream
chopped parsley

PAPRIKA CREAM SCHNITZEL

Fry the chopped bacon gently and set aside. Pound the veal to tenderise and fry quickly in hot oil on both sides to brown. Set it aside also.

Turn down the heat under the pan and add the chopped onion, fry it gently until soft and golden. Return the veal and bacon to the pan. Season well with salt, pepper and paprika. Add the tomato ketchup and sour cream, cover the pan and cook very slowly for 20 minutes, taking care it does not burn. Or it may be baked in a casserole for 1 hour in a slow oven (300°F / 150°C / gas 2). Serve sprinkled with chopped parsley.

You can use 3 fresh tomatoes instead of the ketchup, skinning them in boiling water and scooping out the seeds.

For 6

6 veal cutlets or steaks
2 fl oz / 60 ml olive oil
2 tblsp / 30 ml flour, seasoned with salt and pepper
1 medium onion, cut fine
½ pint / 300 ml chicken or white stock
4 oz / 125 g mushrooms
½ oz / 15 g butter
1 green pepper, cut in strips
6 stuffed olives, sliced (or more if wished)
Marinade
1 tsp / 5 ml salt
1 tsp / 5 ml paprika
4 fl oz / 125 ml salad oil
2 fl oz / 60 ml lemon juice
1 tsp / 5 ml prepared mustard
¼ tsp / 1 ml grated nutmeg
½ tsp / 2 ml sugar
1 clove garlic, crushed

VEAL SCALLOPINI

Mix together all the marinade ingredients and place the cutlets in this for 2 hours.

Heat the olive oil in a heavy, deep pan (which has a lid). Drain the cutlets from the marinade and coat them with the seasoned flour. Fry them quickly on both sides in the hot oil to brown. Set them aside.

Turn down the heat under the pan and gently fry the chopped onion until soft and golden. Add the stock to the onion and bring to the boil. Return the cutlets to the pan, cover it and simmer for 1 hour or until tender.

In a separate pan sauté the mushrooms in the butter and add them to the veal together with the sliced green pepper 5 minutes before serving.

To serve, lay the cutlets along one side of the platter and the strained vegetables along the other. Pour some of the gravy over the meat and sprinkle the sliced olives on top. Decorate with parsley.

BLANQUETTE DE VEAU A L'ANCIENNE

For 8

3 lb / 1½ kg boneless veal
  shoulder cut in bite-size pieces
2½ pints / 1.5 litres chicken
  stock
1 large onion, chopped
2 celery tops
1 leek, white part only
1 tsp / 5 ml dried thyme
1 bay leaf
4 sprigs of parsley
1 tsp / 5 ml salt
20 baby onions
1 lb / 450 g button mushrooms
1 tblsp / 15 ml lemon juice
2 oz / 50 g butter or margarine
1 oz / 25 g flour
2 egg yolks
½ pint / 275 ml double cream
salt and white pepper
chopped parsley to decorate

Blanch the veal: place in a saucepan, cover with cold water and bring to the boil, boiling for 1 minute. Remove the veal immediately.

Wash the saucepan, return the veal to it and add 2 pints / 1 litre of the chicken stock, the chopped onion, celery tops and leeks with the thyme, bay leaf, parsley sprigs and salt.

Bring all this to the boil over a moderate heat. Skim off any surface scum. Reduce the heat and simmer, partially covered, for 1½ to 2 hours.

Half an hour before the meal take the remaining chicken stock, bring it to the boil in another saucepan, add the baby onions, cover and simmer for 20 minutes. Transfer the onions to a large casserole with a slotted spoon and keep warm. Put the mushrooms and lemon juice into the same stock and cook for 5 minutes. Strain and add them to the onions. Add the remaining stock to the veal.

When the meat is cooked, add it to the onions and mushrooms in the casserole, leaving behind the vegetables and the stock it has cooked in. Strain this stock through a fine sieve into another pot, pressing hard on the vegetables, but do not rub them through the sieve. Skim off any fat and boil to reduce the liquid to about 1 pint / 600 ml.

Make a beurre manié with the butter and flour (mashed together until well mixed). Drop this little by little into the boiling stock, whisking it well all the time. Turn the heat down and simmer for 10 minutes, stirring frequently so that it does not burn.

Remove the pot from the heat. Blend the egg yolks well with the cream and whisk into the sauce. Place the pan over a pot of boiling water and stir until the egg is cooked. Taste and season with salt, white pepper and lemon juice.

Pour the sauce over the meat and vegetables in the casserole. Re-heat in a moderate oven for 5 to 10 minutes. It must not boil or the sauce will curdle.

To serve, sprinkle chopped parsley over it. Traditionally, this dish should be served with noodles.

In Britain, where veal is very expensive, you can use pork or turkey breast.

VEAU ÉMINENCE

For 4

1½ lb / 700 g veal cut in thin
    slices from the round
butter and oil for frying
1 tblsp / 15 ml flour seasoned
    with 1 tsp / 5 ml salt and
    ¼ tsp / 1 ml white pepper
4 tblsp / 60 ml grated parmesan
    cheese
1 pint / 600 ml cream

Fry the veal slices on both sides in butter and oil until tender. Sprinkle them with the seasoned flour.

Cover the bottom of a casserole dish with a layer of meat, then a layer of parmesan cheese and repeat the layers ending with the cheese. Pour the cream over the top and place in a moderate oven (350°F / 180°C / gas 4) for half an hour until just brown.

Serve with tomatoes stuffed with chopped eggs, and pasta.

VEAL PROKOFIEV

For 4

1 tblsp / 15 ml oil
1 level tblsp / 15 g butter
1½ lb / 700 g roast of veal
    which has been boned and
    rolled
the bones from the roast
12 small onions
2 tblsp / 30 ml cognac
salt and pepper
½ pint / 300 ml water
2 carrots
4 oranges
1 wine-glass of dry white wine
½ tsp / 3 ml cornflour

Put the oil and butter in a deep flame-proof casserole dish and heat it. Add to it the veal roast and the bones and brown on all sides. Set this aside.

Add the onions to the casserole. When they are golden, return the meat and bones. Add the cognac and flame it with a match or taper. Add some salt and pepper and the water. Peel and cut the carrots into rounds and add them.

Cover the casserole and cook for a good hour on a low heat. Then add the juice of 3 oranges, the white wine and cook for another 20 minutes.

Take out the veal and the bones. Pass the juice through a sieve and return to the casserole. Mix the cornflour in a little water and add it to the juice. Bring this to the boil.

Cut the fourth orange in slices and fry them in a clean pan.

To serve the roast, carve it into slices. Pour the juice over it and decorate with the fried rounds of orange. This is good served with fried rice.

FRIED RICE
1 onion, finely sliced
a little oil for frying
¾ pint / 450 ml rice
1½ pints / 900 ml chicken stock

Fry the onion in some oil until golden. Add the rice and fry it. Add the chicken stock and bring to the boil, then simmer until the water is absorbed. Turn off the heat, cover the pan and keep warm until ready to serve. Before serving, fork it up and turn into a heated dish. Sprinkle with chopped parsley.

STUFFED BREAST OF VEAL

For 6 to 8

Stuffing
1 oz / 25 g butter
½ onion, finely chopped
8 oz / 250 g chopped spinach
1 tsp / 5 ml oregano
salt and freshly ground black
    pepper
8 oz / 250 g sausage meat
1 beaten egg
1 tblsp / 15 ml chopped parsley

3 lb / 1½ kg breast of veal,
    boned
1 tblsp / 15 ml lemon juice
1 oz / 25 g butter or margarine
2 tblsp / 30 ml olive oil

Melt the butter in a saucepan. Fry the onion gently until transparent. Add the spinach, cover and cook it for about 10 minutes on a very low heat. Add the oregano and the seasoning. Tip the sausage meat into a bowl, add the spinach mixture and the beaten egg and parsley. Mix all well together.

Open out the veal breast, skin side down. Lay the stuffing mixture in the centre. Roll it up neatly and tie with string. Put it in a roasting tin and pour over the lemon juice. Dust it with flour and baste it with the butter and oil.

Roast it in a slow oven (325°F / 170°C / gas 3) for about 2 hours, basting frequently with the juices from the pan.

To serve, take out the roast and keep warm. Make a gravy as for the roast pork.

VEAL SHAPE

For 4 to 6

1½ lb / 700 g veal on the bone
8 oz / 225 g gammon steak
1 pint / 600 ml chicken stock
1 lemon
pepper and salt
3 hard-boiled eggs

From my maternal great-grandmother's cook.

Stew the veal and gammon steak in the stock, with a slice of the lemon rind without the pith, for about 2 hours until tender, adding more stock if needed.

Take the meat out of the stock and cut it up into small pieces (about ½" / 1 cm), removing any fat and bone. Grate the remaining lemon rind finely and add it to the meat. Strain the stock into a bowl, skimming off any fat. Add the lemon juice and season to taste. Allow to cool.

Pour enough of the cold stock into a plain, flattish mould to just cover the bottom and put it into the fridge to set. Slice the hard-boiled egg and place on top of the stock which has set. Pour a little more stock over the eggs to hold them in place and allow that to set. Pile the meat gently on top, smoothing it flat, and pour over it the remaining stock. Leave to set for at least six hours or overnight.

When ready to serve, dip the mould for 30 seconds in a basin of hot water, being careful the water does not get into the mould, and invert it onto a platter so that the shape drops out. This can be decorated with watercress around the bottom and served with a salad of sliced tomatoes.

BEEF

My grandmother kept a herd of pedigree Red Poll cattle on Arran. Every year she would send the three-week-old calves which she culled over to the mainland farm at Gartincaber on my grandfather's Buchanan estates to be castrated, fattened and sold at the Stirling Market.

One year Alec Miller, the farm grieve at Gartincaber, received the usual consignment of calves. That evening, going the rounds as he did each night, his eye was caught by one particular bull calf. He called his wife and said to her, 'See, Liz, the way that that wee fellow stands and holds himself. There's no way I'll castrate him!'

So, unbeknownst to my grandmother, Alec took on the calf as his own particular project and Mrs Miller reared him by hand, dosing him with whisky added to his bottle when he became quite sick. Two years later, in 1953, Alec, on his own initiative, entered the bull at the Royal Highland Show and, to his pride and delight – and my grandmother's astonishment – 'Isle of Arran Exile' won the cup as the show's best Red Poll animal.

ROAST BEEF (sirloin or topside)

It is worth buying a good-sized roast, even if it seems expensive, as the next day it is lovely cold, and the following third day can make shepherd's pie.

Either 5 lb / 2.3 kg sirloin – this usually has a bone
or 4 lb / 1.8 kg topside – this has no bone
2 tsp / 10 ml made-up mustard
1 or 2 garlic cloves (optional)
freshly ground pepper
a selection of vegetables for roasting

Pre-heat the oven to 425°F / 220°C / gas 7. Put the joint in a roasting pan and season with about 1 tsp salt and pepper. Smear it with mustard – French or English – or, alternatively, make slits in the meat and push in slivers of cut-up garlic. After seasoning, smear again with oil or dripping.

In our family we love to roast vegetables alongside the meat – half a carrot, half an onion, a Jerusalem artichoke if you have one, or some parsnip or turnip, per person in any selection. Place them around the roast. If they get done too quickly, simply remove them with a slotted spoon to the serving dish and keep warm.

Put the joint into the hot oven and sear (brown) it for 15 minutes to seal in the juices. Then turn the oven down to 325°F / 160°C / gas 3 and roast as directed in the Roasting Table (see p.304), basting it with the fat in the pan.

When the roasting is finished, place the joint on a serving dish, cover and leave it to rest in a warm place. This helps it to finish cooking and to distribute the juices evenly.

Make the gravy. Remove the vegetables from the roasting pan. Pour off any excess fat. Deglaze the pan by pouring stock or water into it and stirring around until all the juice is melted. Taste for flavouring. Add Worcester sauce or a stock cube if necessary, and soya sauce – 2 tblsp / 30 ml for 1 pint / 600 ml. It may also be thickened with cornflour, mixed with a little cold water and then well whisked in.

ROAST POTATOES
6-8 oz / 175-225 g per person according to appetite
4 tblsp / 60 ml dripping or oil

Peel the potatoes. Bring them quickly to the boil in a small amount of water and cook them gently with the lid on for 10 minutes.

Meanwhile, if there is no room in the roasting pan, put the oil in another small pan and put it on the shelf above the roast in the oven. Remove the parboiled potatoes from the water – keep it for the gravy – and place them in the roasting pan, turning them so that they are covered with the oil. Roast for about 1 hour, turning them around at least once while they cook. Then put them in an uncovered dish to preserve the crisp skin.

For 4

6 tblsp / 90 ml plain flour
2 eggs
½ pint / 300 ml milk

YORKSHIRE PUDDING

Sift the flour into a mixing bowl. Make a well in the centre and drop the eggs into it. Add some of the milk. With a wooden spoon start beating them, gradually incorporating the flour. Add about half the milk and beat for about 100 strokes. This will remove any lumps. Add the rest of the milk and set the batter aside to rest for at least half an hour.

When you take the roast out of the oven, turn the oven up to 400°F / 200°C / gas 6. Put a little oil or dripping in the bottom of a square tin or in patty pans and place in the oven to heat for at least 5 minutes.

Take the pan out of the oven and pour in the batter to half fill it. Return at once to the oven and cook for about 15 minutes for the patty pans or 30 minutes for the big pudding, until puffed and golden.

I have put these different elements together so that when you cook a roast dinner, all the recipes are readily available. The method I find best is:

(1.) Turn on the oven.

(2.) Prepare the potatoes.

(3.) Prepare the roast and the vegetables to go with it.

(4.) When the oven is fully heated, put in the roast and vegetables. Remember to turn the oven down after 15 minutes and to baste the joint from time to time while cooking. Add the parboiled potatoes for the last hour of cooking.

(5.) Make the batter for the Yorkshire pudding. Leave it to rest for half an hour before baking it.

BRANDIED PEPPER STEAK

For 4

1½ lb / 700 g good frying steak or T-bone steak
1½ tblsp / 20 ml freshly ground black pepper
2 tblsp / 30 ml olive oil
2 tblsp / 30 ml brandy
1 tblsp / 15 ml Worcester sauce

If you can get a butcher to cut your steak to order, have him cut it 1½" / 4 cm thick. Choose the meat carefully, being sure it is marbled, with flecks of fat through it. This dish is spectacular if cooked in front of the diners. For this you will need an electric frying pan unless you are eating in the kitchen.

Prepare the steak in 4 portions and lay it in a flat dish. Grind the pepper and push it well into the steak. Pour the olive oil over the steak and leave it to marinade for at least half an hour. Cook the steak only when ready to eat it.

Have a hot frying pan ready. Put in the oil from the marinade and, when this is hot, add the steaks. Cook them for 5 minutes on each side if you like them rare, longer if preferred well done. If the steak is cut more thinly, cook for less time.

When the steak is cooked, season with salt, pour the brandy over it and set it alight. Serve once the flames have died down. Deglaze the pan with the Worcester sauce and a little water. Pour this *jus* over the steak. This is delicious served with mashed potato, peas and perhaps mushrooms or tomatoes.

FILET MIGNON

For 6 to 8

2 tblsp / 30 ml chopped parsley
2 oz / 50 g butter
2 ½ lb / 1 kg fillet

Fillet is the most expensive cut of beef. It is taken from the underside of sirloin. If you have a freezer big enough to take a side of beef you will get 1 fillet of about 2½ lb / 1 kg.

salt and pepper
4 oz / 125 g fat bacon
1 tblsp / 15 ml Worcester sauce

First prepare the parsley butter. Beat chopped parsley into the softened butter. Shape it into a roll on greaseproof paper and put it in the fridge to harden while the oven is heating to 400°F / 200°C / gas 6.

Put the fillet in a roasting pan. Season it with a little salt and pepper to taste. Lay the fat bacon over the top to cover it – the bacon itself is a little salty. Set the fillet in the oven and roast for half an hour (more, if you like it less rare). Take it out of the oven and let it rest in a warm place for 10 minutes before carving.

Meanwhile, deglaze the roasting tin with a little water and the Worcester sauce. Serve this in a gravy boat.

To serve, carve the meat ½" / 1.2 cm thick. Top each slice with a pat of parsley butter cut from the roll. The meat should be brown outside and pink inside.

For 8

FILET DE BOEUF WELLINGTON

I served this when my father came to stay with us in the Cape. It was a great success and I was especially pleased as he ran a herd of pedigree beef cattle on his farm in what was then Rhodesia, now Zimbabwe. The dish is more economical than Filet Mignon on its own. It is best prepared in the morning for an evening meal. There are three distinct elements to the dish:
1. 2½ lb / 1 kg fillet
2. 2½ lb puff-pastry, which should be prepared at least 2 hours before needed
3. Forcemeat or stuffing

Have a hot oven (425°F / 210°C / gas 7) ready. Put the fillet in a roasting tin, season it with salt and pepper and smear it all over with 4 oz / 225 g butter. Roast it in the oven 20 minutes for rare, 25 minutes for medium and 30 minutes for well done. Take the fillet out of the oven and leave it aside to cool.

FORCEMEAT/STUFFING
1½ oz / 35 g butter
1 onion, finely chopped
2 spring onions, including the green part, finely sliced
½ lb / 225 g mushrooms, finely chopped
2 slices white bread, crusts removed

Melt the butter in a frying pan. Add the onion and spring onions and cook them gently until soft. Add the chopped mushrooms and cook. Turn off the heat and crumb the bread, adding it to the pan with the chopped ham, tomato purée and basil. Season to taste and leave until cold.

When the meat and forcemeat are cold, take the prepared puff pastry, roll it out to an oblong, wide and long enough to enclose the fillet. Trim off any extra. Drain the fillet or the

3 oz / 75 g minced or finely
chopped ham
3 tblsp / 45 ml tomato purée
1tsp / 5 ml dried basil

pastry may become soggy. Place it in the centre of the pastry. Mound the forcemeat along the top of the fillet. Brush the edges of the pastry with water and fold them up to the top, enclosing the fillet. Seal the ends and crimp along the top edges to form a decorative line.

Roll out any spare bits of pastry, cut them into strips and place them over the roll as decoration. Paint the roll with the beaten yolk of 1 egg and place in the fridge until ready to cook, just before the meal.

Re-heat the oven to the same hot temperature, brush a baking sheet with water and place on it the fillet in its pastry case, making 2 or 3 slits along the top to allow steam to escape, otherwise it will split. Bake for 20 minutes or until golden brown and serve at once. This may sound complicated but it is very simple to do at the end when time counts most.

POT ROASTS

The following recipe comes from Germany, a country to which I owe much – for one thing my great-great-grandmother was German. I first visited Germany in the winter of 1950 to join a group from Caux showing a stage play, on the invitation of industrialists and trade union leaders, all through the cities of that great industrial heartland of the Ruhr. The country was just beginning to get on its feet again, but most of those cities were still in ruins. The play, with humour and depth, dramatised clashes in family and factory and the bridging of division.

So off I set from London together with Betty Belk, the daughter of an American banker. In my innocence I had with me three suitcases and a hatbox! We took the boat to Holland from where we were to get the train to Gelsenkirchen. We spoke not one word of Dutch or German.

We found a train and the ticket collector came round. We showed him our tickets. 'No, no! You are on the wrong train. This one goes to Essen.' So, what to do? We had 7 Dm between us, and our sandwiches, but, naive as we were, no address as we expected to be met at our destination. Finally one of our companions in the compartment of eight spoke up. She was German, married to a British soldier, and was returning on a visit to her family; she was going to Essen and would put us onto the train to Gelsenkirchen. The generosity of that family! She and her parents gave us tea in the station café – served in a tall glass with lemon, and saw us on our way. Later we visited them in their home. They lived in one room up a ruined staircase in a bombed-out house.

Eventually we reached Gelsenkirchen and there were our friends, seven of them, on the platform. They had been meeting every train for two hours! After a meal we were taken to the family with whom we were to stay. He was a foreman in the mines, with his wife and three small boys. They lived in one of the first new houses built after the war. There was a kitchen with a sink on the ground floor, two rooms for the parents and the boys upstairs, and in the attic our room.

Our hostess met us on the doorstep, full of apologies. They had no kopfkissen. What were these? Finally we understood – no pillows. I still remember those beds, with the mattresses made out of three sections pushed together, and the two cotton blankets. The only water was at the kitchen sink. We were lucky compared to some of our friends who had only a curtained-off area of the one room that was the entire family home. It must have been harder for Betty than for me. I at least was used to no heating in Scotland. That family shared with us all they had – from soup with meat in it on Sunday, to bread with, perhaps, a little cheese by the end of the week.

Every night we would show the play and, afterwards, meet and talk with the audience, many of whom were Communists, with all the post-war bitterness. In the mornings there would be schools to visit and, later on in the day, meetings in beer halls to speak at. Others have written better than I can of that time, but I do know what it did for me: taking a young girl excited and looking forward to 'come out' for the London social season and be presented at Court, and showing her what the real world was like.

All during the following summer conferences at Caux in Switzerland, delegations of management and workers would come. We always had extra helpings of food for them. It is hard, today, to grasp the deprivation of that time in Germany, now that it is so prosperous. I will never forget the young people. Everything they had been taught to believe in shattered; all their hopes gone. Could they trust anyone? It was this experience that made me question what I was going to do with my life. I certainly never imagined that cooking was to play such a big part!

BAVARIAN POT ROAST or SAUERBRATEN

The best cut for this is brisket or silverside. The brisket may be on the bone, or boned and rolled. The recipe needs to be planned in advance as it takes 4 or 5 days to marinade the meat before it is cooked. It is an inexpensive joint and can be served for a large crowd – this recipe will serve at least 12 people – but it can be used next day as cold meat.

5½ -6 lb / 2.5-3 kg brisket or silverside

Marinade

1 pint / 600 ml each of vinegar and water
8 cloves, gently bruised
1 scraped parsley root
1 tsp / 5 ml whole peppercorns
2 bay leaves, 2 sprigs green celery leaves, 1 sprig thyme and 2 crushed juniper berries, all tied together in a muslin bag
1 large onion, finely sliced
2 cloves garlic, crushed
1 tsp / 10 ml salt

OTHER INGREDIENTS

1 pint / 600 ml beef stock
1 tblsp / 15 ml brown sugar
8 tblsp / 120 ml tomato purée
1½ pints / 1 litre red wine
1 tblsp / 15 ml lemon juice
2 or 3 strips of lemon peel
4 gingersnap biscuits, crumbled
1 tblsp / 15 ml Worcester sauce

POTATO BALLS

12 large potatoes
1 tblsp / 15 ml flour
1 tblsp / 15 ml farola
3 eggs, slightly beaten
a grating of nutmeg
½ cup crumbed, crisply fried bread
salt

Combine the marinade ingredients in a china, glass or earthenware dish (not iron or aluminium as these will corrode). Add the meat and cover with a tea-towel. Turn it twice a day for at least 4 or 5 days.

Melt some lard, bacon fat or oil and brown the meat on all sides. Meanwhile, put the marinade on to boil and reduce it by half. Transfer the meat to a large, deep casserole. Add the reduced marinade plus all the other ingredients.

Be sure the meat is generously covered with liquid. If it is not, add more stock. Cover the casserole with a lid and set in a warm oven (325°F / 160°C / gas 3) for 3½ to 4 hours. Turn the meat over once during the cooking. You will know it is cooked when a knife goes into it easily. When done, take the meat out and set on a warm platter.

GRAVY

Strain the juice in which the meat has cooked through a fine sieve into a fresh saucepan and bring to the boil. To thicken the gravy, mix 2-4 tblsp / 30-60 ml flour with half a cup of cold water, whisking till smooth. Pour through a sieve into the boiling stock, stirring constantly. Bring it back to the boil.

Carve the meat and pour some of the gravy over it. Put the rest of the gravy into a hot sauceboat to serve separately.

This dish is traditionally served with a side dish of potato balls.

Peel and boil the potatoes. Mash them and let them cool. When cold, add the flour, farola, eggs, nutmeg, fried breadcrumbs and salt to taste. Mix them thoroughly together.

Put a pan of salted water on to boil. Shape the potato mixture into balls the size of a walnut and drop them, a few at a time, into the boiling water. Lower the heat and leave to simmer for 20 minutes.

Sauerbraten can alternatively be served with buttered noodles and red cabbage with chestnuts, and you can, of course, halve the quantities for a smaller number of people.

STOFFATO (An Italian-style pot roast)

For 8

3 lb / 1.2 kg silverside
2 cloves garlic
bouillon or stock to cover the roast
a little oil to fry the meat
12 peppercorns
1 onion, chopped
1 celeriac root, cut up
1-2 leeks, washed and sliced
1 glass red wine
4 tblsp / 60 ml tomato purée
1 sprig thyme
2 tblsp / 30 ml cornflour and cold water to mix
1 red pepper
1 green pepper
1 bunch of parsley

Peel and cut the garlic into slivers. Take a sharp knife and prick the meat, pushing the garlic into the holes. Put the stock on to boil in a large pan with the peppercorns.

Heat the oil in a frying pan. Put the meat in to brown on all sides then transfer it to the boiling stock. Turn the heat down under the frying pan and gently fry the onion, celeriac and leeks until soft, but not coloured. Add them to the meat together with the glass of red wine, the tomato purée and a sprig of thyme. Simmer gently for 2 to 3 hours with the lid slightly lifted to stop it boiling over.

Take the meat out and carve it into slices. Lay it on a platter. Strain off the vegetables. They may be served at the side of the meat.

Thicken the gravy by adding cornflour mixed with cold water to the boiling stock. Check the seasoning and pour the gravy over the meat.

Decorate with chopped red and green peppers and a bunch of parsley.

For 4

cold roast beef
4 large mushrooms, sliced
2 oz / 50 g butter
2 tblsp / 30 ml flour
½ pint / 300 ml consommé or
 stock
2 tblsp / 30 ml lemon juice *or*
 4 tblsp / 60 ml red wine
2 tblsp / 30 ml fine, dried
 breadcrumbs

MIROTON DU BOEUF

This is good for using up nice slices of beef or lamb left from the Sunday roast.

Very thinly slice enough cold roast beef for 4. Lay them in a casserole.

Fry the mushrooms in most of the butter, keeping back a little. When cooked, sprinkle them with the flour. Stir it in and add the consommé with the lemon juice or red wine. Bring it to the boil, stirring it until thickened.

Pour it over the meat slices. Sprinkle the breadcrumbs over the top and dot with the remaining butter. Bake at 350°F / 180° C / gas 4 for about half an hour until nicely browned.

For 6 to 8

2 lb / 1 kg fillet of beef
2 oz / 50 g butter
½ lb / 225 g onions, chopped
½ lb / 225 g mushrooms, sliced
salt
nutmeg
½ pint / 300 ml sour cream

BEEF STROGANOFF

Cut the fillet into 1" / 2.5 cm thick slices. Pound with a wooden mallet or rolling-pin until the slices are very thin. Then cut into neat, finger-long strips.

Melt half the butter in a heavy frying pan. Add the onion and cook it gently until soft and yellow. Set this aside. Turn up the heat under the pan, adding more butter if needed. Cook the meat strips quickly in the pan to brown them on both sides. Push the meat to one side and add the remaining butter and sliced mushrooms. When they are soft, return the onion to the pan. Season delicately with salt and nutmeg. Add the sour cream and check the seasoning. Heat it through.

It may be served on a platter surrounded either with wild or ordinary rice decorated with chopped parsley. A mixture of peas and carrots looks good with this dish.

For 10 to 12

3 lb / 1½ kg lean beef *or* 1 lb / 500 g each of beef, lamb and pork

3 tblsp / 45 ml oil

2 cloves of garlic, crushed

1 lb / 500 g onions

2 tsp / 10 ml paprika

1 pint / 600 ml tomato juice

1 pint / 600 ml stock *or* ½ pint / 300 ml each of stock and Burgundy wine

3 tblsp / 45 ml flour

½ pint / 300 ml whole cooked baby carrots

½ pint / 300 ml cooked onions

½ pint / 300 ml cooked lima beans

1 tsp / 5 ml marjoram

½ pint / 300 ml tomato wedges, skinned

1 tblsp / 15 ml green pepper, chopped

4 fl oz / 125 ml sour cream

MEAT LOAF

1 lb / 450 g steak mince

½ onion, grated

2 slices wholewheat bread, crumbed

a pinch of cayenne

¼ pint / 150 ml milk

1 tsp / 5 ml salt

¼ tsp / 1 ml pepper

BARBECUE SAUCE

¼ pint / 150 ml tomato ketchup

2 tblsp / 30 ml soft brown sugar

1 tblsp / 15 ml Worcester sauce

2 tblsp / 30 ml mustard

HUNGARIAN GOULASH

Use Hungarian paprika if available, but do not use black pepper. I make a lot of stew at one time and freeze the extra in suitable portions for later use.

Cut off any excess fat from the meat and cut the meat into cubes. Heat the oil in a heavy pan and brown the meat well on all sides. Do not put too much meat in at once or it will simply make juice. Lay the meat aside as you brown it. When it is all browned, turn the heat down under the pan, add the onions and garlic, and cook until soft.

Add the paprika and the tomato juice and stock (and Burgundy) to the pan. Bring to the boil. Return the meat to the pan and simmer it slowly until very tender – about 2 hours. Skim off any excess fat from the stew.

About 20 minutes before the end of cooking, add the cooked baby carrots, onions and lima beans, plus the marjoram. It may be thickened with a paste of the flour whisked together with 4 fl oz / 125 ml of water. Pour this paste through a sieve into the boiling stew, stirring constantly.

About 5 minutes before serving, add the tomato wedges, green pepper and sour cream.

Serve with chopped parsley sprinkled on top.

DEVILLED MEAT LOAF WITH BARBECUE SAUCE

Mix together all the loaf ingredients. Shape them into a loaf on a baking tray. Cover with the barbecue sauce, which is made by simply mixing all the sauce ingredients together. Cover the top of the loaf with the sauce and bake for 45 minutes in the oven, preheated to 350°C / 180°C / gas 4. Serve hot.

For 6 to 8

1 lb / 500 g minced steak
1 lb / 500 g minced bacon or
   ham, preferably smoked
12 oz / 350 g soft breadcrumbs
1 tsp / 5 ml pepper
grated nutmeg to taste
2 tsp / 10 ml salt
2 eggs

MEAT ROLL

Mix the meat, breadcrumbs, spices and salt. Add the beaten eggs and mix them in. Knead the meat into a large ball and place in a well-greased pudding basin. Cover with a margarine paper and a cloth, tied down. Place in a pot of boiling water, to which 1 tablespoon of vinegar has been added, to come halfway up the side. Cover the pot with a lid and boil for 3 hours, refilling as necessary.

To serve, remove the butter paper and turn out the roll onto a platter. Pour over it a well-flavoured sauce of your choice (e.g. mushroom, tomato, curry). The dish can be served cold. Pour off excess juice and place a saucer with a weight on it on top and press the meat until cold before turning out.

For 6

1 lb / 500 g shoulder of beef,
   minced (or use good mince)
4 oz / 125 g salt pork, minced
6 slices of wholewheat bread
1 egg, lightly beaten
½ tsp / 3 ml each of sugar, all-
   spice, nutmeg and pepper
a little oil for frying
1 pint / 600 ml well-flavoured
   stock

SWEDISH MEAT-BALLS

Smorgasbord is traditionally ended with a dish of meat-balls served in the stock in which they have been cooked and a dish of boiled potatoes.

In a bowl put the minced pork and beef. Make the bread into crumbs and add to the bowl. Add the egg and all the seasonings and mix well. Shape into balls, walnut-size. Brown these well in a hot pan with a little oil. Have the stock simmering in another pan and, as the balls brown, transfer them to it. Simmer for 1½ hours and serve in their juice.

For 4

1 onion, finely chopped
4 oz / 125 g turnip (swede),
   finely chopped
a little oil for frying
1 lb / 500 g steak mince
1 pint / 600 ml stock
2 tblsp / 30 ml medium-cut
   oatmeal

MINCED COLLOPS (Scottish Mince)

Take a deep saucepan and gently fry the chopped onion and turnip in a little oil until soft but not brown. Add the meat and stir it around until brown. Add the well-flavoured stock to cover the meat. Put the lid on and simmer gently for 1 hour. Sprinkle on the oatmeal to thicken and allow to boil for 15 minutes more. Season to taste.

Meanwhile, poach the eggs. Cut the slices of bread into triangles and fry them. Place the meat in a hot serving dish,

4 eggs
3 slices of white bread
salt and pepper

For 4

8 oz / 225 g onion, finely
    chopped
1 oz / 25 g butter
1 lb / 500 g good minced beef
1 large slice of white bread
½ pint / 300 ml milk
1 tblsp / 15 ml brown sugar
2 tblsp / 30 ml curry powder
a grating of nutmeg
4 oz / 125 g dried apricots or
    apples
4 oz / 125 g raisins
2 bay leaves
2 eggs
½ tsp / 3 ml salt
½ tsp / 3 ml pepper

arrange the poached eggs on top and the bread triangles round the edge, and serve.

BOBOTIE (South Africa)

Fry the onion in the butter until light brown. Put it in a bowl with the meat. Soften the bread in a little of the milk and add it to the meat, together with the sugar, spices and chopped or minced fruit, mixing it well.

Put the meat into a buttered casserole dish, pressing it in, with the bay leaves pushed in on top. Beat the milk up together with the eggs and a little salt and pepper. Pour this custard over the meat to cover it.

Bake in the slow oven (325°F / 160°C / gas 3) for 1½ hours if the meat is raw. If you have used cooked meat, ¾ hour will do.

Serve with yellow rice (see Index), chutneys and a fresh salad of bananas, tomatoes, pineapple and lettuce.

Every South African has their own way of making this dish, so do not argue, as I tried to do once!

We cooked large quantities of Mexican chilli con carne for young people's interracial camps held on the Kingwill farms in the Sneeuberg mountains of the high Karoo, 6,000 feet up.

Among those whom we got to know at the camps was a young man from a radical political family in Soweto. One brother had been a leader of the 1976 student uprising against the system of education imposed on them, while another two brothers were in political exile.

We invited him to stay with us to meet political and community figures in the Cape and to explore the qualities of integrity which will be needed in any new South Africa. He had never before been to Cape Town which was a thousand miles from his home. The first thing he wanted to do was to climb the slopes of Table Mountain from where he could look out across the sea to Robben Island where Nelson Mandela and others whom he regarded as his leaders were still imprisoned.

Catherine also invited him to exchange experiences with her class of seniors in her school which was the first in the city to go multiracial at a time when it was not yet legal. As the questions flew back and forth, one of Catherine's friends made a remark and then, feeling that she had said something silly, blushed furiously. Our Soweto visitor was fascinated. 'I've been reading Jane Austen for my exams,' he exlaimed, 'and about her heroines blushing. Now I know what that is!'

MEXICAN CHILLI CON CARNE

For 4

½ pint / 300 ml brown beans, soaked overnight
1 onion, chopped
1 clove garlic, mashed
¾ lb / 325 g steak mince
½ chilli pepper, chopped or ¼-½ tsp / 1-3 ml cayenne pepper
1 pint / 600 ml tinned tomatoes

Drain the beans and boil them in fresh water until done, about 1½ hours.

Meanwhile, take a deep, heavy saucepan. Fry the chopped onion and the mashed clove of garlic until soft. Add the chilli or cayenne pepper and then the mince, stirring until brown.

When the beans are cooked, drain them and add to the mince, together with the tomatoes and enough of their water to cover. Simmer for half an hour. Serve with rice.

HAMBURGERS

For 4

1½ lb / 675 g steak mince
1 medium onion, finely grated
½ tsp / 2 ml salt
¼ tsp / 1 ml each of pepper and cayenne
1 tsp / 5 ml mixed herbs
¼ pint / 150 ml milk
oil for frying
1 tblsp / 15 ml Worcester sauce

Home-made hamburgers are *so* different.

Mix together the meat, onion, salt, pepper, cayenne and herbs. Add the milk, mixing it well in.

Form this mixture into patties about 1" / 2.5cm thick and fry on both sides in the oil until done.

Push them to one side and deglaze the pan with a little water and the Worcester sauce to make a *jus*.

Serve the hamburgers in buns with a little of the *jus* and onions which have been fried separately. Coleslaw is an ideal side dish.

BOLOGNESE SAUCE

For 4

1 bunch spring onions or 1 big onion
3 cloves garlic
1 lb / 500 g steak mince
2 tblsp / 30 ml oil
1 × 400 g tin of tomatoes
2 oz / 50 g tomato purée
1 green pepper
2 tblsp / 30 ml chopped parsley

Chop the onions finely. Crush the garlic. Heat the oil in a deep saucepan and fry till soft. Add the meat a little at a time to brown it, stirring well to break it up. When it is cooked through, add the tomatoes and tomato purée, salt and pepper. Cover and simmer for 1 hour. Add the chopped and de-seeded green pepper 10 minutes before finishing cooking. Before serving, sprinkle on the chopped parsley.

Serve with spaghetti, 3 oz / 75 g per person, and a dish of grated cheese. A fresh green salad and garlic bread complete the menu.

For 6

9 oz / 250 g dried green lasagne
1 quantity Bolognese sauce as in
   previous recipe
cheese sauce
2 oz / 50 g butter or margarine
1 slice onion, chopped
3 tblsp / 45 ml flour
1 pint / 600 ml milk
7 oz / 200 g grated cheese,
   cheddar and parmesan to
   taste
1tblsp / 15 ml mustard
salt and pepper
pinch of nutmeg

LASAGNE

This can be made ahead of time in quantity and frozen in ovenproof dishes. If they are not freezer-to-table ware but Pyrex, the dish should be removed from the freezer the night before to allow it to defrost to room temperature.

When cooking for the freezer you can double or quadruple the quantities.

Melt the butter or margarine. Add the onion and fry gently until soft. Add the flour and stir it well in. Add the milk, stirring constantly, or whisk it in until it boils. Take it off the heat. Add half the grated cheese, the mustard and the salt, pepper and nutmeg to taste.

Meanwhile, boil the pasta until just done in lots of salted boiling water.

Take a good-sized casserole dish and butter it well. Place half the pasta on the bottom, the Bolognese sauce in the middle and the remainder of the pasta on top. Pour the cheese sauce over everything, making sure the pasta is covered. Sprinkle the remaining cheese over the top and dot it with a little butter or margarine. At this point the dish may be cooled and then frozen for later use.

To cook: Heat the oven to 350°F / 180°C / gas 4. Bake for half an hour if fresh, 1 hour if frozen, until the top is brown and the dish is bubbling.

For 8

1½ lb / 700 g stewing steak
a little oil for frying
8 oz / 225 g onion, chopped
1 pint / 600 ml beef stock
1 lb / 450 g kidneys
2 tblsp / 30 ml flour
1 tsp / 5 ml each of paprika and
   salt
½ tsp / 3 ml pepper
8 oz / 225 g puff pastry
egg yolk beaten with a spoonful
   of milk to glaze the pastry

STEAK AND KIDNEY PIE

Cut the steak into chunks, removing the excess fat. Heat some oil in a deep pot. Fry the steak until brown on all sides and set it aside. Put the finely chopped onion in the pot, reduce the heat and fry the onion until transparent. Return the meat to the pot and add the stock to cover it. A teaspoon of thyme and marjoram may be added if wished. Bring to the boil, cover and simmer very gently for 1½ to 2 hours.

Meanwhile skin and core the kidneys, cutting them into small chunks. Heat some oil in a frying pan and fry quickly without burning. Set them aside.

When the steak is tender, strain off the stock into another saucepan. Bring it back to the boil and add the flour seasoned with the paprika, salt and pepper and mixed to a thin paste with a little cold water.

Take a 2 pint / 1.2 litre casserole. Put the meat and onions in the bottom, the kidneys next, and pour the sauce over it all. Set this aside to cool or till the following day.

Roll out the pastry bigger than you need. Damp the edges of the casserole and first cut long, thin strips of pastry to go right around the edge, dampening them where they join. Try to have the remaining pastry the right size to cover the top.

Dampen the top of the pastry strips and lift the sheet of pastry onto the casserole to cover them, cutting off any excess. With the back of a knife held parallel to the rim, knock right round the edge of the pastry to help it rise.

To decorate, hold your thumb on the top of the pastry edge and cut inwards against the side of your thumb to make a scalloped pattern right round the pie. Any scraps of pastry may be cut into the shape of leaves and placed on top.

Brush the top with the beaten egg and cut 3 slits in it. Place in a hot oven 400°F / 200°C / gas 6 for half an hour until browned.

Note: Keep the filling in the casserole ½ " / 1.5 cm below the top. Put the pie on a baking sheet in the oven to catch drips.

SPICED BEEF

For 20

This dish, suitable for a big reception, takes 8 days to prepare.

4-5 lb / 2-2½ kg topside or silverside without the bone
2 oz / 50 g soft light brown sugar
1 tsp / 5 ml black peppercorns
3 oz / 75 g sea salt
½ oz / 15 g all-spice
12 juniper berries
3 bay leaves

Remove any string tying the meat. Rub it all over with the sugar and place it in a glass or china bowl. Cover it with a cloth and leave it in the fridge for 24 hours.

Next day, grind all the other ingredients together and rub them into the beef. Baste it with its own juice and the spices twice a day for 7 days, turning it each time.

Before cooking, rub off any excess spices and place the beef in a casserole with a lid. Pour in half a pint / 300 ml water or red wine (or a mixture of the two), cover and cook for 4½ hours at 300°F / 150°C / gas 2, being sure it does not dry out. Refill if necessary.

Take the casserole out of the oven and replace the lid with a weighted saucer to press the meat. Leave it in its liquid until cold and chill it overnight. Carve fine slices. Serve cold.

For 8

2 lb / 1 kg topside beef
salt and pepper
all-spice
1 oz / 25 g butter
2 tblsp / 30 ml brandy
5-6 tomatoes
6 slices streaky bacon
3 hard-boiled eggs
¼ lb / 125 g mushrooms
½ lb / 225 g shortcrust pastry

BEEF PIE

Cut the beef into small pieces. Add salt, pepper and a little spice. Heat the butter in a saucepan and brown the meat. Set it alight with brandy. Add the tomatoes, skinned and de-seeded. Put the lid on and simmer gently for 1-1½ hours till tender. Add a little stock if it gets dry.

Take a glass or enamel pie dish. Line it with the bacon. Put in the meat and juices, the hard-boiled eggs, cut in quarters, and the mushrooms. Roll out the pastry and cover the dish, cutting slits in it. Brush with beaten egg and bake in a moderate oven (350°F / 180°C / gas 4) for 1 hour. Turn the oven down if the pastry gets too brown.

Take the dish out. If you have extra stock jelly, pour it into the pie through a funnel placed in one of the slits in the pastry. Leave until cold and then serve.

LAMB

ROAST LAMB WITH ROSEMARY

This may be cooked in one of two ways. The first is hotter, which makes it lovely and brown. The second, cooked more slowly, does not shrink so much.

Hot: Pre-heat the oven to 400°F / 200°C / gas 6. Meanwhile, prepare the roast. A leg or shoulder is good. It has more flavour if cooked on the bone, although it is easier to carve if de-boned and rolled.

Weigh the roast. It will take a total cooking time of 30 minutes per lb / 450 g. Place it in a roasting tin, fat side up. Rub in salt and pepper to taste, and sprinkle with 1 tblsp of dried rosemary for approx. 3 lb / 1½ kg of meat. Baste it well with dripping or oil and roast at the high temperature for 20 minutes.

Meanwhile, prepare the potatoes you wish to roast – at least one per person, according to appetite. Peel and boil them for 10 minutes, and then drain them. If there is room, they may then be roasted around the meat. Otherwise heat some oil in a separate pan and put the potatoes in it and cook on the rack above the meat for about 1 hour.

Prepare the vegetables to cook in the pan with the joint. Allow half an onion and half a carrot per person.

When the roast has cooked for 20 minutes, take it out and turn the oven down to 350°F / 180°C / gas 4. Put the vegetables and potatoes round the roast and baste them and the joint in the juices. Replace in the oven and roast for the required time basting it 2 or 3 times during cooking.

When done, place on a heated serving dish with the vegetables from which the fat has been strained. Keep warm for 20 minutes to complete cooking. Put the potatoes in a separate dish and keep uncovered to preserve crispness.

Gravy: Pour off any excess fat, slowly so as to keep the juices in the pan. Take flour, ½ tblsp / 10 ml per person, and mix into the juices in the pan over a low heat. For 4 people, add ½ pint / 300 ml stock, or water flavoured with a stock cube, whisking it until boiling. Flavour to taste with Worcester sauce or lemon juice and soya sauce, salt and pepper.

Cool cooking: Heat the oven to 325°F / 150°C / gas 3 and allow 35 minutes per lb / 450 g. The potatoes may need to finish browning after the meat is taken out.

Lamb is traditionally served with either mint sauce or redcurrant or mint jelly.

CROWN ROAST OF LAMB
(A dinner party special)

For 8 to 12

Ask the butcher to crown 2
   sections of best end of neck
14 oz / 411 g tin of apricots

Apricot stuffing
4 oz / 125 g dried apricots,
   soaked overnight then
   chopped
1 tblsp / 15 ml parsley,
   chopped
1 tsp / 5 ml rosemary
1 small onion, finely chopped
3 oz / 75 g fresh white
   breadcrumbs
rind of 1 lemon, grated
juice of half a lemon

Place the crown roast in the roasting tin, tied in a ring so that all the ends of the chops point upwards. Season with salt and pepper. Wrap tinfoil round the end of each chop so that they do not burn.

Mix all the stuffing ingredients together and place in the centre of the joint. Dot it with butter. Brush the joint with cooking fat. Cover the stuffing with butter paper or tinfoil so that it does not dry out. Put 1″ / 2.5 cm of water in the bottom of the pan. Roast at 375°F / 190°C / gas 5 for 1½ hours.

To serve, remove the foil and stick apricot halves on the end of each chop. Serve with new potatoes, peas, carrots and a light gravy.

LAMB CUTLETS ON BROWN RICE

For 8

1 pint / 600 ml brown rice
2 pints / 1.2 litres stock
3 rashers of bacon
1 medium onion, chopped
6 mushrooms, chopped
1 clove garlic, finely chopped
oil for frying
1 egg

Put the rice on to boil in the stock, cover and simmer for about 45 minutes. It should absorb all the stock. (Brown rice takes longer to cook than white.)

Put the cut-up rashers of bacon, the chopped onion, the mushrooms and the garlic in a pan and fry gently in some oil until soft. Add all this to the boiling rice for its last half hour of cooking. Add a little stock as it cooks, if it dries out too much.

1 tblsp / 15 ml milk

8 lamb or mutton cutlets (chops) trimmed

flour seasoned with salt and pepper

4 oz / 125 g dried breadcrumbs

6 chicken livers

3 oz / 75 g butter

1 tblsp / 15 ml chopped parsley

Beat the egg. Mix in the milk. Dip each of the cutlets first in a little seasoned flour, and then in the beaten egg and milk, and finally in the breadcrumbs, covering well. Fry in hot oil or fat for 7-10 minutes on each side, but do not brown too much. Put them aside and keep warm.

Sauté the livers separately in the butter and chop them small. Add them at the last minute to the rice.

To serve, place the rice down one side of the platter and the chops down the other. Sprinkle the rice with chopped parsley.

COTELETTE D'AGNEAU (Lamb Chops)

For 6

A recipe from my maternal grandmother, Evelyne Sellar.

½ oz / 12 g butter

1 tblsp / 15 ml oil

6 lamb cutlets

8 oz / 225 g onion, chopped

½ pint / 300 ml stock

seasoning

1 tsp / 5 ml basil

2 large potatoes

1 lb / 450 g Jerusalem artichokes

1 tsp mustard

¼ pint / 150 ml cream

3 oz / 75 g mushrooms, finely chopped

1 tblsp / 15 ml flour

2 tsp / 10 ml tomato purée

lemon juice

This is cooked in 3 sections:

(1.) *The cutlets*. Melt the butter and oil in a pan. Put in the cutlets with a lid over them to whiten them. When whitened, take them out and keep them warm. Add the chopped onion to the pan and cook gently until transparent, but not brown. Return the cutlets to the pan, add the stock, season to taste with salt, pepper and the basil. Cover the pan with greaseproof paper and a lid and cook either in the oven at 350°F / 180°C / gas 4 or on top of the stove over a very low heat for 30-40 minutes.

(2.) Peel, cut up and put the artichokes and potatoes in a pan. Add cold salted water halfway up. (Artichokes, like potatoes, turn brown if left in the air, so put them in water as you peel them.) Bring to the boil and cook for 20-30 minutes, until tender. Strain them dry and sieve them or put them through a moulin-légume. Add some mustard to taste and the cream.

(3.) *The gravy*. Melt 1 oz / 25 g butter in a pan. Add the chopped mushrooms and fry them quickly for a moment or two. Sprinkle the flour over them and stir it in. Strain off the juice from the cutlets and stir it into the flour mixture together with the tomato purée and a little lemon juice to taste. Boil it all well together to reduce the gravy to about a cupful. Season to taste.

To serve: Pile the artichoke purée down one side of a large serving dish and the cutlets in a line down the other side. Pour the gravy over them.

SOSATIES (South African kebabs)

For 12

4-5 lb / 2 kg leg of lamb, cut
    into bite-size pieces
6 medium onions, sliced in rings
4 oz / 125 g dried apricots
    soaked overnight in water

Marinade
2 onions, chopped
2 tblsp / 30 ml curry powder
2 tblsp / 30 ml apricot jam
2 tblsp / 30 ml fruit chutney
3 tblsp / 45 ml sugar
8 fl oz / 225 ml each of vinegar
    and water
2 tsp / 10 ml cornflour

Make the marinade first. In a saucepan fry the chopped onions in a little oil until soft. Add the curry powder, jam, chutney and sugar with the vinegar and water. Boil this for 10 minutes and then add the cornflour mixed in a tablespoon of cold water. Bring it back to the boil to thicken it before setting aside to cool.

When cold, pour this marinade over the meat and sliced onions and leave for at least 24 hours, turning occasionally. Keep it covered.

Take 24 skewers. If they are wooden, soak them in cold water for 1 hour. Thread the meat and onion rings alternately on the skewer, ending with an apricot.

Have ready some red-hot embers in the barbecue. Place the skewers on the rack and grill, turning from time to time.

The marinade makes a good sauce if heated.

Note: For a barbecue, you can make a rich scone dough (see Index). Form it into balls and cook over the fire on the end of sticks. When done, take off the stick and put butter and honey in the hole. Eat while hot. Scrumptious!

STEW OF SPRING LAMB

For 4

2 tblsp / 30 ml oil
1½ lb / 700 g stewing lamb,
    trimmed of excess fat and cut
    in bite-sized pieces
¼ lb / 125 g onion, chopped
1½ pints / 900 ml stock
½ lb / 250 g baby carrots – if
    unavailable, use slices of larger
    carrots
½ lb / 250 g baby onions
salt and freshly ground pepper
½ lb / 250 g peas
½ lb / 250 g cauliflower florets
sprig of mint
1 tsp sugar
1 tblsp / 15 ml butter and
    1 tblsp / 15 ml oil
½ lb / 250 g button mushrooms
1 tblsp / 15 ml lemon juice

Heat the oil in a deep heavy pan (with a lid). Add the meat in portions and brown it on all sides, setting each portion aside as done. When the meat is all set aside, add the chopped onion to the pan and fry gently until transparent but not brown. Return the meat to the pan with the onions. Add the stock and bring quickly to the boil. Turn the heat down and simmer, covered, for a total of 2 hours.

After the first hour add the prepared carrots and baby onions. Season with salt and pepper and continue cooking.

About 15 minutes before serving, put on 2 pans, each with a little salted water, and bring to the boil. Put the cauliflower in one, and the peas in the other. Turn the heat down and steam the vegetables for about 10 minutes.

In another pan melt the tablespoon of butter and oil. Add the whole button mushrooms and fry gently until done (about 5-10 minutes). Sprinkle them with lemon juice.

To serve: take a large, heated platter. Put the peas on one side at the end, the mushrooms at one side in the middle and the cauliflower at the other end.

Thicken the stock in which the meat is cooking by mashing together 1½ tablespoons of butter or margarine with 2 tablespoons of flour. Stir this a little at a time into the boiling stew just before serving. Put the stew down the other side of the dish.

It is good served with minted, new potatoes.

IRISH STEW

For 6

This is one dish at which my husband, Peter, is the master. Being Irish, he is always the one to cook it.

3 lb / 1½ kg best end neck of mutton or lamb
stock from cooking the meat
salt and pepper
6 carrots cut into bite-sized chunks
6 onions, peeled and quartered
3 lb / 1½ kg potatoes (you use more than you might expect)
chopped parsley

The day before, put the meat in a saucepan, cover well with water and bring to the boil. Simmer for about 1 hour. Take the pan off the stove, turn the contents into a bowl, cool and then leave in the fridge overnight.

Next day, take the bowl from the fridge. The fat will have hardened on top. Skim this off with a slotted spoon. (If you have a bird-table, the birds will love this.)

Put the meat and stock into a very large saucepan and bring to the boil. Add salt and pepper and carrots. Continue simmering and, about half an hour later, add the onions and the potatoes, cut in halves. Add more water to cover everything and more seasoning if necessary. Simmer for about a further 1½ hours. The meat should be coming away from the bones and the potatoes should almost be disintegrating into the stock.

Sprinkle with parsley and serve from the pot into heated soup plates. (An empty plate in the centre of the table can be useful for discarded bones.)

When we lived in South Africa some friends were complaining that it was impossible to entertain because of the high cost. We suggested that it was not necessary to serve expensive cuts of meat and invited them to a dinner of Irish Stew, followed by apple pie. It was a great success.

LAMB MOUSSAKA

For 4

2 aubergines, sliced
1 oz / 25 g butter
2 cloves garlic, peeled and crushed
2 medium onions, sliced

Blanch the aubergine by sprinkling salt over the slices and leaving in a strainer for 20 minutes.

Melt the butter in a flameproof casserole. Add the prepared garlic, onions and aubergine. Cook them gently for 10 minutes, stirring well. Add the tomatoes, meat, herbs, salt

101

14 oz / 400 g tinned tomatoes
12 oz / 350 g cooked minced
    lamb
½ tsp / 3 ml dried oregano
1 tsp / 5 ml fresh rosemary
salt
freshly ground black pepper
3 egg yolks
½ pint / 300 ml yoghurt
1 tblsp / 15 ml grated parmesan
    cheese

and pepper. Cover and cook slowly for 10 minutes.

Beat the egg yolks and add them to the yoghurt. Pour this over the top of the casserole. Sprinkle the parmesan cheese on top and bake in the oven (preheated to 350°F / 180°C / gas 4) for 30 minutes.

Serve with a green salad and French or garlic bread.

For 8 to 10

JORDANIAN VINE LEAVES

The wife of the Jordanian Military Attaché in Washington showed me how to make this dish. Now that we have planted a vine in our conservatory at home in Ireland, I am able to make it again. It takes a good deal of work beforehand, but the final serving is easy.

A lot of young, but good-sized
    vine leaves, blanched in
    boiling water for a minute

The filling
3 lb / 1½ kg leg of lamb
1 pint / 600 ml long-grain rice
1 stick of cinnamon
6 oz / 175 g peeled almonds
4 oz / 125 g butter
3 oz / 90 g peeled pistachio or
    pinenuts
4 oz chicken liver (if available)
2 onions, chopped
1 tsp / 5 ml salt
½ tsp / 3 ml each of black
    pepper and nutmeg

Cut the meat off the lamb bone into small diced pieces. Boil up the bone in 2½ pints / 1½ litres water to make a good stock. Cook for a couple of hours.

Strain off the bone and cook the rice with the stick of cinnamon in the 2 pints / 1.2 litres of stock which should be left.

Split the almonds and fry them in butter until brown and put aside. Fry the pistachio or pinenuts and put them aside.

Fry the lamb until cooked and the juice gone. Fry the liver and chop it very finely. Lastly fry the onion until soft.

Combine the fried meat and liver, the cooked rice, the salt, pepper and nutmeg, the onion and the nuts, mixing them well.

Place a spoonful of filling in each vine leaf and fold it over to enclose it. A teaspoon will be enough as the leaf has to fold right over on itself.

Take a large saucepan and place the filled leaves, folded side down, neatly round the base of the pan, covering the bottom. Build it up until the pan is ¾ full. Keep it neat.

Cover the vine leaves with boiling chicken stock flavoured with cinnamon and nutmeg. Put the lid on the pan and simmer for half an hour.

To serve, strain off the juice, keeping it warm. Invert the saucepan onto a platter and lift it off, keeping the vine leaves in the shape of the pan. Pour the juice around it. Try not to touch the parcels of vine leaf with a spoon as they break easily and then it will look messy.

This is a complete meal. It is good with a crusty French bread.

For 4

1 large onion, chopped
2 cloves garlic, crushed
2 tblsp / 30 ml olive oil
1 oz / 25 g butter
½ pint / 300 ml long-grain or basmati rice
4 oz / 125 g mushrooms, quartered
2 tsp / 10 ml herbs of your choice
1 tin of tomatoes made to 1¼ pints / 750 ml with stock or water
4 oz / 125 g grated cheese
8 oz / 225 g cold meat, cut in pieces
½ cucumber, de-seeded and diced
1 green pepper (optional)

RISOTTO

Gently fry the onion and garlic in the olive oil and butter until transparent.

Add the rice and fry until it turns milky in colour. Add the mushrooms, herbs, tomatoes, stock and water and simmer until the rice is level with the liquid.

Add the meat, diced cucumber and green pepper. Put the lid on the saucepan, turning the heat right down so that the risotto may just steam.

To serve: fork up the rice to mix everything. The grated cheese is served separately, with garlic bread and a fresh green salad.

SWEETBREADS, LIVER AND KIDNEY

After my father had bought his first farm in Rhodesia - now Zimbabwe - in the 1930s, a mining company came in and pegged his best land for gold. As Rhodesia was established to favour mining, he could do nothing to alter this. One claim, however, was incorrectly pegged, so he and my mother were able to reclaim that piece. Having no capital to start a mine himself, he set up a butcher's shop on this piece of land to serve the miners next door. Thereafter he was able proudly to put on his passport under 'Occupation' – 'Butcher'.

My mother used to tell me of the drama of my grandparents' first visit to stay with them in the bush. With them were Jean, my father's teenage sister, a valet and my grandmother's lady's-maid. I was only four years old at the time and we had been living in grass huts on the shoulder of the kopje while my father worked on building our first proper house. This was a lengthy process as he had to bake his own bricks from the clay on the farm. All, however, was nearly completed for the arrivals. Our boiler was a 40-gallon petrol drum on bricks outside the back of the house, with a fire underneath. My mother had cleaned wooden boxes and decorated them with pretty curtains to serve as chests of drawers. The walls were painted. Only the doors remained to be hung and the outside drains finished.

When the party arrived from their 100-mile drive from town, it was a disaster. A dog from the kraal had got into the house through the unfinished doors and was attacked by Sinbad, our Doberman pinscher. The fight in my grandparents' room had left the walls splattered in blood. Eventually that was cleaned up, and everyone fed and settled in.

Next morning my grandmother arrived at breakfast holding up a pile of her underclothes. My cat, Peggy, had had kittens among them. Undaunted, my grandfather, who had gained his Able Seaman's Certificate on a voyage before the mast on a sailing ship from Australia to Britain, set to with his valet to dig the drains.

My father and mother then decided to show them the local sights. They reached the butcher's shop as the men were about to slaughter a bullock. Normally very skilled and quick, their attention was distracted and the animal escaped. A chase ensued, with much shouting, axes flying and hysterics all round. It was enough. Next day they left for town!

CALVES BRAIN FRITTERS

Naturally, having a butcher's shop, my mother used all parts of an animal. This is one of her recipes from that time.

For 2 or 3

1 set calves brains
1 tblsp / 15 ml lemon juice
2 slices onion
3 cloves
½ a bay leaf

Fritter batter
4 oz / 125 g flour
1 tsp / 5 ml baking powder
¼ tsp / 1 ml salt
1 egg
3 fl oz / 75 ml milk

Soak the brains for 1 hour in enough cold water to cover. Drain them and parboil for 20 minutes in clean water with the lemon juice, onion slices, cloves and bay leaf. Drain them again, remove all the skin and blood clots and cut them into pieces.

Prepare the batter. Sift the flour, baking powder and salt together. Make a well in the centre, drop in the egg and add the milk. Take a wooden spoon and beat them together, gradually drawing in the flour. Beat until smooth.

Add the brains to the batter. Take a frying pan, set muffin rings in it with a generous amount of fat or oil. Heat till smoking and drop spoonfuls of the mixture into each ring. Cook on one side, remove the rings and turn the fritters over.

Drain them on a paper towel and serve with a cold sauce tartare or a lightly seasoned tomato sauce, sharpened with lemon juice.

We often used to tease my brother, Seumas, that he nearly became Tarzan.

Above us on the kopje lived a troop of baboons. They used to maraud over my father's fields, making off with his pumpkins. My father shot one of the baboons to try and scare them away. The workers living nearby asked if they could take it to their village as it made good eating.

Unfortunately, the way to the village led right past our house. The baboons came down from the hill looking for their dead comrade, but all they encountered was my baby brother asleep in his pram under a shelter outside the house. Everybody was away except for the cook who, luckily, saw them dancing around the pram, about to make off with the baby. With great presence of mind he gathered all the saucepans he could and threw them, making a colossal clatter. He saved the day – and Seumas!

HAGGIS

A traditional Scottish dish served on national occasions such as Burns Night (25 January) and St Andrew's Day (30 November).

One one occasion a telegram was received at the Caux conference just before St Andrew's Day announcing the arrival of the former Lord Provost of Glasgow, SIR PATRICK DOLAN AND A HAGGIS. Two rooms were reserved for them, much to the merriment of us Scots!

We like to tell people that haggis is a bird that flies backwards over the heather. But for those who want to know, here is my recipe for a party.

1 sheep's paunch
1 sheep's heart
1 lb / 450 g minced mutton
½ lb / 225 g lamb's liver
2 sheep's kidneys
1 onion, chopped
12 oz / 325 g oatmeal (not rolled oats)
2 tsp/ 10 ml mixed herbs

Soak the paunch for 4 hours in well-salted water. Then turn it inside out and wash it well in several changes of water. Turn it back again ready for use.

Boil the heart for 1 hour. Mince the raw mutton/lamb, the liver, kidneys and the cooked heart with the onion. Put all these in a big basin. Add the oatmeal together with the herbs, salt, pepper and suet and mix well.

Stuff the paunch three-quarters-full with this mixture. Prick it and tie it in a cloth. Place it in a pan of boiling water

1 tsp / 5 ml black pepper
2 tsp / 10 ml salt
2 oz / 50 g suet

and boil for 3 hours.

Drain it and serve on a platter on a clean napkin – to the accompaniment of bagpipes. As the first cut is made, the hosts asks the honoured guest to deliver the toast to the haggis.

Serve with chappit tatties (mashed potatoes) and bashed neeps (mashed turnip or swedes).

Note: if you cannot get a paunch, steam the haggis in a pudding basin, covered with a butter paper and tied down with a cloth.

OX TONGUE

1 ox tongue
a bouquet garni (3 sprigs
  parsley, 1 of rosemary, 2 of
  thyme, 1 dried bay leaf, all
  tied in muslin)
8 peppercorns
1 carrot
1 onion, quartered
2 sticks celery
2 tsp / 5 ml salt

Sauce
2 oz / 50 g horseradish
½ pint / 300 ml of the hot stock
½ oz / 15 g melted butter
1 tblsp / 15 ml soft white
  breadcrumbs
4 tblsp / 60 ml whipping cream
1 big or 2 small egg yolks
1 tsp / 5 ml dry mustard
1 tblsp / 15 ml vinegar
seasoning

Put the meat, herbs, vegetables and seasoning in a pot. Add enough water to cover well. Bring slowly to the boil and skim off any scum. Turn the heat down and allow the tongue to simmer for about 4 hours.

Take out the tongue and skin it, removing any bones in the base. It may then be served hot as is, or with the addition of the sauce.

To make the sauce, put the grated horseradish and the stock on the stove and simmer gently for 20 minutes. Remove from the heat and add the melted butter, the breadcrumbs and the cream. Replace the pan on the heat and simmer again until it thickens.

Strain this through a sieve. Add the egg yolk, the dry mustard dissolved in vinegar, with salt and pepper to taste. Re-heat gently, stirring constantly until the eggs are cooked.

Carve the tongue onto a hot platter and pour the sauce over it.

An alternative is to serve the tongue cold. Push the hot tongue into a bowl as tightly as possible. Cover it with its stock. Put a saucer on top with a weight on it and allow to cool. Ideally keep in the fridge overnight before carving and serving the next day.

For 4

LIVER WITH ORANGE

1 lb / 450 g lamb's liver, cut in
  slices (more if wished)
3 tblsp / 45 ml flour seasoned
  with paprika, salt and pepper

Dip the liver slices in the seasoned flour. Melt half the butter. Add the oil and fry the liver until just tender and brown on both sides. Place it in a hot casserole.

Turn down the heat under the frying pan. Add the

1 oz / 25 g butter / margarine *and* 2 tblsp / 30 ml oil
1 onion, finely chopped
1 small clove garlic, crushed
1 tblsp / 15 ml parsley, finely chopped
pinch of dried thyme
½ pint / 300 ml chicken or beef stock
2 oranges

chopped onion and garlic and fry gently until soft with a little more butter if needed. Add the parsley, thyme and any remaining flour. Stir it well, add the stock and bring to the boil.

Grate the rind and squeeze the juice from one orange. Add it to the sauce and pour it all over the liver.

Clean and dry the pan. Melt in it the remaining butter. Slice the second orange and fry the slices quickly on both sides. Sprinkle with a little sugar and arrange on top of the liver.

Place all in the heated oven (350°F / 180°C / gas 4) for about 20 minutes till really hot.

For 4

6 lamb kidneys *or* 1 ox kidney
3 tblsp / 45 ml flour, seasoned with salt, pepper and thyme
a little butter for frying
6 medium onions, sliced
3 tblsp / 45 ml each of Worcester sauce and tomato ketchup
1 tblsp / 15 ml mushroom ketchup
½ pint / 300 ml beef or chicken stock
4 fl oz / 125 ml sour cream

DEVILLED KIDNEYS

Skin and slice the kidney, removing the core. Dip the slices in the seasoned flour and fry in the butter quite quickly. Set aside in a casserole, keeping it warm.

Turn the heat down and fry the onions gently until transparent. Sprinkle over them any remaining flour, stir it in and then pour over the Worcester sauce, the ketchups and enough stock to make a good gravy. Bring this to the boil, stirring.

Take the pan off the stove, stir in the cream and pour it over the kidneys in the casserole.

Serve with triangles of crisply fried bread for a supper dish. Or, for a lunch, with plain boiled rice and a vegetable.

SWEETBREADS

1 pair of sweetbreads, should do about 4 people
½ pint / 300 ml stock
1 tblsp / 15 ml sherry
½ lemon
½ onion, chopped
1 small carrot, sliced
1 bay leaf
1 oz / 25 g butter
2 tblsp / 30 ml flour
4 fl oz / 125 ml sour cream
salt and pepper

These need careful preparation if not already cooked by the butcher. First they must be soaked in frequent changes of cold water for 4 hours until there is no trace of blood. Second, they must be blanched in a pan of cold water which is brought slowly to the boil and cooked for 3 minutes. Drain the sweetbreads and rinse in cold water.

Cut up the sweetbreads, removing the skin and membrane. Place them in a saucepan with the stock to cover. Add the sherry, the juice of the lemon, the onion, carrot and bay leaf. Simmer all together for 15 minutes.

Melt the butter in another pan over a low heat, stirring in the flour. Strain the stock from the sweetbreads over this roux, stirring while bringing to the boil. Take it off the heat, add the sour cream, the sweetbreads and vegetables.

Serve on buttered toast or in vol-au-vent pastry cases, decorated with chopped parsley.

POULTRY

HOWTOWDIE (roast chicken)

For 6

This name is from the Old French *hutaudeau*, meaning a pullet / chicken.

3 lb / 1.4 kg chicken
2 oz / 50 g butter
12 button onions
a pinch of mace
10 whole cloves
1 pint / 600 ml stock made from
   the giblets
seasoning

Preheat the oven to 400°F / 200°C / gas 6. Prepare the stuffing by melting the butter and frying the shallot. Take it off the heat, add the parsley, tarragon and the breadcrumbs. Moisten it slightly with the milk (not soggy) and stuff the bird.

To cook the pullet, put the butter in a casserole in the oven and let it melt. Then add the onions and let them brown gently. Put the chicken in the centre of the casserole and roast it for 20 minutes until lightly browned. Add the mace, cloves, seasoning and stock. Cover the casserole and cook for 40 minutes or until the chicken is done. Remove the pullet to an ashet and keep it warm.

Stuffing
1 oz / 25 g butter or margarine
1 shallot chopped
1 tsp / 5 ml each fresh tarragon
   and parsley, chopped
2 oz / 50 g soft breadcrumbs
a little milk to moisten

GRAVY
the liver from the chicken
stock from the chicken
2 tblsp / 30 ml cream
salt and pepper

Cook the liver for 3 minutes in the stock. Take it out and mash it so that it absorbs the liquid. Skim off any excess fat from the stock. Add the cream and the mashed liver, with salt and pepper to taste.

Serve with 2 lb / 1 kg cooked spinach, fresh if possible, chopped and cooked in its own juice for 5 to 10 minutes. Dress the spinach round the chicken, pouring gravy over the top.

COCK-A-LEEKIE

For 8

a big boiling fowl, about 5 lb /
   2½ kg
1 dozen dried prunes, soaked
   overnight

Put the bird in a big pot with all the ingredients. Cover with water. Bring slowly to the boil, turn the heat down and simmer for about 2 hours.

Dish up on an ashet. Surround with a mixture of freshly

1 carrot
1 onion
3 or 4 leeks
salt
bouquet garni of thyme, parsley,
    bay leaf, sprig of rosemary,
    6 peppercorns and a piece of
    celery, all tied in a muslin bag

boiled vegetables, such as carrots, beans and leeks with the prunes from the pot.

Make a gravy with 1 pint / 600 ml of the stock, thickening it with 2 tblsp / 30 ml cornflour, seasoned to taste.

Mask the chicken by pouring some of the gravy over it. Serve the rest in a sauceboat. A dish of mashed potatoes is a good accompaniment.

Scots cooks traditionally use the word ashet for a platter, derived from the French *assiette*.

SOUTHERN FRIED CHICKEN

For 4

1 chicken, cut in pieces
3 tblsp / 45 ml flour
½ tsp / 3 ml salt
½ tsp / 3 ml paprika
¼ tsp / 1 ml pepper
1 egg
2 tblsp / 30 ml milk
oil for frying

Cut the chicken into pieces (I get 9 pieces – 2 legs, 2 thighs, 2 wings, the wishbone, 2 sides of breast). In a plastic bag put the flour and seasoning. Add the chicken pieces and shake the bag, covering the chicken in the seasoned flour. Remove from the bag, shaking off any excess.

Beat the egg and milk together in a bowl. Dip the floured chicken pieces into this, making sure they are well covered.

In a separate bowl put the same measurements of flour, salt, paprika and pepper that went in the plastic bag. Dip the egg-covered chicken into this new seasoned flour, again coating well.

In a deep pan heat enough oil to cover all the chicken pieces and fry them gently for about half an hour. When cooked, drain them on kitchen paper and keep them hot. Serve as soon as possible.

This chicken is traditionally accompanied by the following:
(1.) Gravy made with cream and fried and cut-up chicken liver.
(2.) Whole fresh green beans, boiled together with diced bacon.
(3.) Apple jelly, sweet potatoes and spoon bread (see Index).

CHAMPAGNE CHICKEN

For about 10

4 oz / 125 g clarified butter,
    made by melting 6 oz / 175 g
    of butter. Leave it till cold.
    Discard the sediment on the
    bottom, using only the clear
    fat on top

Heat the clarified butter in a heavy frying pan. Shake the chicken in a plastic bag with the seasoned flour. Remove the chicken from the bag and brown it in the pan.

Remove the chicken to a casserole. Add half the champagne, put on the lid and cook in the oven (350°F / 180°C / gas 4) for about 1 hour until the chicken is tender.

Meanwhile, prepare the fruit: melt half the butter with the

5 lb / 2½ kg chicken pieces
4 tblsp / 60 ml seasoned flour
½ bottle champagne
4 oz / 125 g fresh butter
4 oz / 125 g icing-sugar
2 fl oz / 50 ml water
4 oz / 125 ml seedless white
    grapes
6 fresh peaches or table pears,
    halved and peeled
3 oranges, sectioned
4 tblsp / 60 ml redcurrant jelly or
    bar-le-duc (see Index)
1 fl oz / 25 ml curaçao
1 tblsp / 15 ml lemon juice
1 tsp / 5 ml Bovril

icing-sugar and the water until the sugar has dissolved. Add the grapes and cook until heated through. Drain them and keep them warm. Add the stoned peaches or cored pears and cook for about 8 minutes until just soft, turning once only. Drain them, fill the hollows with the bar-le-duc and keep them warm on a plate. Add the orange segments and heat through in the same syrup. Drain and keep warm.

When the chicken is cooked, take out the pieces and place them down one side of a large platter. Arrange the fruit on the other side. Serve with boiled rice.

Add the remaining champagne to a saucepan together with the curaçao, Bovril, lemon juice and the juices from the pan. Boil this to reduce it to half the quantity. Cut up the remaining fresh butter into the gravy and swirl it around until melted, but do not boil. Serve in a gravy boat.

The syrup from cooking the fruit may be used for a fruit salad.

For 8

2 × 2 lb / 1 kg chickens or 4 lb /
    2 kg chicken pieces
3 tblsp / 45 ml flour, seasoned
    with salt and pepper
3 oz / 75 g butter
2 tblsp / 30 ml oil
1 small onion, finely chopped
1 tblsp / 15 ml paprika
1 tsp / 5 ml salt
¼ tsp / 1 ml pepper
8 fl oz / 225 ml chicken broth
    made from the giblets and
    bones
8 fl oz / 225 ml sour cream
½ tsp / 3 ml lemon juice
2 tblsp / 30 ml chopped parsley

CHICKEN PAPRIKA

Cut up the chickens into 9 pieces each and dredge them lightly in the seasoned flour.

Heat 2 oz / 50 g of the butter and the oil in a heavy frying pan with a lid. Fry the chicken until nicely brown. Add the onion, paprika, salt and pepper. Cover the pan and cook gently in its own juice for about 45 minutes until the chicken is tender. Dish up on a platter and keep warm.

Add the broth to the pan and cook for 1 minute. Remove from the heat and stir in the cream, the remaining 1 oz / 25 g of butter, and the lemon juice. Check the seasoning. Pour over the chicken, sprinkle with chopped parsley and serve at once.

Note: I always buy whole chickens rather than the chicken pieces so as to make stock from the bones.

For 4

2 lb / 1 kg chicken, cut into 8
    pieces
3 tblsp / 45 ml flour
salt and pepper

CHICKEN ALLA CACCIATORE

Put the flour, salt, pepper and paprika in a plastic bag. Add the chicken pieces and shake vigorously to coat the chicken. Remove from the bag.

Heat the olive oil or butter in a deep, heavy-bottomed

paprika
4 tblsp / 60 ml olive oil or butter
1 large onion, chopped
1 stalk celery, stringed, chopped
4 oz / 125 g mushrooms
1 green pepper, de-seeded,
    diced
1 clove garlic, pressed or
    chopped
1 sprig rosemary and thyme and
    a bay leaf in a bouquet garni
½ tsp / 3 ml sugar
a pinch of all-spice
2 fl oz / 50 ml sherry *or* 4 fl oz /
    125 ml dry white wine
½ pint / 300 ml tomato juice *or*
    3 large tomatoes, skinned and
    chopped
1 tblsp / 15 ml parsley, chopped

pan. Brown the chicken pieces all over and set aside.

Add the onion, celery, mushrooms, green pepper, garlic and the bouquet garni to the pan, reducing the heat and stirring gently until the onion is transparent but not brown. Add the sugar and all-spice. Mix them in and then return the chicken to the pan.

Add the wine or sherry, cook and stir for 5 minutes. Add the tomatoes or tomato juice. Cover the pan and simmer for about 1 hour until the chicken is tender.

Skim off any excess fat and serve with chopped fresh parsley sprinkled over it. Being an Italian recipe, it should be served with pasta or rice, though mashed potato is also good.

For 4

6 oz / 175 g white meat of
    chicken (or rabbit can be
    used)
2 eggs, separated
½ pint / 225 g whipping cream
salt and pepper

CHICKEN CREAM TETEBURY

Pass the uncooked meat through a mincing machine several times, and then rub through a sieve, separating any gristle from it.

Add the yolks of the 2 eggs and the cream. Beat the whites stiff and add to the mixture.

Put in a well-buttered pudding basin, cover with a butter paper and tie a cloth over it. Steam for 1 hour in a big saucepan with water and a spoonful of vinegar halfway up the bowl.

Turn out and serve hot with new potatoes and creamed spinach.

I can remember my grandmother, Evelyne Sellar, giving this to us as children in her lovely small flat in London. It was a favourite.

POULET À LA KIMBOLTON

For 4

My Hamilton great-grandmother, 'Tat', daughter of the seventh Duke of Manchester, came from Kimbolton. This was her recipe.

1 × 2 lb / 1 kg chicken
2 oz / 50 g butter
2 onions, 1 sliced and 1 chopped
1 pint / 600 ml chicken stock
2 egg yolks
5 fl oz / 150 ml whipping cream
1½ lb / 700 g potatoes
8 rashers of bacon, rolled and fried

Fry the chicken in the butter in a heavy saucepan to brown it. Take it out, add the sliced onion to the pan and cook until transparent. Add the stock and return the chicken. Simmer for 1 hour. Remove the chicken to a platter and keep warm.

Skim the fat off the stock and boil until reduced by half. Pour it over the beaten egg yolks in a bowl and add the cream. Lay the sliced chicken on a platter and pour the sauce over it.

Meanwhile, boil the potatoes and then cut them into small cubes and fry until crisp and brown with the chopped onion. Fry the bacon rolled up and held with cocktail sticks. Serve the fried potatoes and the bacon alongside the chicken.

MEDAILLONS DU VOLAILLE À LA CRÈME

For 6

1 large fowl
1 mirepoix (1 onion, 1 carrot, 2 sticks celery and 1 tsp / 5 ml mixed herbs, chopped)
salt and pepper
1 fl oz / 25 ml strong chicken stock
5 fl oz / 150 ml vegetable stock
2 truffles and 4 oz / 125 g mushrooms *or* 8 oz / 225 g mushrooms
8 slices of cooked tongue
3 oz / 75 g butter
1 tblsp / 15 ml sherry
mashed potato for 6
2½ fl oz / 60 ml béarnaise sauce
4 fl oz / 125 ml whipping cream

Separate the main portions of meat from the bones of the fowl. Take off the skin and sinews. Flatten each piece with a wetted cutlet bat or rolling-pin and pare into oval shapes.

Prepare the mirepoix and fry gently in a flameproof casserole with a little butter until soft. Put the fillets on top. Season with salt and pepper and moisten with the chicken stock and half the vegetable stock. Cover with butter paper and a lid and cook for 45 minutes in the oven, pre-heated to 325°F / 160°C / gas 3.

Cut the truffles, mushrooms and tongue into julienne strips (matchstick size) and heat up in the butter with the rest of the stock and the sherry.

As soon as the fillets are done, remove them, straining and keeping aside the stock. Dress the fillets in a circle on a thin border of mashed potato round a dish. Fill the centre with the prepared garnish of truffle, tongue and mushrooms.

Have ready some heated béarnaise sauce (see Index). Incorporate the set-aside chicken stock and the cream gradually into it. Pour the sauce over the garnish and serve.

For 4

ORIENTAL CHICKEN WITH FRIED RICE AND PEACHES

1 good-sized chicken, cut into
   joints

Marinade
4 tblsp / 60 ml soya sauce
4 tblsp / 60 ml sherry
½ tsp / 2½ ml ground ginger
½ tsp / 2½ ml cinnamon
2 tblsp / 30 ml brown sugar
¼ tsp / 1 ml ground black
   pepper

Fried rice
½ pint / 300 ml basmati rice
1 pint / 600 ml chicken stock
2½ oz / 60 g mushrooms, sliced
1 tblsp / 15 g butter
3 rashers of bacon, cut into small
   pieces
1 onion, sliced
1 tblsp / 15 ml parsley,
   chopped

Peaches
6 or 8 tinned peach halves
4 fl oz / 125 ml of the juice from
   the tin
2½ fl oz / 60 ml vinegar
4 cloves
3 tblsp / 45 ml raisins
¼ tsp / 1 ml ground ginger
1 tblsp / 15 ml coconut
1 tblsp / 15 ml chopped walnuts
a pinch of nutmeg
1 glacé cherry for each fruit
   half

Mix together all the marinade ingredients and pour over the raw chicken pieces. Leave the chicken in the marinade for 2 hours.

Heat a little oil in a saucepan and add the chicken. Brown the chicken pieces on all sides. Turn the heat down, add the marinade and simmer gently for about an hour until done.

Boil the rice gently in the chicken stock, without the lid, until the liquid is absorbed. Put the lid on, turn the heat off and leave the rice to steam in its own heat for 15 minutes.

Next, fry the mushrooms lightly in the butter. Add the bacon and onions and fry them too. Put aside. Now heat the cooked rice thoroughly in the frying pan. Add the bacon, onion and mushrooms and toss it all together.

Boil the peach juice, vinegar and cloves for 5 minutes and pour over the fruit halves. Mix together the raisins, ginger, coconut, walnuts and nutmeg. Moisten the mixture with some of the hot, spiced liquid and, when ready to serve, fill the hollows of the fruit halves and decorate each with a cherry on top.

Place the rice down the centre of a large platter, with a line of chopped parsley along the top. On one side place the cooked chicken pieces, and on the other, the spiced fruit, with a large bunch of parsley at one end.

For 4 to 6

GRACE'S CHICKEN

As a student, Professor Chris Greyling of Durban Westville University played an unexpected part in building reconciliation with President Jomo Kenyatta amid the trauma of the independence struggle in Kenya. In later years, often when it was unpopular, he and his wife, Grace, have been among the senior Afrikaners who have taken a lead in building towards the new South Africa. Something of this is told in my husband's book, *Southern Africa: What Kind of Change?* Grace entertained us one day with this dish.

1 chicken, cut into portions
1 onion, sliced
mayonnaise, chutney and
    tomato ketchup

Put the onion in the bottom of a wide casserole dish. Place the chicken pieces on it in one layer, skin side up. Put some mayonnaise, chutney and tomato sauce on each piece.

    Place the covered casserole in the oven at 350°F / 180°C / gas 4 for about 1 hour. For the first 40 minutes keep the lid on. Then take it off for the last 20 minutes to allow the chicken to brown.

For 6

CHICKEN PIE

1 good-sized chicken
1 onion, quartered
2 carrots, sliced
a bouquet garni (a sprig of
    thyme and parsley, a bay leaf,
    2 cloves, and 4 peppercorns,
    all in a muslin bag)

vegetables
½ lb / 250 g baby onions
¼ lb / 125 g carrots
2 oz / 50 g margarine
¼ lb / 125 g button mushrooms

sauce
4 tblsp / 60 ml fat from the
    stock
4 tblsp / 60 ml of flour
1 pint / 600 ml chicken stock
2 tblsp / 30 ml lemon juice
½ pint / 300 ml milk

Put the chicken, onion, 2 carrots and bouquet garni into a saucepan and cover with boiling water. Simmer for about 1¼ hours until the chicken is cooked.

    Prepare the vegetables. Cook the onions and carrots in a little water to which half the margarine has been added. When tender, allow the water to boil away so that the vegetables begin to brown. Slice the mushrooms and cook them in the rest of the margarine.

    When the chicken is cooked, remove it from the stock. Take the meat off the bone, removing any fat or skin. Cut the chicken into neat portions and lay it in a 2 pint / 1.2 litre casserole. Put the cooked vegetables on top. This can be left to cool while the sauce is made.

    Skim 4 tblsp / 60 ml of the fat off the stock. Put it in a saucepan and heat gently. Stir in the flour and the pint of chicken stock. Add the lemon juice and milk. Bring this to the boil, stirring constantly. It will thicken. Pour this over the chicken pieces in the casserole and set aside until cold.

    To make the pastry, sift together the flour and the salt. Grate in the cold margarine and lard and very lightly rub it into the flour until it resembles coarse breadcrumbs. Use only your fingertips as the palm of your hand will be too hot and it needs to keep light and cool. Now take a knife and mix in

pastry
1 pint / 600 ml plain flour
1 tsp / 5 ml salt
4 oz / 125 g margarine
4 oz / 125 g lard or white fat
4 oz / 125 ml water

just enough water to bind it. Roll into a ball and let rest for half an hour before rolling it out.

On a floured surface roll out the pastry a little larger than the pie dish. Brush the edges of the dish with water. Cut strips of pastry to go right round and brush them on top with water. Roll up the pastry onto your rolling-pin and unroll it over the pie. Cut off any excess. With the knife horizontal, knock 4 lines right round the edge of the pastry to encourage it to rise. Finally, holding the knife perpendicular to the pie, press your thumb on top of the pastry against it to form a scalloped edge right round.

The pastry trimmings can be rolled out and cut to make leaves and roses as decorations. Brush the top with a little beaten egg. Cut a cross in the centre to make a hole for the steam, and a slit on either side.

Put the pie on a baking sheet in the oven (preheated to 400°F / 200°C / gas 6) and cook for 45 minutes until the pastry is risen and brown.

For Creamed Chicken cook the chicken and the sauce as for the pie. Combine them and serve hot, with rice.

For 4

14 oz / 400 g cooked chicken or
    turkey cut in cubes
6 tblsp / 90 ml mayonnaise
3 pineapple slices, cut up
3 tblsp / 45 ml pineapple juice
2 tblsp / 30 ml curry powder
2 oz / 50 g salted peanuts
maraschino or glacé cherries and
    watercress, for decoration

SWISS CURRIED CHICKEN SALAD

Mix together the mayonnaise, pineapple, juice and curry powder. Combine it with the chicken and nuts. Pile onto a serving dish and decorate with the cherries and a bunch of watercress.

For 6

1 large boiling hen or capon,
    about 5 lb / 2½ kg
chicken stock to cover it
1 large onion, quartered
bouquet garni (sprig of thyme
    and parsley, a bay leaf,
    6 peppercorns)
salt

COLD CHICKEN SOUFFLÉ

It is best to take 2 days to prepare this. Put the hen in the boiling stock with the onion, the bouquet garni and salt. Simmer for 2 hours or until tender.

Soufflé
the white meat of the hen
½ pint / 300 ml aspic (see
    Index)
½ pint / 300 ml reduced stock
1 tblsp / 15 ml gelatine
8 fl oz / 225 ml cream
2 fl oz / 30 ml tarragon vinegar
1 tsp / 5 ml mustard
salt and pepper
8 oz / 225 g cooked ham

Take all the meat off the bone. Set aside the brown parts to be used for a different dish such as pilau.

Prepare a ring mould and line it with some of the aspic, leaving it aside to set. If you have no ring mould, stand a jam jar filled with water in the centre of a soufflé dish or china bowl.

Return the bones to the stock and continue boiling until it is reduced to about 1 pint / 600 ml, almost glazed. Strain the liquid off the bones, skim off all the fat and add the gelatine to the hot stock. Let it cool but be sure it does not set before you want to use it.

Pound the white meat and push it through a wire sieve or chop it in the food processor.

Whip the cream and season it with salt, pepper, the tarragon vinegar and the mustard. Mix the pounded meat with this.

Take the gelatine stock, fold it into the meat mixture and put it in the ring mould, smoothing out the top. Put it aside to set until the next day.

Chop the cooked ham, mix it with the remaining aspic and leave it aside to set.

To serve, turn the chicken out of the mould, chop up the ham and aspic and pile it in the centre of the mould. A tomato salad is good with this.

For at least 12

ROASTIT BUBBLY JOCK (roast turkey)

The Scottish name comes from the gobbling sounds of a turkey. Prepare the turkey and stuff it the day before cooking.

1 × 12 lb / 5½ kg turkey
5 tblsp / 75 ml oil or poultry fat
4 onions, quartered
4 carrots, quartered
salt and pepper
paprika

Sausage meat stuffing
1 lb / 450 g sausage meat
2 apples, peeled, cored, grated
2 slices day-old bread, made into
    breadcrumbs
1 tsp / 5 ml each of chopped
    thyme, parsley, celery leaves
1 tsp / 5 ml grated lemon rind

The sausage meat stuffing is for the neck end of the bird. Mix all the ingredients for it together in a bowl. Lift up the flap of skin where the neck has been cut off and push in the stuffing. Fold the flap down over it and secure with cocktail sticks or sew it.

Next, prepare the chestnut stuffing. Make the bread into crumbs. Grind the cooked chestnuts in a food processor or through a sieve. Melt the margarine in a large pan. Add the chopped onions and fry gently until transparent. Add the herbs. Remove the pan from the heat and add the chestnuts and breadcrumbs. Check for seasoning and stuff the body of the turkey.

Preheat the oven to 400°F / 200°C / gas 6. Place the turkey and oil in a large roasting tin, surrounded by the carrots and onions. Sprinkle liberally with salt, pepper and paprika.

*Chestnut, sage and onion
    stuffing*
8 large peeled chestnuts, ground
    up, or tinned chestnuts
8 slices day-old white bread,
    with the crusts
4 oz / 225 g margarine
3 onions, chopped
2 tsp / 10 ml dried thyme
3 tsp / 15 ml dried sage
2 tblsp / 30 ml chopped parsley
salt and pepper

Giblet stock
Boil the neck, wingtips and
    giblets in 2 pints / 1.2 litres
    water with an onion. Do *not*
    include the liver as this will
    make the stock bitter.

Put about 1" / 2.5 cm water in the bottom of the roasting tin. Cover the breast and legs with butter paper and then the whole with tinfoil, fastening it well down.

Place this in the hot oven for 20 minutes. Then turn the heat down to 325°F / 160°C / gas 3 and cook until done. Total cooking time will be about another 5 hours. After 4 hours remove the tinfoil and paper. Take out the onions and carrots and keep them warm. Baste the turkey and cook for another hour to allow it to brown.

Cooking should be finished about half an hour before the meal to allow time to make the gravy etc.

Gravy: Pour off most of the fat from the roasting pan, leaving the juices. Gently fry the turkey liver and chop it finely. Add to the juices and liver 8 tblsp / 100 ml flour.

Add 2 pints / 1.2 litres of the giblet stock. Use extra water and a stock cube if necessary and whisk it in. Season with salt and pepper, bring to the boil and add 1 tblsp / 15 ml lemon juice and redcurrant or rowan jelly to taste, about 4 oz / 125 g. Serve in a hot gravy boat.

Bread sauce is traditionally served with this, separately, in a gravy boat (see Index).

Roast Potatoes: Peel 6½ lb / 2½ kg of potatoes, cut them into even-sized pieces, and boil them in salted water for 10 minutes. Strain them off (I use the water to make stock). Heat 5 fl oz / 150 ml oil in a second roasting tin. Put in the parboiled potatoes, turning them in the oil. Place the tin on the rack above the turkey and roast for at least 1 hour.

Brussel sprouts and roast chestnuts go with this (see Index).

Also served with redcurrant jelly, rowan jelly or cranberry relish.

Present the turkey on your biggest platter, surrounded by the roast vegetables and roast potatoes.

GALANTINE OF TURKEY

I made this for my daughter Catherine's 21st birthday, and the following year for her wedding. It makes a fine centrepiece for a cold buffet. We had three Turkeys Galantine, as well as other things, for a wedding party of 200, and there was lots left over.

First de-bone the turkey (I used one weighing 21 lb / 9½ kg). Perhaps the butcher will do this for you if you ask nicely. I have chosen to do it myself.

Lay it on its breast on a board, slit the skin right down the backbone and then, with a sharp knife, work the meat away from the back down each side of the bird. De-bone the legs by cutting off the bottom joint and then work the meat away from the thigh bone from the inside, gradually pulling the leg inside out until you can free the meat from the lower bones. For the wings, cut off the lower joint and then gradually work down the wings from the inside, turning them inside out as you go. Try not to break the skin.

When all the bones are out, prepare the stuffing.

stuffing

4 lb / 1.8 kg sausage meat

1 lb / 450 g soft white breadcrumbs

1 lb / 450 g dried apricots

1 lb / 450 g onions, chopped and fried

the grated rind and juice of 1 lemon

2 tblsp / 30 ml mixed dried herbs

6 tblsp / 90 ml chopped parsley

3 eggs

8 fl oz / 225 ml white wine to moisten the stuffing

1 tblsp / 15 ml salt

1 tsp / 5 ml pepper

8 truffles *or* 8 oz / 225 g button mushrooms

1½ lb / 700 g each of sliced cooked ham and cooked tongue

2 lb / 900 g boneless turkey roast of white meat

Mix together the sausage meat, breadcrumbs, chopped apricots, parsley and fried onions, the lemon juice and rind, the herbs, raw eggs, white wine, salt and pepper.

Slice the truffles or mushrooms, the ham, tongue and turkey breast.

Lay the turkey out flat. Put half the sausage meat mixture down the centre of the bird. On top of this put half the sliced turkey meat, followed by half the sliced ham and tongue. Lay the truffles or mushrooms down the centre, and repeat the layers in inverse order – the tongue and ham next, ending with the sausage meat. Draw the sides and ends of the turkey over the stuffing, enclosing it. With a needle and strong linen thread sew the skin together over the stuffing, being sure it is completely enclosed. Turn the bird over.

Dust the bird with flour, salt, pepper and paprika. Smear it with butter and oil. Place it in the roasting pan. It is excellent if you can find a turkey bag big enough to hold it as then no water is required for roasting. Otherwise, cover the turkey breast with butter paper, put 2" / 5 cm water in the bottom of the pan and enclose it in tinfoil.

Roast in a slow oven (325°F / 180°C / gas 3) basting occasionally. I had thought it would take 8 hours, but found it was almost too well done in 5 hours. Take the turkey out of the oven and leave it on a rack in a draught to cool as quickly as possible before refrigerating it.

Meanwhile, boil up the turkey bones to make a stock. The juices from the pan may be added to it. Cool this and refrigerate also. Next day the fat can be lifted off.

CHAUDFROID SAUCE

1 pint / 600 ml milk
4 oz / 125 g carrot
4 oz / 125 g onion
1½ bay leaves
9 peppercorns
4 fl oz / 125 ml white wine
    vinegar
1 tsp / 5 ml each of tarragon
    and chervil
2 oz / 50 g butter
4 tblsp / 60 ml flour
2 egg yolks
1 tblsp / 15 ml gelatine in 2
    tblsp / 30 ml cold water or
    stock
½ pint / 300 ml aspic jelly made
    from the turkey stock clarified
    as for beef consommé (see
    Index)
4 fl oz / 125 ml cream

To serve, the bird may be masked in a chaudfroid sauce.

In one saucepan simmer the milk, covered, with the carrot, onion, bay leaves and peppercorns for 10 minutes.

In a second saucepan, likewise simmer the vinegar with the chervil and tarragon.

In a third saucepan, melt the butter and stir in the flour. Strain the milk off the carrots etc into this. Whisk it until smooth and bring it to a good boil. Then whisk in the egg yolks. Place the pan over hot water and stir until the sauce has heated again and the yolks have cooked. Stir in the softened gelatine and the aspic over the heat until they have dissolved into the sauce. Remove it from the heat. Strain the vinegar and add it, stirring until smooth.

Leave the sauce aside. When it has cooled but not set, stir in the cream. Mask the turkey with this before it sets and leave to set before applying any decoration. I used sliced tomato and cucumber to represent flowers and leaves, with narrow strips of cucumber skin for stalks. Cover with 1 or 2 layers of the aspic to prevent drying out.

This sauce may also be used to mask a cold salmon, using fish aspic instead of chicken aspic.

For a dinner party of 8

2 ducks, stuffed and roasted

stuffing
4 oz / 125 g butter or margarine
1 onion, finely chopped
8 oz / 225 g white bread with
    the crusts removed
1 tsp / 5 ml salt
2 tblsp / 30 ml sage
1 tblsp / 15 ml chopped parsley
the raw ground liver from the
    duck
2 eggs

orange garnish
2 oranges
8 oz / 225 g sugar
8 fl oz / 225 ml red wine
glacé cherries

FARMYARD DUCK À L'ORANGE

Melt the butter in a pan and gently fry the onion until soft. Soak the bread in water. Squeeze it dry and crumble into the cooked onions. Season to taste. Add the sage and parsley, then the raw ground liver and lastly stir in the raw eggs.

Stuff the ducks, folding the skin over and securing with toothpicks, and place them in a roasting pan in about 1" / 2.5 cm water. Brush them with melted butter and roast them in the oven heated to 350°F / 180°C / gas 4 for about 1½ hours. Baste them frequently with the juices in the pan, adding more water if it looks like drying out. When cooked, make gravy from the juices in the pan.

Cut each duck into 6 portions. Put the stuffing down the centre of the platter, dress the portions round the side, glaze them with the syrup from preparing the oranges (see below) and put 1 orange slice on each piece topped with half a glacé cherry.

To make the garnish, slice the oranges, discarding the ends. Heat the sugar gently in the wine. When dissolved, bring the syrup to the boil and poach the orange slices in it for 15 minutes until transparent. When ready, set them out on greaseproof paper.

Boil up the syrup until reduced by half. Glaze the duck portions with this and decorate with the orange slices topped with the cherries.

This dish is delicious served with wild rice and a green vegetable. Duck is very rich, so a plain starter such as melon balls is good.

STUFFINGS

These are either cooked inside the bird or, separately, in a loaf tin, covered with a butter paper. They will take about an hour in a moderate oven.

SAGE AND ONION STUFFING

2 onions, finely chopped
4 oz / 125 g margarine
1 tblsp / 15 ml dried sage
1 tblsp / 15 ml chopped parsley
½ tblsp / 7 ml dried thyme
4 oz / 125 g soft breadcrumbs
   from day-old bread
salt and pepper

Melt the margarine in a frying pan and gently fry the onions until transparent. Add the herbs. Turn off the heat and add the breadcrumbs. Season to taste with salt and pepper. This will be enough to stuff one medium chicken. For a turkey, double or triple the measures according to size.

CHESTNUT STUFFING *see* Roast Turkey

SAUSAGE MEAT STUFFING *see* Roast Turkey

TARRAGON STUFFING *see* Roast Chicken

AMERICAN DUCK STUFFING

2 oz / 50 g onion, finely chopped
1 oz / 25 g margarine
4 oz / 125 g diced apple
2 oz / 50 g raisins
1 tblsp / 15 ml dried sage
4 oz / 125 g soft breadcrumbs
½ tsp / 3 ml salt
a pinch of pepper

Fry the onion lightly in the margarine. Add the apples, raisins and sage. Turn this together for a moment. Remove from the heat and add the breadcrumbs and seasoning. This goes very well with Duck à l'Orange. It can also go with pork.

PENNSYLVANIA DUTCH STUFFING

6 medium potatoes
3 oz / 75 g butter
¼ pint / 150 ml milk

Boil the potatoes in their skins, peel and sieve them, mashing them with the milk and 2 oz / 50 g of the butter.

3 slices bread, cut in cubes
1 onion, chopped
1 tblsp / 15 ml chopped parsley
1 stalk celery, diced
1 green pepper, diced
½ tsp / 3 ml each of pepper and
   paprika
1 beaten egg
salt to taste

Meanwhile, melt the rest of the butter in a saucepan and fry the bread cubes until crisp. Set them aside and fry the onion until soft, adding more butter if needed. Add the parsley, celery and green pepper. Cover and cook gently until soft. Add the paprika and pepper. Stir into the mashed potato with the beaten egg.

Put the mixture into a bread tin or earthenware casserole, cover with a butter paper and bake in the oven (350°F / 180°C / gas 4) for about 1 hour, removing the paper for the last 20 minutes to brown it. In Pennsylvania this is served with turkey.

DUMPLINGS

8 oz / 225 g plain flour
4 tsp / 20 ml baking powder
½ tsp / 3 ml salt
2 oz / 50 g suet/margarine
1 tblsp / 15 ml each of mixed
   dried herbs and chopped
   parsley
1 beaten egg
4 fl oz / 125 ml milk, approx.

Sift together the flour, baking powder and salt. Add the suet or margarine and work in with your fingertips. Mix in the dried herbs. Make a well in the centre and add the beaten egg and enough milk to make a firm dough.

Form the dough into balls. These may then be cooked either by dropping them into boiling water for about 20 minutes – they will rise to the surface when done. Or they may be cooked on top of a stew in the oven for the last half hour of the stew's cooking time.

SAUCES

BARBECUE SAUCE

1 onion, finely chopped
1 oz / 25 g butter
4 tblsp / 60 ml vinegar
6 tblsp / 90 ml tomato ketchup
2 tblsp / 30 ml French mustard
a pinch of pepper and celery salt
2 tblsp / 30 ml brown sugar
1 tblsp / 15 ml Worcester sauce
4 tblsp / 60 ml water
½ tsp / 3 ml salt

Sauté the onion in the melted butter. Blend in the other ingredients, stirring them well. Bring the sauce to the boil, reduce the heat and simmer for 30 minutes until the sauce thickens.

This can be varied by adding 2 tblsp / 30 ml of chutney instead of the same quantity of the ketchup.

BREAD SAUCE

½ pint / 300 ml milk
½ onion, studded with 6 cloves
4 slices white bread, crusts
   removed
1 oz / 25 g butter
salt and white pepper

Put the milk on to simmer slowly with the studded onion. Simmer for 10 minutes. Cut the bread into cubes. Add to the milk together with the butter. Let it stand on a very low heat until simmering, for 15 minutes. Remove the onion before serving, and add a little more milk if the sauce is too stiff. It should be the consistency of porridge. Season to taste with salt and pepper.

CUMBERLAND SAUCE

1 orange
6 tblsp / 90 ml redcurrant jelly
½ tsp / 3 ml English mustard
a few drops Worcester sauce
4 fl oz / 125 ml water

Cut off the zest (the orange peel with none of the white pith) from the orange. Cut this into fine slices and blanch it in boiling water for 5 minutes. Drain it and return to the pan. Add the redcurrant jelly, mustard, Worcester sauce and the water. Stir until dissolved. Squeeze the orange and add its juice to the sauce. Serve warm. It is delicious with venison or mutton.

CURRY SAUCE

2 tblsp / 30 ml oil
1 onion, chopped finely
1 clove garlic, crushed
1 tblsp / 15 ml curry powder
1 sharp apple, cored, skinned
    and cut up
1 tsp / 5 ml garam masala *or* ½
    a stick of cinnamon, 2 cloves
    and ½ tsp / 3 ml cumin seeds
1 pt / 600 ml vegetable stock
1 tblsp / 15 ml cornflour
salt

Heat the oil in a pan and fry the onion and the crushed garlic gently until soft. Add the curry powder and fry it for a few moments. Add the apple, the garam masala (or alternatives) and the vegetable stock. Bring to the boil, cover and simmer for 15 minutes. Mix the cornflour with a little cold water and add it to the boiling sauce, stirring until it boils again. Taste for seasoning.

HOLLANDAISE SAUCE

4 oz / 125 g butter
3 fl oz / 75 ml water
2 tblsp / 30 ml lemon juice
3 egg yolks

This is a delicate sauce and needs careful handling. Heat the butter, water and lemon juice together until boiling. Remove from the heat. Beat the egg yolks well in a separate bowl. Pour a little of the boiling sauce onto the egg yolks, stirring well. Then return this to the butter, water and lemon juice in the first saucepan, whisking it in. This should prevent curdling. Leave it to sit in a warm place for a few minutes to thicken. If it does not thicken, put it over boiling water. Stir it while watching carefully that it does not curdle. Serve immediately while warm, so that the butter does not harden.

MADEIRA SAUCE

the meat juices in the pan
6 fl oz / 175 ml Madeira
1 pint / 600 ml beef stock
1 tblsp / 15 ml tomato purée
salt and pepper
1 tblsp / 15 g butter

Skim the fat off the meat juices. Pour the Madeira onto the meat juices in the pan in which the meat has been cooked and boil until reduced by half. Add the stock and tomato purée and boil this for 5 minutes. Season it. Remove from the heat and stir in the butter just before serving. Do *not* boil again. This was often served at my grandparents' house with roast beef.

MINT SAUCE

3 tblsp / 45 ml water
1½ tblsp / 22 ml sugar
4 fl oz / 125 ml vinegar
8 tblsp / 120 ml finely chopped
  fresh mint leaves

Heat the water and dissolve the sugar in it. Add the vinegar and bring to the boil for 5 minutes. Pour over the mint and serve hot or cold.

SPINACH AND MUSHROOM SAUCE

2 oz / 50 g onion, finely
  chopped
¾ pint / 450 ml chicken or
  vegetable stock
8 oz / 225 g sliced mushrooms
4 oz / 125 g chopped spinach
1 tblsp / 15 ml cornflour
2 fl oz / 50 ml red wine
4 fl oz / 125 ml whipping cream

Boil the onion in the stock. After 5 minutes add the mushrooms and spinach and simmer with the lid on for a further 5 minutes or so until they are cooked. Liquidise or process them finely. Return them to the pan and bring back to the boil. Mix the cornflour with a little cold water and whisk it into the boiling sauce. Add the wine, if used. Just before serving, add the cream and re-heat but do not boil.

PARSLEY BUTTER

2 oz / 50 g butter
2 tblsp / 30 ml finely chopped
  parsley

Beat the chopped parsley into the butter. Form it into a roll and wrap in greaseproof paper. Put it in the fridge to harden. When serving with steak or chops, cut it into thick pats and place on top of the meat.

RAISIN SAUCE

¼ pint / 150 ml water
8 oz / 225 g soft brown sugar
1 oz / 25 g butter
¼ tsp / 1 ml ground cloves
8 oz / 225 g raisins
1½ tblsp / 22 ml brown vinegar
1tblsp / 15 ml Worcester sauce
½ pint / 300 ml redcurrant jelly

Boil the water and sugar together for 5 minutes. Add all the other ingredients and bring to the boil. It is ready to serve.

Note: I have often substituted apple jelly for redcurrant. I always make a lot because it keeps in the store cupboard.

SWEET AND SOUR SAUCE

½ onion, chopped
1 tblsp / 15 ml oil
9 fl oz / 250 ml crushed
  pineapple
½ tsp / 2.5 ml ground ginger
½ a red and ½ a green pepper,
  diced
3 tblsp / 45 ml vinegar
2 tblsp / 30 ml tomato ketchup
1 pint / 600 ml water
2 tblsp / 30 ml soya sauce
2 tblsp / 30 ml cornflour

Fry the onion in the oil until soft. Add all the other ingredients except the cornflour. Bring to the boil and simmer for 5 minutes until the peppers are cooked. Mix the cornflour with a little cold water and stir into the sauce. Bring back to the boil and it is ready to serve.

TOMATO SAUCE

1 onion, finely chopped
2 tblsp / 30 ml salad oil
1 clove garlic, crushed
14 oz / 400 g tomatoes, tinned
  or fresh
1 bay leaf
1 tsp / 5 ml each of oregano and
  tarragon
½ pint / 300 ml vegetable stock
1 tblsp / 15 ml sugar
salt and pepper

Heat the oil in a deep pan and fry the onion gently until transparent. Add the crushed garlic and the tomatoes. If the tomatoes are fresh, peel them and scoop out the seeds before adding them to the onions. Add the herbs, vegetable stock and sugar; salt and pepper to taste. Cover and simmer for about 20 minutes.

Before serving, if you wish it smooth, liquidise the sauce. To thicken, add 1 tblsp / 15 ml cornflour mixed first in a little cold water and bring it back to the boil while stirring. This will prevent the solids sinking to the bottom.

BASIC WHITE SAUCE

1 oz / 25 g butter or margarine
2 tblsp / 30 ml flour
½ pint / 300 ml milk
salt and pepper
a pinch of mace

Melt the butter in a saucepan. Add the flour, mixing it until smooth. Add the milk a little at a time, stirring each addition with a wooden spoon until boiling point is reached. Season with the salt, pepper and a pinch of mace.

An alternative method is to melt the butter and add the flour to make your roux, as above. Then add all the milk at once, whisking with a wire whisk to remove the lumps. Continue stirring until boiling. Season as before.

Note: White sauce is measured by the quantity of milk used.

The next sauces are all variations of the basic white sauce.

BÉCHAMEL SAUCE

1 pint / 600 ml milk
1 bay leaf
6 peppercorns
a pinch of all-spice
2 oz / 50 g butter
4 oz / 125 g each of carrot and
   onion, finely chopped
4 tblsp / 60 ml flour
salt

Put the milk, bay leaf, peppercorns and all-spice in a pan. Very slowly bring it to simmering point.

In another pan melt the butter. Add the onion and carrot. Partially cover the pan and very gently let the vegetables sweat in their own juices and butter for about 10 minutes. They must not brown. Take off the lid, add the flour and allow to cook for a moment or two, while stirring.

Strain the simmering milk into the flour mixture using either method as for white sauce. Bring it back to the boil and it is ready to serve.

BÉARNAISE SAUCE

½ pint / 300 ml white or
   Béchamel sauce, made as above
4 egg yolks
4 fl oz / 125 ml white wine
   vinegar
2 oz / 50 g butter
4 shallots
1 tsp / 5 ml each of tarragon
   and chervil
salt and pepper

Put the Béchamel / white sauce in the top of a double boiler and heat it over gently boiling water with the egg yolks beaten into it. Stir until it is hot and the yolks cooked. Add half the vinegar. Stir in the butter, a little at a time. Do not allow the sauce to boil or it will curdle.

Cut up the shallots and put them in another pan with the remaining vinegar. Cover them and simmer very gently until cooked – about 4 minutes. Add them to the sauce together with the herbs. Season with salt and pepper and serve hot.

CAPER SAUCE

½ pint / 300 ml white sauce
2 tblsp / 30 ml brown vinegar
4 tblsp / 60 ml capers
1 tsp / 5 ml mustard

Make the white sauce as explained above and add the other ingredients. Bring to the boil and serve hot. This is often served with boiled ham, boiled mutton or fish.

EGG SAUCE

½ pint / 300 ml Béchamel sauce
2 hard-boiled eggs, chopped

Make the Béchamel sauce as described above, adding seasoning to taste. When the sauce is cooked, stir in the chopped eggs.

PARSLEY SAUCE

½ pint / 300 ml Béchamel sauce
2 tblsp / 30 ml chopped parsley

Make the Béchamel sauce as described above, adding seasoning to taste. Just before serving, stir in the parsley.

Note: the egg or parsley sauce is good with smoked haddock or other fish. Use the milk in which the fish has been cooked as part of the milk for the sauce.

CURRY SAUCE

1 large onion, finely chopped5
    tblsp / 75 ml ghee or oil
2 cloves garlic, peeled and
    crushed with 1 tsp / 5 ml salt
1 tsp / 5 ml ground ginger
½ tsp / 5 ml each of cayenne
    pepper, cumin and turmeric
¾ tsp / 4 ml ground coriander
14 oz / 400 g tinned or fresh
    peeled tomatoes

For 10

2 lb / 900 g of mutton or
    chicken
8 tblsp / 120 ml oil
5 onions, finely sliced
3 cloves garlic, crushed
1 small root ginger, skinned and
    ground to paste or 2 tsp / 10
    ml powdered ginger
3" / 7.5cm stick of cinnamon
2 pods of cardamom
½ tsp / 2 ml chilli powder
1 lime or lemon
3 big tomatoes, skinned and
    sliced
8 fl oz / 225 ml yoghurt
2 pints / 1.2 litres water
2 tsp / 10 ml salt
1 pint / 600 ml basmati or long-
    grain rice
2 tsp / 10 ml chopped mint

Fry the onion and garlic gently in the ghee until golden. Add the spices and fry until the fat runs. Add the tomatoes and cook for 10 minutes. Add 2 cups of cold water and bring to the boil.

Drop the koftas into this sauce and simmer for 25 minutes to complete the cooking. Serve with rice.

CHICKEN OR MUTTON PILAU

This recipe was given me by the wife of the Pakistan Military Attaché in Washington.

Cut the meat into bite-sized pieces. If using chicken, cut it into small joints. Heat the oil in a deep heavy saucepan. Brown the meat and set it aside. Turn down the heat and fry the onion in the same oil until transparent. Add the garlic and return the meat to the pan. Add the ginger paste and mix in well. Then add the cinnamon stick, the seeds from the cardamom pods and the chilli powder. Stir well and add 6 fl oz / 175 ml water. Cover tightly and simmer for about 15 minutes.

Add the juice from the lemon or lime, the tomatoes and salt to taste. Cover again and cook slowly until done, stirring occasionally. This should take 1 to 1½ hours. Add a little more water if it gets too dry. About 15 minutes before the meat is done, add the yoghurt.

While the curry is cooking, prepare the rice. Bring the 2 pints / 1.2 litres of water to the boil. Add the salt and then the rice, with the mint leaves on top. Cook on a moderate heat with the lid off until the water is absorbed and the rice barely cooked. Add this to the meat in the saucepan.

Remove the saucepan from the heat, seal the lid tightly with a paste of flour and water, and cover with a blanket to keep it hot. Leave for 1 hour before serving.

CHICKEN CURRY

As taught to me by the Maharanee of Kutch.

1 large chicken, cut in pieces
3 onions, sliced
4 tblsp / 60 ml oil or white fat

Masala
2 heaped tsp / 14 ml coriander
1 heaped tsp / 7 ml chilli (less, if
    you like it milder)
1 heaped tsp / 7 ml cumin
1 heaped tsp / 7 ml mixed spice
¾ tsp / 4 ml turmeric

3 cloves garlic, crushed
½ pint / 300 ml stock or water
1 tsp / 5 ml salt
4 cardamoms
1 pint / 600 ml thick-set yoghurt
4 tblsp / 60 ml coconut

Fry the onions gently in the oil until soft but not brown. Add the masala and fry with the onion for a minute or two until the fat runs. Add the chicken pieces and fry them gently until sealed.

Add the garlic, stock, salt and cardamoms, emptying the seed out of the cardamom pods beforehand. Cover the pot and simmer gently for about 1 hour until the chicken is tender. Add more stock if needed.

Ten minutes before serving, add the yoghurt and coconut to the chicken. Heat but do not boil. Serve with plain boiled rice.

The next recipe for Tandoori chicken holds special memories for me from the months which I spent with Rajmohan Gandhi and his friends, crisscrossing the country and everywhere welcomed in Indian homes.

I remember the Christmas which we spent in Bombay when we visitors decided to give a party for our hosts. I volunteered to cook the Christmas dinner. A comment afterwards from one of our Hindu guests moved me very much: 'I didn't know that Christ came for all of us. I thought he was just for you Christians.' We ended those two weeks in Bombay when Rajmohan led a meeting for 10,000 on the beach front in which he outlined his challenge to his country.

While in Bombay I was introduced to the Maharanee of Gwalior, with her son the young Maharaja, and his sister. She asked me if I liked riding. I said that I loved it. 'Well, come and exercise the horses tomorrow,' she said, 'at the racecourse.'

Next morning, in borrowed trousers, I turned up at this oasis of a green heaven, such a contrast to the dust and the beggars outside. Given a horse, I set off around the track – and I really disgraced myself. I lost my stirrups, just being able to cling on around the horse's neck. Managing to regain my stirrups, I cantered in at a sedate pace to be met by gales of laughter. 'We always give that horse to our guests.

It changes its leading leg. Come tomorrow and we will give you a better one.' I later learnt that they ran one of the top stables in India and had entertained our Queen.

I learnt a few words of Hindi, thinking that 'Challo!' might be useful in dealing with those marvellous taxis – three-wheeled scooters with a canopy. 'Challo! Challo!' I called out to my driver as we shot around corners. Only on arrival did I discover that, instead of asking him, as I thought, to go more slowly, I was actually urging him to greater speed.

From Bombay on to Bangalore where, with the background of my grandfather's service in the army in India, I was fascinated to be entertained for dinner in the Officers' Mess and to find that all the silver and the traditions had been carried over by the Indian Army from the old imperial days.

Then to Madras, and by bus to Kerala, a state Christianised by 'Doubting Thomas', the disciple who would not believe that Christ had risen unless he put his hand into the wound in his side. We were shown the tomb where he was buried after his martyrdom.

I was asked to help set up a camp for younger people at Panchgani, in the hills above Pune (Poona). The cooking on that occasion was done by army cooks on open fires, with metal sheets over them. After the camp the elders of Panchgani requested a meeting with Rajmohan and offered him a piece of land if he would build a permanent centre there. This was the birth of 'Asia Plateau' which has become a focus of hope for India and Asia. It has just celebrated its 25th anniversary.

I will never forget India's wonderful hospitality. On our arrival in one city two of my friends were given the address of the family where they were to stay. That evening they arrived at the door, introducing themselves as the guests who had come for the week. They were shown into the house and seated. After a longish wait they were taken to their room. At the end of the week a neighbour came round and asked, 'Where are my guests? I've been expecting them all week.' They had gone to the wrong house, but been welcomed none the less!

In Delhi we were shown with pride the Red Fort, built in Mogul times, with, in the courtyard, the iron pillar which has never rusted. A family took us out to a tandoori restaurant where we were served the traditional chicken with naan, an Indian bread. I asked to see how it was cooked and was fascinated with the tandoori ovens, deep holes in the ground with a narrow opening at the top and a fire of charcoal at the bottom. The chicken was fixed to great long skewers and put in the hole. Then the naan, made of yeast dough, was rolled out and slapped against the sides where it stuck until cooked, taking about ten minutes.

My recipe for tandoori chicken is as near as I can get to the real thing!

TANDOORI CHICKEN

1 large chicken (2½ lb / 1.3 kg) cut in pieces
¾ pint / 450 ml yoghurt or buttermilk
1 tsp / 5 ml curry powder
1 tsp / 5 ml turmeric
1 tsp / 5 ml chopped garlic
1 tsp / 5 ml salt
2" / 5 cm fresh ginger root, chopped
½ tsp / 3 ml chilli powder
½ tsp / 3 ml cumin
10 black peppercorns
4 tblsp / 60 ml tomato ketchup
3 cloves
1 bay leaf
4 tblsp / 60 ml ghee or oil
juice of 1 lime or lemon

Mix all the ingredients well in the yoghurt. Leave the chicken pieces to marinade in it for 6 hours or overnight.

Failing a tandoori oven, build your own barbecue fire and reduce it until the flames have gone and the embers are red-hot. Heat the wire grill on top. Remove the chicken from the sauce and place it on the grill, turning regularly until done – about half an hour. It is important to cook it slowly so that it is done right through. Dust it with paprika. Serve the marinade separately as a sauce.

Alternatively, the chicken may be cooked under the grill or in the oven at medium heat (350°F / 180°C / gas 4) for about 1¼ hours. In this case, cover it with tinfoil for the first hour, taking it off for the final 15 minutes for the chicken to brown. Dust with paprika.

Traditionally this dish is served with naan, the North Indian yeast bread. We have found that baked potatoes and various salads are excellent with it.

For 6

Pastry

4 oz / 125 g each of
   wholewheat and plain flour
1 oz / 25 g softened butter
5 fl oz / 150 ml (approx.) water

Filling

8 oz / 225 g minced meat or
   4 oz / 125 g each of potato
   and cauliflower

Masala

1 large onion, chopped
½ tsp / 3 ml each, turmeric,
   coriander, cumin, ginger
1 clove garlic, crushed
½ a red pepper, cut up and de-
   seeded

SAMOSAS

First make the pastry. Mix the 2 flours and rub in the butter with your fingertips. Add enough water to make a stiff but pliable dough. Knead this hard for 15 minutes by hand. Lay the dough aside under an airtight cover for 1½ hours – not in the fridge. This allows the flour to swell and become light.

Prepare the filling. Gently fry the onion in a little oil until soft and just turning colour. Add the masala spices, garlic and pepper and fry for a moment. Add the meat or vegetables and cook gently until just dry and soft before setting it aside to cool.

When the dough is ready, take it and knead it again briefly. Divide it into small balls about the size of a walnut. Keep these from the air under an upturned bowl so that they do not dry out. Knead each ball in turn to a smooth round and roll into a circle as thin as possible without tearing the dough. Cut each round in half. Dip your finger in a cup of cold water and wet half the straight edge of one section. Fold this over against the dry part of the straight edge and press them together, forming a cone. Spoon in your filling, dampen the top edges and fold them in on each other to enclose the filling, pressing them well together.

As each is ready, deep fry in a pan of hot oil until golden brown. Take them out and drain on kitchen paper.

For 4

2 onions, finely sliced
1 clove garlic, crushed
4 tblsp / 60 ml oil
14 oz / 400 g tinned or skinned
   fresh tomatoes
8 fl oz / 225 ml thick-set
   yoghurt
6 eggs

Masala

1 tsp / 5 ml turmeric
½ tsp / 3 ml coriander
½ tsp / 3 ml each, cumin, chilli,
   ginger

EGG CURRY

Fry the onions and garlic gently in the oil in a saucepan until light brown. Add the masala and cook well for about 3 minutes. Add the chopped tomatoes, cover and cook for about 30 minutes. Add a little water if needed. Add salt to taste and the yoghurt when the cooking is almost finished.

The eggs may be poached in this sauce or you can hard-boil them. If hard-boiled, make 6 or 8 cuts in the white around the yolk, put them in the sauce and bring to the boil.

AVIAL VEGETABLE STEW

For 4

2 lb / 1 kg vegetables selected
from the following: egg-plant
(aubergine), green beans,
carrots, peas, potatoes,
cauliflower florets
8 tblsp / 120 ml oil
2 tsp / 10 ml cumin seeds
6 tblsp / 90 ml coconut
1 tsp / 5 ml chilli powder
½ pint / 300 ml of the water
from cooking the vegetables
4 tblsp / 60 ml tomato ketchup
8 tblsp / 120 ml thick-set
yoghurt

Cut the vegetables into pieces roughly the same size. Parboil these in a little salted water for about 10 minutes and set aside.

Heat the oil in a saucepan and fry the cumin seeds and chilli for about 3 minutes. Drain the vegetables and add them. Let them cook for about 5 minutes to absorb the spices.

Add the coconut, the vegetable water and the tomato ketchup. Cook until the vegetables are done and add the yoghurt just before serving.

VEGETABLE CURRY

For 4

1 tblsp / 15 ml mustard seeds
6 tblsp / 90 ml oil
2 onions, finely sliced
8 oz / 225 g carrots, sliced
8 oz / 225 g cauliflower florets
14 oz / 400 g tinned or skinned
and chopped fresh tomatoes
8 oz / 225 g peas

Masala
1 tblsp / 15 ml ground ginger
1½ tsp / 8 ml turmeric
1 tsp / 5 ml each of coriander
and chilli powder
1 tblsp / 15 ml cumin seeds

Fry the mustard seeds in hot oil in a covered saucepan until they pop – 3 to 4 minutes. Lower the heat and fry the onions gently until soft. Add the masala and cook for about 3 minutes.

Add the carrots, cauliflower and tomatoes with a little extra water. Cover again and cook until still a little crunchy. Just before the end add the peas. Season to taste with salt.

BEAN AND BANANA CURRY

For 4

2 red chillis *or* ½ tsp / 3 ml chilli powder
pinch of asafoetida (optional)
1 tblsp / 15 ml ghee or oil
½ tsp / 3 ml turmeric
1 lb / 450 g fresh green beans, cut in pieces *or* 1 cup dried beans, soaked overnight and boiled for 1 hour
4 bananas, sliced
1½ tsp / 7 ml sugar
4 fl oz / 125 ml buttermilk or yoghurt

In a saucepan fry the chilli and asafoetida in the oil for a moment. Add the turmeric and fry until the fat runs.

Add the raw green beans or the cooked dried beans and fry for 5 minutes. Then the bananas, salt and 1 cup of water. Cover tightly and cook until done. The green beans should still be a little crunchy. Add the yoghurt last. Heat through and serve.

CABBAGE AND MUSTARD SEEDS

For 4

2 tblsp / 30 ml mustard seeds
4 tblsp / 60 ml oil
1 lb / 450 g shredded white cabbage
4 oz / 125 g fresh or dried shredded coconut (optional)

Fry the mustard seeds in the oil in a heavy saucepan with the lid on until they pop – about 4 minutes. Add the shredded cabbage and turn it around in the oil. Replace the lid and cook gently for up to 10 minutes. The cabbage should still be crunchy. Shredded coconut may be added before serving.

FRIED POTATO CURRY

For 4

1 lb / 450 g potato, peeled and cut in 8
4 tblsp / 60 ml oil
1 tblsp / 15 ml mustard seeds
½ tsp / 3 ml chilli powder

Boil the potatoes in salted water until done. Drain and fry them in the oil together with the chilli and the mustard seeds until crisp and golden.

PEA AND POTATO CURRY

For 4

1 large onion, finely sliced
3 cloves garlic, crushed
3 tblsp / 45 ml ghee or oil
2 green chillis, finely cut *or* 1 tsp /
   5 ml chilli powder
1 tsp / 5 ml turmeric
2 tsp / 10 ml coriander
1 lb / 450 g potatoes
2" / 5 cm piece of fresh ginger
   root, peeled and chopped *or*
   1 tsp / 5 ml ground ginger
8 oz / 225 g peas
½ pint / 300 ml water
juice of 1 lemon or lime

In a saucepan fry the onion and garlic slowly in the oil until soft and brown. Add the chilli, turmeric and coriander and fry gently for 3 to 4 minutes. Add the potatoes and chopped ginger and fry for 15 minutes. Then add the peas and water. Cover and cook until done. Stir in the juice of the lime or lemon just before serving.

STUFFED POTATO CURRY

For 6

½ medium onion, chopped
2 tblsp / 30 ml oil
6 oz / 175 g peas
1 green chilli *or* ½ tsp / 3 ml
   chilli powder
juice of ½ lemon
½ tsp / 3 ml salt
6 large potatoes

CURRY
1 medium onion, finely sliced
3 tblsp / 45 ml oil
½ tsp / 3 ml chilli powder
1 tsp / 5 ml turmeric
14 oz / 400 g tinned or fresh
   tomatoes, skinned and
   chopped
juice of ½ a lemon
1 tsp / 5 ml salt

Fry the onion in the oil until soft. Crush the peas coarsely and mix together with the chilli, onion and lemon juice, with salt to taste.

Peel and cut the potatoes in half vertically. Scoop out the centres and replace them with the stuffing mixture. Place the 2 halves of the potato together and fasten shut with cocktail sticks.

Deep fry them in hot oil until brown – about 15 minutes – then drain and cook them in the curry, prepared ahead.

In a deep saucepan fry the onion in the oil gently until soft. Add the spices and fry for about 3 minutes. Add the tomatoes, lemon juice and salt. Cook for about 20 minutes or until the tomatoes are done.

Add ½ pint / 300 ml of water and the stuffed potatoes. Put the lid on the pan and cook until soft – about another 20 minutes.

DAL

This is a standard dish to go with curry, especially vegetarian curries.

12 oz / 350 g red lentils or dried
   peas
2 onions, finely sliced
1 tsp / 5 ml turmeric
1 tsp / 5 ml cumin seeds
2 tsp / 10 ml coriander
1 tsp / 5 ml chilli powder
4 tblsp / 60 ml tomato ketchup
salt to taste

If using dried peas, soak them in water overnight. Cook the lentils or soaked peas in 1¾ pints / 1 litre of water. Simmer until soft with the lid on. The lentils take about half an hour, the peas longer – 1½ hours to 2 hours. Stir from time to time so that it does not stick to the bottom, adding more water if needed. When done, it will have the consistency of porridge.

Meanwhile, in a deep saucepan, slowly fry the onions in a little oil until brown. Add the turmeric, cumin, coriander and chilli and fry them together for about 3 minutes. Add the ketchup. Stir into the cooked lentils or peas, season with salt and serve.

POORIES

An unleavened Indian bread which goes with all curries.

6 oz / 175 g plain flour
½ tsp / 2 ml salt
1 tblsp / 15 ml melted ghee or
   oil
4 fl oz / 125 ml cold water
oil for deep frying

Sieve the flour and salt together. Make a well in the flour and add the water and ghee or oil. Mix together and knead the dough until smooth – about 10 minutes. The dough should be stiff enough to make a smooth ball without sticking to your fingers. Set aside under a damp cloth for at least 1 hour.

Break off small walnut-size pieces of the dough. Do not cut them as they will stick to the knife. Knead each piece in turn into a round smooth ball, roll out thinly and fry immediately in hot oil, turning once. They should puff up. Drain on kitchen paper, keeping each poorie hot while you repeat the process.

BHUGIAS (Vegetable Fritters)

4 oz / 125 g plain white flour *or*
   chana gran flour
1 tsp / 5 ml chilli powder
1 tsp / 5 ml baking powder
1 tblsp / 15 ml turmeric
3 tblsp / 45 ml oil

Mix the dry ingredients together. Form a well and add the oil and enough water to make a runny dipping batter.

Dip neatly cut-up vegetables into this batter and deep fry in hot oil until crisp. Drain dry on paper towels and serve hot. These are often served before the main meal, with drinks.

Suggested fillings
bananas, split lengthways and sliced into ½" / 1½ cm
   pieces
cauliflower florets
green pepper, cut in rings
egg-plants (aubergines), sliced thinly
potatoes, sliced or cubed
spinach leaves, torn in pieces
onion rings

One memorable occasion was the banquet given to our party in Madras by Shri Rajagopalachari, first Indian Governor General and Rajmohan Gandhi's maternal grandfather.

We were seated in a shamayana, a canopy put up under the palm trees. The night was magical – brilliant stars – and our music the accompaniment of frogs and crickets. We were greeted in the traditional Indian manner – hands together as if in prayer, and a bow of the head.

Before the meal, each guest was provided with a bowl of water and a fresh towel to wash and dry our hands. Seated on cushions at long, low tables, our plates were banana leaves. On these, at the top, were little piles of Indian chutneys, hot and spicy, with sweet sliced bananas and coconut.

Then the meal was served – a vegetable pilau with chappatis. This was eaten with two fingers of your right hand. A glass of water was placed by your left hand. The food was handed round again and again until I could manage no more. Then the banana leaves were simply folded over.

Below are a couple of desserts from my hostess in Madras.

GULAB JAMUN

8 cups of milk
2 tblsp / 30 ml cornflour
1 tblsp / 15 ml cold milk

Syrup
1½ lb / 700 g white sugar
½ pint / 300 ml cold water
3 drops rosewater or vanilla
   essence

Boil the 8 cups of milk gently until all the water has evaporated and it thickens to a creamy consistency. It will be a light brown colour. You must stir it all the time. This can take up to 2 hours. Let it cool for a few minutes.

When ready, add the cornflour to the 1 tblsp of cold milk. Mix well and add to the evaporated milk. Cook very gently, stirring well, until it is thick enough to roll into round bite-sized balls. Set these aside.

Boil together the sugar and water slowly until the sugar

melts and then more quickly to a thin syrup. Take it off the heat and cool. Then add the flavouring.

Fry the milk balls in ghee – clarified butter. Put them in the syrup and leave for several hours until cold. Serve in the syrup.

SEVIYAN

1 tblsp / 15 ml ghee
3 white cardamoms
2 oz / 50 g very fine vermicelli –
    Indian only
1½ pints / 900 ml boiled milk
4 oz / 125 g sugar
1¼ oz / 35 g blanched almonds
1 tsp / 5 ml rosewater

Melt the ghee and fry the crushed cardamoms. Add the vermicelli and fry very slowly and carefully so that it neither breaks nor burns, until it is a golden brown. Add the milk and sugar. Cook very carefully on a low heat.

When the mixture thickens, in about 20 minutes, add the almonds and the rosewater and put it in your serving dish. Leave until cold.

In India, for a party, desserts are often covered in a fine silver leaf which is then eaten.

WEST AFRICAN DISHES

I spent two months in West Africa in 1954 as one of a party of fifty of all ages invited by Nigerians and Ghanaians, who were seeking independence without violence and a society free of corruption. It was a fascinating time to be there. The air was full of hope and expectancy – and it was an introduction for me to a new part of the continent where I had been born.

We began in Lagos, presenting two stage plays. As props girl for the plays I had to explore the whole town searching for material. Those wonderful markets full of noise, food, exotically patterned cloth, brass and leather work and so on – everything you needed. I learnt that much of what I had known as Moroccan leather in fact originated in Nigeria and had been trekked across the Sahara in camel trains. I came to enjoy the fun of bargaining – a game you were expected to play.

Then three weeks on a train whose three carriages were our home, six to a compartment, as we toured the country. Ibadan in the west, with its university, the roads lit at night by the candles on hundreds of little stalls. Kaduna, the administrative capital of the north, and then to the thousand-year-old walled city of Kano, ruled by its Emir.

I was invited to stay with a Lebanese family. Their home was amazingly cool with its thick mud walls and high ceilings, despite the heat outside. There was lovely Lebanese food – rice and lamb, cooked with olive oil and spices.

The plays were put on in an open-air cinema. Building the stage from scratch, our crew could only work at night as the scaffolding would burn them by day in the sun's intense heat. A bus was hired to take us to the theatre on the opening night. Arriving to find thousands gathered outside, we were rather nervous of what the throng would make of us whites – there had been riots the year before. But as we got off the bus, a way opened in the crowd and we were clapped in.

We played in that theatre for a week. On the last night the rains were coming – and a tropical storm stops everything. One man said to us, 'If it does not rain tonight I will truly believe that God is with you.' The wind came and all hands were musterred to hold down the scenery. Then there was that distinctive hot damp smell of water on the dry earth that comes with the rain. In the interval, Ivan and Elsie Menzies, former D'Oyley Carte opera singers, entertained and held the audience. At the end of the show we struck and packed the stage and scenery in five minutes flat, an out-and-out record – usually we took two hours. As I closed the lid of the props trunk the first drops fell.

We were invited to a reception at the Emir's palace. Crossing first the outer courtyard, then the middle and inner courts we finally came to the palace itself where the Emir graciously received each one in the luxuriant greenery of his garden. I still remember his comment when introduced to Mrs van Beunigen, a senior Dutch lady who had courageously saved the lives of thousands of prisoners during the Nazi occupation of her country. 'Such a woman is worth a hundred men,' he said.

The Emir showed us his throne room, amazingly decorated in bold zigzag patterns of black and sparkling mica. The British Resident of the Colonial Service, who accompanied us, had lived in Kano for years but had himself never been inside the palace. When we left the city, the Emir sent his Chief Minister in his ceremonial robes of white cotton and black velvet to bid us farewell at the

EMIR'S PROCESSION, KANO

station. It was for me an introduction to an ancient and very dignified civilisation.

From Kano we went to Enugu in eastern Nigeria where I left the party to go with a small advance group to prepare the arrival in Ghana. In Accra, for transport for the 50 of us we had one Volkswagen Beetle. There were no buses, so we went everywhere on foot. Two of us girls were welcomed in the home of an Ashanti chief. His youngest wife came to town to look after us. The recipe for groundnut stew which follows is one she made.

We lived about two miles from the city centre. It was hot walking that distance, though fun as the children played tag with us and the workmen sitting at the corner would offer to share their fufu and chilli soup. I'm afraid I never quite dared to sample it!

We got tired one day and my friend said she had heard where we could hire ladies' bicycles. So we explored a maze of streets to find this shed in the heart of the town, next to Kwame Nkrumah's headquarters. The bargaining successfully concluded, we set off on our bicycles, enjoying our new-found freedom.

But now a new hazard. No one had ever seen a white woman on a bicycle before, so we became the target of all the lorry drivers with their mammy wagons painted with slogans, 'God's Time is Best', 'In God We Trust'. And so it had to be! For fun, they would drive as close to us as possible, passing us with cheers but threatening to push us into the deep, open drains along the roadside. Finally the Chief Justice came to Bremer Hofmeyr, leading our party, and said, 'For God's sake get those girls off those bicycles before we have an incident!' We were relegated once more to our feet.

That summer, 30 from Africa were at the Caux conference. There the idea came that Africa could speak to the world with an answer – and that it would come in the form of a play. Three of the men we had met, a Ghanaian MP, the leader of the Nigerian university students, and the vice-president of the African teachers of South Africa, sat down together and wrote Freedom, describing what they saw as the challenge for their continent. It was later made in Nigeria into a full-length colour feature film and was used by President Kenyatta and many others in Africa to help in their struggle for the full meaning of freedom.

I have only room here to record a couple of the recipes which I enjoyed in Nigeria and Ghana.

AKARA (Fried Beancakes)

8 oz / 225 g black-eyed beans
1 onion
½ a red and ½ a green pepper
salt to taste
1 egg (optional)
vegetable or palm oil for frying

Soak the beans in a large bowl of warm water for 10 minutes and then scrub them hard in several changes of water to remove the skins. Grind the beans to a paste in a liquidiser with the minimum of water.

Chop the onion and peppers finely and stir them by hand into the paste with the salt. A beaten egg may be added if wished.

Heat the oil in a pan. Form the paste into small balls and fry on both sides in deep oil until golden brown.

Rosa Amata, who gave me this recipe, says, 'West Africans eat these balls with corn or maize porridge in the morning or as a fast food at the office.' They make a delicious savoury snack or are an excellent supper dish with salad.

JOLLOFF RICE (Nigeria)

For 8

Chicken
3 lb / 1½ kg chicken pieces
3 onions, finely sliced
groundnut oil for frying
1 tsp / 5 ml cayenne pepper
stock or water to cover chicken

Rice
3 onions, chopped
4 tblsp / 60 ml groundnut oil
3 tomatoes, skinned and
    chopped
2 green, 1 red bell peppers,
    ground in a processor, seeds
    and all
4 fl oz / 125 ml tomato paste
2 tsp / 10 ml salt
1 tblsp / 15 ml African red
    pepper or cayenne (hot)
1 pint / 600 ml basmati or long-
    grain rice
2 pints / 1.2 litres chicken or
    meat stock
4 oz / 125 g butter
1 tsp / 5 ml of either thyme or
    nutmeg (optional)

Chicken In a deep saucepan fry the onions for the chicken until soft. Add the chicken and fry that with the cayenne pepper. When it is browned, cover the chicken with stock or water and simmer for about 1 hour until tender.

Drain the stock off the chicken and use the required quantity to cook the rice. Keep the chicken hot.

Rice In a deep saucepan fry the onions in the oil until soft. Add the tomatoes and bell peppers and cook for 10 minutes until their water has gone. Add the tomato paste, red pepper or cayenne, salt, the rice and the stock. Stir in the butter, the thyme or nutmeg if used, and bring to the boil. Cook for 15 minutes or until the rice has absorbed all the stock. Turn off the heat, put on the lid and leave to steam in its own heat for another 15 minutes.

To serve, put the rice down one side of a big platter and the chicken down the other. Served with pineapple and fried plantain if available, or bananas, and a green vegetable.

Note: this recipe is very hot as eaten in Nigeria. If you like it milder, use half the quantity of red pepper or cayenne.

For 8

GROUNDNUT STEW (Ghana)

I watched my hostess in Accra making this. She took me out to the courtyard behind her home to a shed where she had a stone shelf and a stone rolling-pin. There she rolled and crushed the lightly roasted groundnuts (peanuts) until they were almost like peanut butter. She then cut up the meat and other vegetables. She called a child to fetch a brazier and placed a pot of the prepared stew with vegetables on it. The child's job was to fan the brazier and keep the live coals burning until the stew was cooked.

2½ lb / 1 kg good stewing beef, cut in cubes
peanut oil for frying
2 onions, cut finely
3 lb / 1½ kg tomatoes, skinned and chopped
1 tblsp / 15 ml red pepper or cayenne
½ lb / 225 g crunchy peanut butter
2 lb / 1 kg mixed vegetables (e.g. okra, carrots, green beans, courgettes)

In a large saucepan, fry the meat in the peanut oil in batches until browned. Set this aside and fry the onions until soft. Add the tomatoes and return the beef to the pan. Bring to the boil and simmer until nearly tender, adding more water if needed. Add the red pepper or cayenne (halving the suggested amount if you prefer it milder).

Half an hour before serving add the neatly cut-up vegetables and the peanut butter, stirring until well mixed. Cook until done.

This is served with foufou – pounded yam or cassava – but rice or baked potatoes may be more available!

A most delicious groundnut stew was prepared for me by a delegation of French-Cameroon women who were visiting the United States. I found myself, with my schoolgirl French, having to act as their interpreter.

CHINESE DISHES

I developed a taste for Chinese food when looking after a delegation of a hundred young people brought to Europe from China.

CHINESE SWEET AND SOUR FISH

A favourite with our children.

1 lb / 500 g frozen fish in batter
   or fish fritters (see Index)
2 tblsp / 30 ml cooking oil

Heat the oil in a pan and fry the fish until lightly brown and crisp. Use more oil if needed. Drain on a piece of paper towel and keep warm. Serve with a sweet and sour sauce (see Index) and Chinese rice.

CHINESE RICE

½ pint / 300 ml basmati rice
1 pint / 600 ml water
4 oz / 125 g bacon rashers,
   diced
a little oil for frying
2 onions, finely sliced
1-2 tblsp / 15-30 ml soya sauce
2 eggs
4 spring onions, finely sliced
chopped parsley

Cook the rice in the water. When the water is almost absorbed put the lid on the saucepan and, if the stove is electric, turn it off. The residual heat will finish the cooking. Keep the rice hot until needed.

Meanwhile, fry the bacon until transparent. Remove it from the pan and put it on a plate. Heat the oil and fry the onion, adding the soya sauce. Put it aside with the bacon. Scramble the eggs in the same pan. Cut them up and fork them into the rice along with the bacon and onion.

Just before serving, add the spring onion and toss it through. Sprinkle the parsley over the top.

Note: An added novelty is to have, as a side dish, some puffed noodles: drop a nest of fine egg noodles into hot smoking oil and fry for a moment until puffed and brown. Take them out and drain them on a paper towel.

PRAWNS AND FRIED NOODLES

For 4

1 pint / 600 ml peanut oil
6 oz / 175 g Chinese noodles
3 large Pacific prawns *or* 1 lb /
    450 g lobster, tinned or frozen
1 bamboo shoot, chopped up
1 water chestnut, sliced
1 cucumber, peeled, de-seeded
    and diced
2 tblsp / 30 ml cornflour
½ pint / 300 ml chicken stock
1 tsp / 5 ml soya sauce
2 spring onions

Heat the oil for the noodles. You will know it is hot enough when a cube of bread will brown in 30 seconds. Take a frying basket and, with the noodles in it, lower it into the oil and fry steadily until golden brown. Drain on paper.

In a separate pan heat 2 tblsp / 30 ml oil; add the prawns or lobster and fry for 1 to 2 minutes; add the bamboo shoot, water chestnut and cucumber. Cook for 1 to 2 minutes.

Blend the cornflour with the chicken stock and the soya sauce and stir into the pot. Taste for seasoning and cook until thickened. Dish up and garnish with sliced spring onions. Serve the noodles separately.

PRAWN PANCAKES

For 4

4 oz / 125 g plain flour
2 oz / 60 g cornflour
¾ pint / ½ litre water
a pinch of salt

Filling
1 oz / 25 g lard or oil
1 onion, chopped
4 oz / 125 g raw pork or beef,
    minced
3 oz / 80 g shelled prawns
1 tin bean sprouts
seasoning
a few drops of soya sauce

Mix the flour, cornflour, water and salt together and beat until smooth. Set aside for half an hour.

Take a frying pan the size you wish the pancakes to be. Melt a little lard in the pan and, when hot, add just enough pancake batter to cover the bottom, tilting the pan to ensure this. Fry the pancake *on one side only* until quite dry but *not* golden in colour. Place on a clean tea-towel and continue until the batter is nearly used up, stacking the pancakes in the towel. Keep some batter back to use later when filling and sealing the pancakes.

To complete the filling, fry the onion gently in the lard or oil until transparent. Add the minced meat, 2 oz / 50 g of the prawns, chopped, and the remaining 1 oz / 25 g prawns kept whole. Add the drained bean sprouts, the seasoning and the soya sauce. Cook for 1 to 2 more minutes. Drain any excess lard.

Now take a pancake and place 2 tblsp / 30 ml of the prawn mixture into it. Fold in the ends and roll up, using the remaining batter to seal. Fill all the pancakes.

Put about 2" / 5 cm oil in a wide pan, heat well, and fry each pancake for a few minutes until really hot right through. Drain on a paper towel and serve.

RICE AND PASTA

PLAIN RICE

For 4

1 onion, chopped
2 oz / 50 g butter
½ pint / 300 ml long-grain rice
1 pint / 600 ml water

Sauté the onion in the butter in a saucepan. Add the rice together with the water and 1 tsp / 5 ml salt. Bring to the boil, stir once and then simmer until the water has just been absorbed. Turn off the heat and allow to steam in its own heat with the lid on. Do not stir until ready to serve. Before serving, fluff up the rice with a fork.

YELLOW RICE (South Africa)

For 4

1 pint / 600 ml water
2 tblsp / 30 ml brown sugar
2 oz / 50 g butter
½ tsp / 3 ml turmeric
1½ tsp / 7 ml salt
1 stick of cinnamon
½ pint / 300 ml long-grain rice

Put the water into a saucepan with the sugar, butter, turmeric, salt and cinnamon. Bring to the boil. Add the rice and simmer until the water is absorbed. Cover the pan, turn the heat off and steam in its own heat for 10 minutes.

In South Africa this is served with bobotie (see Index).

CRISP FRIED RICE

Heat 1 tblsp / 15 ml oil in a frying pan until hot and smoking. Put about 2 tblsp / 30 ml uncooked long-grain rice in a single layer on the bottom. It will puff up almost immediately. Take it out and drain it on a paper towel. Delicious served as a side dish with curry.

SPICY VEGETABLE RICE

For 8

1 pint / 600 ml long-grain rice
2 pints / 1.2 litres water
6 tblsp / 90 ml melted butter
1 large onion, sliced finely

Cook the rice in the water until done.

Heat the butter in a saucepan and sauté the onion until soft. Add the vegetables to the onion, then the ginger, garlic, curry powder and salt to taste. Cover and cook until done.

1 lb / 500 g frozen mixed
    vegetables
1 oz / 25 g fresh ginger root
    peeled and chopped finely
3 cloves garlic, mashed to a
    paste with 1 tsp / 5 ml salt
1 tblsp / 15 ml curry powder
salt
6 tblsp / 90 ml each of yoghurt
    and milk, mixed together
1 tblsp / 15 ml lemon juice
2 hard-boiled eggs

Toss the rice together with the cooked vegetables and add the yoghurt and milk, the lemon juice and the cut-up eggs. Re-heat and serve.

For 4

2 tblsp / 30 ml mustard seeds
a little oil for frying
1 tsp / 5 ml turmeric
2 red chillis, chopped finely
1 pint / 600 ml water
½ pint / 300 ml basmati rice
¼ pint / 150 ml grated
    coconut
2 oz / 50 g cashew nuts

COCONUT RICE (Madras)

Fry the mustard seeds in oil until they pop, keeping them covered. Add the turmeric, chillis, water and rice and simmer until the water is absorbed.

Meanwhile, fry the coconut and cashew nuts until lightly browned and then fork them into the cooked rice.

For 4

½ pint / 300 ml wholegrain
    brown rice
2 medium onions, chopped
2 tblsp / 30 ml oil
8 oz / 225 g chopped
    mushrooms
8 oz / 225 g grated cheddar
    cheese
2 tsp / 10 ml marmite
2 eggs, beaten
salt and pepper
3 tomatoes, skinned and sliced
tomato sauce
3 tblsp / 45 ml tomato ketchup

RICE, MUSHROOM AND
TOMATO LOAF

Put the rice on to boil in 1¼ pints / 750 ml water (brown rice takes longer to cook and needs extra water). Simmer for about 40 minutes.

Meanwhile, fry the onions gently in the oil. Add the mushrooms and cook until tender. Take off the heat and stir in the cheese, marmite, beaten eggs and seasoning.

Mix this in with the cooked rice. Grease a 2 lb / 1 kg loaf tin. Put half of the sliced tomatoes in the bottom of the loaf tin, then half the mixture and a further layer of sliced tomatoes. Fill the tin with the remaining mixture. Cover with a butter paper and tinfoil and bake at 370°F / 190°C / gas 5 for 35 minutes. When done, take out of the oven and leave aside for 5 minutes.

Turn it out of the tin onto a platter and cover with the

1 tsp / 5 ml mustard
1 tblsp / 15 ml brown sugar
4 fl oz / 125 ml tomato juice or
   vegetable stock

tomato sauce, which is made by simply boiling together the ketchup, mustard, sugar and stock or tomato juice.

RICE AND LENTIL CUTLETS

For 4

4 oz / 125 g each of short-grain
   rice and brown lentils
1 onion, chopped
2 cloves garlic, chopped
a little butter for frying
1 tsp / 5 ml each chopped
   tarragon, parsley and thyme
flour
1 egg
4 oz / 125 g dried breadcrumbs

For this recipe you need a short-grain, sticky rice such as is used in puddings.

Boil the rice and lentils separately in salted water until tender. Lentils take about 1 hour. Drain them.

Fry the onion and garlic gently in a little butter. Add the herbs, the rice and the lentils. Check for seasoning. Form into balls, golf-ball size, and dip each first in flour, then in raw egg mixed with a little milk, and finally in the dried breadcrumbs. Fry them in a mixture of butter and oil until brown and crisp. Serve with tomato or barbecue sauce.

RISOTTO GRANDMÈRE

For 4

2½ oz / 60 g butter
2 onions, chopped
½ a cucumber
4 oz / 125 g mushrooms, sliced
1 tsp / 5 ml salt
2 tsp / 10 ml chopped mint
2 tblsp / 30 ml parmesan cheese
½ pint / 300 ml long-grain rice
1¼ pint / 700 ml stock or water
4 tblsp / 60 ml red wine

Melt 2 oz / 50 g of the butter in a wide saucepan. Fry the onion gently for 5 minutes with the lid on.

Slice the peel of the cucumber into fine shreds. Split the cucumber lengthwise and de-seed. Dice the cucumber flesh.

Add the mushrooms, cucumber skin and pieces, and the mint to the onion. Cover the pan and simmer for a further 3 minutes.

Add the rice, turn it for a minute over the heat and then add the stock and wine. Simmer until the risotto is a creamy consistency. When the grains are tender, remove the pan from the heat. Scatter the cheese over the top with the extra butter. Cover and steam in its own heat for 10 minutes. Stir quickly once or twice with a fork and turn into a hot dish. Serve with a bowl of grated cheese.

SPÄTZLI (Swiss Noodles)

For 4

1¼ lb / 550 g flour
1 tsp / 5 ml salt
3 small eggs
8 fl oz / 225 ml water
1 oz / 25 g butter

Sift the flour and salt. Make a well in it and break in the eggs. Add the water and mix the water and eggs together, gradually drawing in the flour. Leave aside to swell for an hour.

Have ready 2 big saucepans of boiling salted water. Place the dough – it is very soft – on a wetted board. With a knife scrape thin pieces off the board into the first pot. When it comes back to the boil, remove the spätzli with a slotted spoon and put it into the second pot.

Boil it for about 10 minutes until done. Then drain it and put in a bowl with the warmed butter.

Spätzli may be served as an accompaniment to a main course, or eaten as a dish on their own with grated Swiss cheese and chopped parsley.

GNOCCHI

For 4

An Italian dish which can be used instead of spaghetti.

1 pint / 600 ml milk
4 oz / 125 g semolina
pinch of grated nutmeg
salt and pepper
2 beaten eggs
2 oz / 50 g each of grated
   parmesan and Swiss cheese

Bring the milk to the boil in a saucepan. Sprinkle in the semolina, stirring constantly. Add the nutmeg, salt and pepper to taste. Simmer until thickened – about 5 minutes.

Remove from the heat and beat in the eggs. Pour into a well-greased baking tin and spread it out to about ½" / 1 ½ cm thickness.

When quite cold, cut into shapes. Arrange these in a buttered casserole. Sprinkle liberally with cheese, dot with butter and grill for 5 minutes till golden brown. Serve with tomato sauce.

MACARONI D'ITALIA

For 4

8 oz / 225 g macaroni
1 large onion
8 oz / 225 g courgettes, cut up
4 tomatoes, peeled and diced
1 tsp / 5 ml sage
salt and pepper
4 fl oz / 125 ml whipping cream
4 oz / 125 g grated cheese (less
   if it is parmesan)

Boil the macaroni in a large pot of water until it is *al dente* (i.e. cooked but still firm).

Meanwhile, fry the onion gently in a deep saucepan. Add the courgettes. Put the lid half on and let the vegetables sweat for about 5 minutes. Then add the tomato, sage and seasoning to taste. Cook for 10 minutes.

When the macaroni is ready, drain it and put it into a buttered casserole in layers alternately with the vegetables and half the grated cheese. Pour the cream over the top and finish with the rest of the grated cheese. Add some dabs of butter. Bake in the oven at 400°F / 200°C / gas 6 for about 20 minutes until the cheese melts and browns.

PASTA AND TUNA CASSEROLE

8 oz / 225 g pasta
8 oz / 225 g shallots
4 oz / 125 g mushrooms, sliced
2 oz / 50 g butter
8 oz / 225 g tinned tuna
½ tsp / 3 ml celery salt
½ tsp / 3 ml salt
pepper
8 fl oz / 225 ml each of sour
   cream and creamed cottage
   cheese
4 oz / 125 g mature cheddar
   cheese

Boil the pasta in salted water until tender. Drain it.

Sauté the shallots and mushrooms in the butter. Add the tuna, breaking it up, the celery salt and seasoning to taste. Heat through.

Combine the sour cream and cottage cheese in another bowl or in a food processor and beat until smooth.

Layer the pasta, vegetables and tuna in a buttered casserole, ending with pasta. Pour on the cream and cheese mixture. Sprinkle the grated cheese on top. Bake in the oven at 350°F / 180°C / gas 4 for half an hour. Ham or chicken can be substituted for tuna.

EGG AND CHEESE DISHES

For 4

6 eggs
6 tblsp / 90 ml cold water
½ tsp/ 3 ml salt
¼ tsp / 1 ml pepper
1 oz / 25 g butter or margarine

BASIC OMELETTE

Crack the eggs into a bowl and beat them up with the water, salt and pepper.

Take a heavy-duty frying pan or omelette pan. Melt half the butter in this and let it turn light brown. Add half the egg mixture. As it sets, lift the edges so that the raw egg can run underneath.

When just about set, flip one half over the other. Cook a moment more and flip it upside down onto a heated serving plate. Repeat the process for the second half of the mixture.

An omelette should not be cooked until it is dry. The centre should be only just set.

CHEESE OMELETTE

Grate 2 oz / 50 g of cheese. Spread half the cheese over the first omelette before flipping one half over on the other. Repeat for the second omelette.

4 oz / 125 g mushrooms, sliced
butter or margarine for frying
1 oz / 25 g chopped onion

MUSHROOM OMELETTE

In a separate pan fry the onion until soft. Add the mushrooms and, when cooked, add them to the omelette as for the cheese recipe.

1 onion, skinned and sliced
1 clove garlic, chopped (optional)
4 tomatoes, skinned and cut up
olive oil for frying

ONION AND TOMATO OMELETTE

Gently fry the onion and garlic until soft. Add the tomatoes. Season with salt and pepper, and sugar if desired. Leave to simmer while you are cooking the omelette. Before bringing the omelette to the table pour the tomato sauce over it.

1 tblsp / 15 ml mixed dry herbs
   or 2 tblsp / 30 ml fresh herbs

OMELETTE AUX FINES HERBES

Mix this into the eggs for the plain omelette before cooking.

HAM OMELETTE

If you have pieces of leftover ham to use up, make a light Béchamel sauce (see Index) and, when cooked, add the chopped ham to this. Spread half of this over the first omelette and then flip the one half over on the other. Cook a moment longer and turn upside down onto a heated plate. Repeat for the other omelette.

SPANISH OMELETTE

2 oz / 50 g butter or margarine
½ a large onion, chopped
2 boiled potatoes, sliced
½ a green pepper, chopped
2 tomatoes, skinned, sliced
6 eggs
6 tblsp / 90 ml water
1 tblsp / 15 ml chopped parsley
  or chives
seasoning

Melt the butter in a large, heavy-duty frying pan. Fry the onion gently until beginning to brown. Push to one side, turn the heat up and add the potatoes. When they are beginning to brown add the green pepper and tomatoes. Mix everything together and cook for a moment more.

Mix together the eggs, water, parsley or chives and seasoning in a bowl. Pour all this over the fried vegetables in the pan and, as it cooks, push the edges into the middle so that the raw egg runs underneath. When almost ready, put the pan under a hot grill for a moment to set the omelette.

For 4

BAKED EGGS

1 oz / 25 g butter
4 eggs
4 tblsp / 60 ml whipping cream
salt and pepper

Butter 4 ramequin dishes with half the butter. Drop a raw egg into each dish. Put 1 tblsp / 15 ml cream on top of each, with salt and pepper and a dot of the remaining butter.

Bake in the oven at 350°F / 180°C / gas 4 for about 15 minutes. The white should be set and the yolk runny, unless you prefer it hard.

This recipe may be varied by baking the eggs on top of cooked mushrooms, spinach or tomato sauce.

DRAPPIT EGGS (Poached eggs on spinach)

8 oz / 225 g spinach
4 eggs
2 pints / 1 litre stock
4 slices toast in rounds, buttered

First cook the spinach in its own juice for about 10 minutes (I never add water). Season to taste with salt, pepper and nutmeg.

Poach the eggs in stock or water.

To serve, divide the spinach between the rounds of toast. Drain the eggs and place 1 on top of each round.

EGGS BENEDICT

Poached eggs, on a bed of spinach over a slice of ham placed on a round of toast or a toasted English muffin. Mask the whole with Hollandaise sauce (see Index).

For 4

OEUFS POCHES TALLYRAND

(Eggs and Mushrooms in Potato Cases)

1 lb / 450 g potatoes
4 oz / 125 g butter
2 egg yolks
salt and pepper
4 slices of bread
4 oz / 125 g mushrooms
2 tblsp / 30 ml white wine
1 tsp / 5 ml lemon juice
4 eggs
a dash of vinegar
4 oz / 125 g grated cheese
4 fl oz / 125 ml whipping cream

Boil the peeled potatoes in salted water until done, and then mash them very well. Add 1 oz / 25 g of the butter, then 2 egg yolks, salt and pepper and stir vigorously until fully blended. A little milk may be added if needed.

Cut the bread into rounds and fry in a little butter until crisp and golden brown.

Place the mashed potato in a piping bag fitted with a star tube and pipe 4 rounds on top of each other on the rounds of bread, leaving a hole in the centre. Put them in the oven at 350°F / 180°C / gas 4 for 10 minutes.

Toss the mushrooms in the pan with a little butter to cook. Add the white wine, lemon juice and seasoning and keep warm.

Poach the eggs in salted water with a dash of vinegar until

the whites are set, but not the yolks. The water should be nearly, but not, boiling.

Put the mushroom mixture inside the potato cases and place a poached egg on top of each. Divide the cream between the cases. Sprinkle them well with grated cheese and return to the oven for 2 minutes or until the cheese is melted.

SCOTCH WOODCOCK

(Scrambled Eggs with Anchovies)

For 4

8 anchovies
½ oz / 15 g butter
4 slices of toast
4 egg yolks
4 fl oz / 125 ml single cream
pinch of cayenne pepper and
    salt
1 tblsp / 15 ml chopped parsley

This was one of my grandfather's favourites. He always preferred a savoury to a sweet.

Pound the anchovy fillets into the butter. Spread the toast with this mixture. Put the slices on a plate and keep warm.

Beat the egg yolks, cream, salt and cayenne over boiling water in a double boiler until thickened. Add the parsley and divide this between the slices of toast. Serve at once.

SAVOURY FRENCH TOAST

4 slices white bread
1 tblsp / 15 ml each of tomato
    ketchup and milk, mixed
1 egg
¼ tsp / 1 ml thyme
1 tsp / 5 ml parsley
a little butter for frying

Cut the bread into triangles and brush each side with the tomato ketchup mixture. Beat the egg together with the herbs and seasoning. Dip the prepared bread into the egg mixture and fry in butter.

Dress in a ring with crisply fried onions, tomatoes or mushrooms in the centre.

CHEESE SOUFFLÉ

For 6

2 oz / 50 g butter
4 tblsp / 60 ml flour
12 fl oz / 350 ml milk
4 oz / 125 g each of grated
    cheddar and parmesan cheese
6 eggs, separated
1 tsp / 5 ml salt
dash of pepper and paprika
1 tsp / 5 ml English mustard

Tie a greaseproof paper around the outside of an unbuttered soufflé dish, so that the paper comes well up above the top. This is to hold in the risen soufflé.

In a saucepan melt the butter. Add the flour and then gradually stir in the milk, whisking to make sure there are no lumps. Bring this to the boil, stirring constantly.

Take off the heat and add the grated cheese. Then stir in the beaten egg yolks. Add the seasoning and mustard.

Beat the egg whites stiffly but not dry. First fold in a

spoonful of the egg white (this makes it easier to mix). Then fold in the rest of the whites with a metal spoon.

Pour the mixture into the soufflé dish. It should be no more than three-quarters full. Take a knife and cut a circle in the mixture halfway inside the dish to help raise a 'hat' when it cooks. You will not see any line once you have withdrawn the knife.

Put the soufflé in the oven (preheated to 420°F / 220°C / gas 7) for 15 minutes – no longer. It should be well risen but still a little runny inside. The company should be seated at the table before you bring in the soufflé. If kept waiting it will fall.

When serving soufflé for a light lunch or supper, I like it with potato crisps, spinach and a tomato sauce.

QUICHE LORRAINE

For 8

1 lb / 450 g shortcrust pastry (see Index)
4 eggs
2 oz / 50 g melted butter
¾ pint / 450 ml milk
1 onion, grated
1 tsp / 5 ml salt
a good pinch of pepper
a dash of cayenne pepper
4 oz / 125 g grated cheese, half parmesan, and half cheddar

Line 1 big pie plate or 2 smaller ones with the shortcrust pastry. Pinch the pastry all round the edge with your thumb and forefinger to scallop it.

Separate 1 of the eggs and whisk the white lightly. Brush the pastry shells with this.

Beat the yolk and the 3 remaining eggs together. Mix in the melted butter, milk, onion and seasonings.

Divide the grated cheeses between the pies and pour the egg custard over them. Bake in the oven at 400°F / 200°C / gas 6 for 10 minutes to set the pastry. Then turn the heat down to 300°F / 150°C / gas 3 and continue cooking slowly until firm – about 45 minutes. The time depends on the size of the dish. Test with a skewer, which will come out clean when ready. Do not allow the pie to boil.

This basic recipe may be varied in many ways by putting a mixture of the following in the pie before pouring on the quiche custard.
  blanched cauliflower
  blanched spinach
  blanched courgettes and fried onions
  cooked carrots
  fried mushrooms
  cooked, chopped-up bacon

MUSHROOM AND TOMATO FLAN

For 4 to 6

Pastry
4 oz / 100 g plain flour
pinch of salt
1 oz / 25 g rolled oats
1 oz / 25 g each of margarine
    and lard or white fat
1 egg yolk
4 tblsp / 60 ml cold water

Filling
1 large onion, sliced
2 oz / 50 g butter
4 oz / 125 g sliced mushrooms
2 tomatoes, skinned and sliced
½ pint / 300 ml milk
2 eggs, beaten
salt and pepper
herbs to taste
3 oz / 75 g grated cheese

Sift the flour and salt together. Add the oats. Rub in the fats lightly and gently with your fingertips.

Make a well in the centre and put in 1 egg yolk and the water. Cut this in with a knife and then knead it lightly into a ball of firm dough. Set this aside to rest, covered, for half an hour.

The filling
Gently fry the thinly sliced onion in the butter until soft. Add the mushrooms and tomatoes and cook until soft.

In another bowl mix together the milk, beaten egg, cheese and seasonings. Mix in the cooled vegetables.

Roll out the pastry and line the pie dish, pinching the edge to scallop it. Whisk the extra white of egg a little and brush it over the base of the pastry in the dish. What remains may be added to the filling.

Bake a pie in the oven at 400°F / 200°C / gas 6 for 10 minutes. Then reduce the heat to 300°F / 150°C / gas 3. Cook for about 45 minutes altogether. Test with a skewer which will come out clean when it is cooked. Do not let it boil or it will go watery.

EGG AND BACON PIE

For 4

8 oz / 225 g shortcrust pastry
    (see Index)
6 big rashers of bacon, with the
    rind removed
2 oz / 50 g grated or cream
    cheese
2 eggs
8 fl oz / 225 ml whipping cream
    or evaporated milk
salt and pepper

Line the pie dish with the pastry, as in the recipe above. Brush the base with a little lightly whisked egg white taken from the eggs.

Fry the bacon and chop it small. Spread it over the bottom of the pastry shell. Over it spread the cheese.

Whisk the eggs together with the cream or evaporated milk. Season with pepper (you may not need salt because of the bacon). Pour this mixture into the pie dish and bake in the oven at 400°F / 200°C / gas 6 for 10 minutes. Then reduce the heat to 300°F / 150°C / gas 3. Cook for a further 30 minutes. Test with a skewer for readiness.

For 4

1 recipe for choux pastry before it is baked (see Index).

GOUGÈRE

Butter a pie dish well. Put in the choux pastry and push it well up the sides. In the centre put the filling of your choice – e.g. leeks in cream sauce, etc – and bake for 45 minutes in a hot oven (400°F / 200°C / gas 6) until the pastry is puffed and golden.

CHEESE FRITTERS

2 tblsp / 30 ml plain flour
1 tsp / 5 ml English mustard
4 fl oz / 125 ml milk
2 oz / 50 g grated parmesan
   cheese
pinch of salt
2 egg whites
oil for frying

Whisk in the flour with the mustard and milk until all lumps are removed. Add the cheese and salt.

Beat the egg whites until very stiff and fold gently into the cheese and milk mixtures with a metal spoon.

Have ready a large pan with hot oil about 2" / 5 cm deep. Drop spoonfuls of the fritter mixture into this and brown on all sides. Drain the fritters on kitchen paper and serve on a napkin.

3 medium-sized pies

MONACO PIZZA PIE

1 oz / 25 g fresh yeast *or* 1 tblsp /
   15 ml dried yeast
½ tsp / 3 ml sugar
12 oz / 350 g plain flour
salt
3 fl oz / 75 ml olive oil

Dissolve the yeast in a little tepid water with the sugar. After 10 minutes, when it has frothed up, put it into a well made in the centre of the sieved flour and salt. Add the olive oil and enough warm water – about ¼ pint / 150 ml – to moisten the dough.

Knead all this together until the dough is elastic. Roll it into a ball and put in a bowl covered with a plastic bag and a blanket to keep it warm. Set it aside to rise until doubled in bulk. This will take 1 to 2 hours. (I put it in the airing cupboard where it is not too hot.) When ready, turn the oven on to 350°F / 180°C / gas 4.

Divide the dough into 3. Knead each into a round and then roll it out flat on a floured surface. Place each round on a baking tray, prick it all over and leave it to 'prove' – a second rising – for about half an hour.

Cook these in the oven for about 10 minutes until nearly done. They are then ready for the topping.

The toppings listed are the basic ingredients. To them you can add olives and anchovies for 1 pie, sliced mushrooms for another, and sweetcorn and salami for the third.

PIZZA TOPPINGS
6 onions, sliced finely
2 cloves garlic, crushed
9 large tomatoes, peeled
12 oz / 350 g mozzarella cheese

Fry the onions in oil until soft. Add the garlic and chopped tomatoes. Divide this between the pies. Cover with the other ingredients of your choice. Finish with grated mozzarella

163

VEGETABLE DISHES

GREEN BEANS WITH CHEESE

For 4

1 lb / 450 g fresh or frozen
  French cut green beans
4 oz / 125 g grated Swiss cheese
8 fl oz / single cream or a white
  sauce

If the beans are fresh, cook them for 2 minutes in boiling salted water before putting them into a buttered casserole. If frozen, put them straight into the casserole, layered with the grated cheese. Pour the cream over the top, with a final layer of cheese.

Bake in the oven at 350°F / 180°C / gas 4 for half an hour.

CORN FRITTERS

For 4

½ pint / 300 ml tinned creamed
  corn
3 eggs, separated
1 oz / 25 g plain flour
½ tsp / 3 ml salt
¼ tsp / 1 ml pepper
oil for shallow frying

Mix together the corn, egg yolks, flour, salt and pepper.

Whisk the egg whites until stiff and fold them into the mixture.

Have a frying pan ready with a little hot oil. Drop the mixture by spoonfuls into the pan, turning them once. Cook for about a minute on each side until just turning colour. Do not overcook.

These can be served with chicken or they make a light supper dish.

SCALLOPED CORN

For 4

4 oz / 125 g soft breadcrumbs
1 oz / 25 g butter
14 oz / 400 g tinned sweetcorn
3 tblsp / 45 ml double cream
1 tsp / 5 ml sugar
1 tsp / 5 ml salt
¼ tsp / 1 ml pepper

Fry the breadcrumbs in the butter until crisp. Butter a casserole and sprinkle half the breadcrumbs around the bottom and sides, reserving some for the top.

Mix together the corn with 3 tblsp / 45 ml of the liquid from the tin. Add the cream, sugar, salt and pepper. Add this to the casserole. Sprinkle the remaining breadcrumbs on top and bake in the oven at 350°F / 180°C / gas 4 for about 30 minutes.

This can be made with 6 freshly boiled cobs of corn which you strip first with a knife and then with the prongs of a fork.

For about 8

1 marrow
2 apples, peeled and sliced
1 lemon
2 onions, finely chopped
2 oz / 50 g butter
1 lb / 450 g corned beef
14 oz / 400 g tin baked beans
1 tsp / 5 ml each of sage and
    thyme

STUFFED VEGETABLE MARROW

Cut the marrow in half lengthwise. Scoop out all the seeds. Mix together the apple and the juice and grated rind of the lemon.

Fry the onion gently in the butter. Add the apple and lemon mixture, the chopped corned beef, the baked beans, sage and thyme. Remove from the heat and pile into the hollow in the marrow, well heaped up. Replace the other half of the marrow on top and tie together with tinfoil and string.

Place in a roasting pan, half-filled with water. Cover the pan with tinfoil and bake in the oven at 350°F / 180°C / gas 4 for 1 hour until well done. Lift the marrow onto a serving plate before folding back the foil.

MUSHROOMS

These are delicious in stews. They are also very good as a savoury snack or entree dish.

1 oz / 25 g butter
4 tblsp / 60 ml white wine
8 oz / 225 g mushrooms
2 fl oz / 50 ml fresh or sour cream
chopped parsley

STUFFED MUSHROOMS
2 or 3 large open mushrooms
    per person
sage and onion stuffing (see
    Index).
1 slice of cheese for each
    mushroom

(1.) For 4 people, fry ½ lb / 225 g mushrooms in 2 oz / 50 g butter for about 5 minutes, turning them from time to time. Serve on hot buttered toast.

(2.) Melt the butter in a saucepan. Add the wine and the mushrooms. Cover and simmer slowly for 10 minutes. Just before serving add the cream. Serve on toast or in ramequin dishes with a sprinkling of parsley.
You could also sprinkle 2 oz / 50 g cheese over the top and then lightly grill.

(3.) Chop the stalks of the mushrooms finely and add them to the stuffing.
Butter a large flat casserole dish. Lay the mushrooms in this, gills up. Put a dab of butter in each cap and place in the oven at 350°F / 180°C / gas 4 for about 10 minutes.
Pile the stuffing into each cap. Put a slice of cheese over the top of each and bake for a further 15 to 20 minutes.

(4.) As a filling for vol-au-vent pastry cases, use recipe 2, mixed with ½ pint / 300 ml Béchamel sauce (see Index), taking the liquid from the mushrooms to make the sauce. Add 1 tsp / 5 ml thyme for flavouring. Put this into the cases and re-heat in a moderate oven for 10 minutes just before serving.

BAKED STUFFED POTATOES

The traditional method is to prick the potatoes and bake in the oven heated to 400°F / 200°C / gas 6 for an hour. This, however, is expensive unless the oven is already on. I now have an electric frying pan and find this is ideal. Put a metal sheet in the bottom of the pan, cut the potatoes in half, rub a little fat on the cut side and bake for 30 minutes with the vent open to allow the steam to escape. Fillings can be many and various, added when cooked. Some suggestions:

(1.) Crush 1 or 2 garlic cloves with butter. Cut a cross in the potato, press it open and push in a generous pat of the garlic butter.

(2.) Take 2 or more slices of cheese for each potato. Cut a cross in each potato, press open and push the cheese in. Bake for a further couple of minutes to melt the cheese.

(3.) Cut a lid off the cooked potato. Carefully scoop out the potato and mash it with milk and butter, seasoning it well. Return it to the shell as is, or mixed with chopped ham, cooked bacon or shrimps. Garnish with chives or chopped parsley.

CHANTILLY POTATOES

For 4

1½ lb / 700 g potatoes, boiled, mashed and flavoured to taste
8 fl oz / 225 ml whipping cream
4 oz / 125 g grated cheese

Spoon the potatoes into a buttered casserole. Whip the cream until stiff and gently fold in the grated cheese, seasoning to taste. Spread this over the potatoes and bake in the oven at 350°F / 180°C / gas 4 for 30 minutes.

CRÊPES DE POMMES DE TERRE

For 8

8 oz / 225 g cream chese
2 tblsp / 30 ml plain flour
salt and pepper
6 oz / 175 g Swiss cheese, diced
2 lb / 1 kg raw, peeled potatoes
2 eggs, beaten together
3 tblsp / 45 ml double cream
1 oz / 25 g each of butter and oil

Blend together the cream cheese, flour and seasoning to taste. Stir in the diced cheese.

Grate the potatoes roughly, twisting them in a towel to remove moisture and stir them into the mixture with the eggs. Add cream until it becomes the consistency of creamy coleslaw.

Heat the butter and oil in a frying pan. Ladle in spoonfuls of the potato batter and cook as for pancakes, turning them once.

For a light meal, serve with a sauce of your choice.

POMMES DAUPHINES

For 4

4 oz / 125 g butter or margarine
4 fl oz / 125 ml water
4 tblsp / 60 ml plain flour
2 medium eggs
8 oz / 225 g mashed potato
oil for deep frying

In a saucepan heat the butter and water together until boiling. Remove from the heat and add the flour all at once, beating it in. Return to the heat and stir until the mixture comes into a ball away from the sides of the pan.

Remove from the heat and allow to cool a little before beating in the eggs, one by one. Now add the mashed potato, beating it in.

Have ready a pan of hot, deep fat and drop in spoonfuls of the mixture, turning them over to brown on both sides.

Drain on paper towels and keep hot. Serve as soon as possible. A nice change from chips!

For a light supper dish, mix in 4 oz / 125 g grated cheese to the mashed potato mixture, fry as before and serve with a tomato sauce.

RÖSTI (a delicious Swiss dish)

For 4

4 large potatoes
1 large onion
2 oz / 50 g butter
salt and pepper

Steam the unpeeled potatoes until just cooked. Peel and roughly grate them.

Fry the onion gently in the butter. Add the grated potato, sprinkling with salt and pepper. Cover with a lid or plate and fry slowly for 20 minutes until brown. Remove from the heat, invert the pan onto a plate and slide the potatoes back into the pan to fry for a further 10 minutes until brown on the other side.

To serve, cut the rösti like a cake. This is often eaten with a fresh tomato salad and Swiss cheese as a meal on its own.

THUMP (a Scots recipe)

For 4 to 6

2 lb / 1 kg freshly boiled
   potatoes
8 fl oz / 225 ml milk
4 oz / 125 g butter
8 oz / 225 g spring onions,
   sliced

Mash the potato together with the milk, butter and spring onions. Beat until light and fluffy, adding more milk if needed. (Excluding the onions, this is the way to make ordinary mashed potato.)

To serve, put a dollop on your plate, make a well in the centre and drop some parsley butter into it.

To be traditional, serve buttermilk to drink.

169

SPINACH WITH CHEESE

For 4

1 lb / 450 g fresh spinach
1 large onion, chopped
4 slices buttered toast
2 oz / 50 g cheese, sliced

Cook the fresh spinach and chop it up. Gently fry the onion in a little butter and mix it into the spinach with a little cream if available. Season to taste with salt, pepper and nutmeg. Pile the spinach onto the toast. Cover well with cheese and heat under the grill until the cheese is melted.

Note: You may put 2 fried rashers of bacon on the toast under the spinach and/or a poached egg on top for a quick meal.

SALSIFY ITALIENNE

For 4

My grandmother's recipe.

8 roots of salsify
juice of ½ a lemon
1 oz / 25 g butter
1 onion, chopped
4 chopped mushrooms
1 oz / 25 g cooked ham
1 tblsp / 15 ml plain flour
1 tsp / 5 ml tomato purée
1 tsp / 5 ml mixed herbs
5 tblsp / 75 ml each of white
    wine and good stock
2 tomatoes, skinned, quartered
1 tblsp / 15 ml chopped parsley
a dish of parmesan or grated
    cheese

Wash and scrape the salsify. Simmer in salted water with the lemon juice for 40 to 60 minutes until tender. Then drain it.

In a fireproof casserole melt the butter. Add the chopped onion and soften it. Then add the mushrooms and the chopped ham. Cook slowly, stirring frequently for 7 to 10 minutes.

Remove from the heat and stir in the flour, tomato purée and the dried herbs. Pour on the wine and stock and simmer for about 5 minutes, till thickened. Add the salsify and the tomatoes. Cook for another 5 minutes. Serve in the casserole sprinkled with chopped parsley.

The cheese is served separately.

SCALLOPED TOMATOES

For 4

4 oz / 125 g onions, finely
    chopped
2 oz / 50 g butter or margarine
8 oz / 225 g soft breadcrumbs
1 tblsp / 15 ml sugar
1 tsp / 5 ml salt
¼ tsp / 1 ml pepper
dash of cayenne
1 pint / 600 ml tinned tomatoes

Gently fry the onion in the butter until soft. Add three-quarters of the breadcrumbs, the sugar, salt, pepper and cayenne. Butter a 2 pint / 1.2 litre casserole and layer the tomatoes and the breadcrumb mixture alternately, finishing with the remaining breadcrumbs.

Bake in the oven at 350°F / 180°C / gas 4 for 45 minutes and serve.

RATATOUILLE

4 fl oz / 125 ml olive oil

1 clove garlic, sliced finely

3 large onions, sliced

4 green peppers de-seeded and
sliced

1 medium egg-plant
(aubergine), sliced ¼" / 1 cm
thick and quartered

5 medium tomatoes, skinned,
de-seeded and cut up

Heat the olive oil in a saucepan. Add the garlic and then the vegetables in alternate layers, with a little salt and pepper on each layer, until the pan is filled.

Add a few more drops of olive oil to the surface and then simmer over a low heat for 30 to 35 minutes, gently moving the contents from time to time. For the final 10 minutes remove the lid so as to reduce the juice to the required consistency.

This is delicious served with fried fish, or any dry meat – steak, chops, fried chicken, etc.

BAKED TOMATOES

I often serve these as a second vegetable. Choose large tomatoes – 1 between 2 people plus an extra couple if served as a second vegetable.

Halve the tomatoes and place them on a baking tray. Sprinkle them with salt, sugar and pepper. Cover them with dried breadcrumbs and a dab of butter on the top.

Bake them at 350°F / 180°C / gas 4 for about 15 minutes until cooked, but still holding their shape.

Delicious served with fish, steak, chops, or any dry meat.

VEGETABLE STEW

Good on a winter's day with cold meat.

2 lb / 900 g mixed vegetables
for 4 people (onions, carrots,
turnips, artichokes, potatoes,
etc.)

1 tsp / 5 ml sugar

1 tsp / 5 ml dried thyme or other
herbs

salt and pepper

Peel some pickling onions if you have them – otherwise quarter some large onions. Cut up carrots, turnips, potatoes or other vegetables of your choice. Put them in a saucepan with a well-fitting lid, together with a knob of butter, sugar, salt and pepper. Add some water – not too much – and steam them until tender. Serve them in their juice.

VEGETABLES

Vegetables can make or mar a good meal. If possible I choose fresh vegetables and, if serving several, select them to complement each other in colour and texture as well as in taste.

At a talk on waterless cooking to which I went, the lecturer asked us how we made tea. You soak the leaves in boiling water and then drink the water. The same thing happens with vegetables. Much of the good can come out into the water. Since then I use the minimum amount of water possible. Sometimes, it is true, they boil dry and burn a little; but if you watch carefully you can preserve their full taste and value. And now that I have a vegetarian daughter, it is even more important.

This lesson was emphasised for me by a medical nurse responsible for the health of all who came to the Moral Re-armament conference centre at Mackinac Island, Michigan, in the United States. We were talking about the Californian farmers who, for two years, had been sending a lorry-load of fresh vegetables to the conference every two weeks. The nurse remarked that, in contrast to previous years, the incidence of minor ailments such as colds had dropped by two-thirds. Cause and effect?

Mackinac, set in the heart of the Great Lakes, is a unique place. The only cars allowed on the island are the ambulance and the fire engine. Public transport is by horse-drawn 'surrey with a fringe on top', or by bicycle. During the summer the island is awash with tourists and holiday-makers, but in winter the lakes freeze over, the snow comes four feet deep and the island returns to its inhabitants. Skis are then the order of the day. I lived on the island right through one winter, cooking while a studio was built and a feature film made of the play The Crowning Experience with which I had earlier been in Atlanta, Georgia. We cooked in shifts. I loved the breakfast shift when I would wake at 4 a.m. and go across to the kitchen under the brilliant starry sky, the snow crunching, fresh and untouched, underfoot.

The ice on the lakes was too rough for skating because of the strong currents, so we made an ice-rink by flooding a flat piece of ground down by the shore. First it would be the turn of the figure-skaters. Then the rink would be cleared and swept for furious games of ice hockey. Before nightfall we would flood the rink again, ready for the next day's sport.

The island, in American Indian legend, is the home of the Great Spirit. We used to ski to visit our friends in the Indian village in the centre of the island. And, in the summer, along with the hundreds of international visitors to the conference, leaders of their people would come – Chief Walking Buffalo with his unforgettable head-dress of buffalo horn, and many others.

When I finally came to leave the United States it was in midwinter by the little three-seater aeroplane taxi from the island. It was the only way out unless you were brave enough to risk the shifting ice bridge. I felt I was in a flying cardboard box tied together with string, taking off from that clearing in the woods. We seemed to head straight for the pine trees – and then we were up and I was lost in wonder, looking down at the frozen lakes and the pattern of their ever-changing ice floes.

I was on my way home to Scotland for the first time in eight years.

My measurements in this vegetable section are for the weights of peeled and cleaned vegetables. With peas or broad beans in their pods, for instance, you will need to buy double the weight you finally want.

Note: Root vegetables should always be put on to cook in cold water. Leaf vegetables are put straight into boiling water.

ARTICHOKES, JERUSALEM

These were a favourite of my mother. She was slowly perfecting growing a knobless variety by keeping and growing only those with no knobs. I use ones from her stock.

To prepare: peel and slice the artichokes and keep them in water with a little lemon juice. Put them in a saucepan, which has a well-fitting lid, with a little cold water. Add a couple of slices of onion and a knob of butter. Bring to the boil and then turn down the heat. Simmer gently until all the water has evaporated. The butter will prevent the artichokes from burning when it starts to sizzle. The artichokes should then be ready. Do not allow them to sizzle for more than a few moments or they will burn.

ARTICHOKES, GLOBE
(see under Entrées)

BEANS, BROAD

If you grow broad beans yourself you can eat them really young.

To prepare: steam them in a little salted boiling water for 5 to 15 minutes, depending on their age. They are especially good served with lots of butter.

BEANS, GREEN

4 oz / 125 g per person.

To prepare: if the beans are fresh, top and tail and string them. If they are large, slice them.

For French beans, slice them diagonally along the length, or break them in approximately 1″ / 2.5 cm pieces.

Cook the beans, covered, in about 1″ / 2.5 cm boiling salted water over a low heat (so that they do not boil dry) for 10 minutes. Drain and serve them with some dabs of butter.

They are also good served with sliced mushrooms mixed through them. If the beans are young, they can be served whole with onion, chopped and softened in butter.

In the southern United States they are cooked with chopped ham or bacon mixed through them.

BROCCOLI

Allow approximately 4 oz / 125 g per person.

To prepare: cut off any hard stalk ends. Stack the broccoli in a saucepan, stalks down. Pour over them a little boiling water. Add salt.

Bring back to the boil, cover and cook for about 10 minutes when they should be tender but still firm. Drain and serve with melted butter.

BRUSSELS SPROUTS

Allow approximately 4 oz / 125 g per person.

To prepare: wash them and peel off any discoloured leaves. Make a cross in each stalk to help it cook quickly.

Put the sprouts in a little boiling, salted water and cook gently for about 15 minutes. They should retain their shape. Serve with butter.

Sprouts should be picked after a frost as this improves their flavour.

FOR A FESTIVE DISH
Roast chestnuts for 10 minutes in a moderate oven until the shell cracks, or boil them for 20 minutes. Peel and chop them and mix them in with the sprouts before serving.

Allow 2 oz / 50 g per person.

CABBAGE, PLAIN

Allow about 4 oz / 125 g per person.

Slice the cabbage finely into a colander and wash it under cold running water. Put it in the saucepan with the water adhering to the leaves. This should be enough water for cooking.

Add a knob of butter, a grating of nutmeg and some salt and pepper to taste and simmer for 10 to 15 minutes on a low heat. It should be crisp but tender and the leaves a good colour. (The cooking time refers to a hard cabbage. Green cabbage leaves may take less time.)

CABBAGE, RED

For 4 to 6

1 onion, chopped
1 tblsp / 15 ml butter or bacon fat
6 tblsp / 90 ml brown sugar
3 tblsp / 45 ml vinegar or white wine
1 tblsp / 15 ml caraway seeds
2½ pints / 1½ litres, approximately, red cabbage, sliced fine
1 apple, grated (optional)

Fry the onion lightly in the melted butter. Add the sugar, vinegar or wine, and caraway seeds. Then add the cabbage and apple and cook gently with the lid on but stirring frequently for about 25 minutes.

For 4

1 lb / 450 g carrots
1 onion, finely chopped
1 oz / 25 g butter or margarine
salt
1 tblsp / 15 ml sugar
chopped parsley

For 4

CARROTS, TYROLEAN

Slice the carrots finely in rounds. Soften the onion in the butter in a saucepan over a low heat. Add the carrots and salt and cover tightly with the lid. Simmer gently until tender, shaking frequently to prevent sticking. Then sprinkle the sugar over to glaze them. Serve garnished with parsley.

CAULIFLOWER

Strip off all the outer leaves of the cauliflower. You can leave on the small young ones. Wash thoroughly.

Cut a cross in the stalk to help cooking. Put the cauliflower right way up in a saucepan with a little salted, boiling water in it. Put the lid on and steam for about 20 minutes, being careful it does not boil dry. It should then be tender but not falling apart.

CREAMED CAULIFLOWER

Prepare a Béchamel sauce (see Index), using some of the cauliflower water mixed with milk as the liquid. Pour this over the cooked cauliflower.

CAULIFLOWER CHEESE

Add 4 oz / 125 g cheddar cheese to the Béchamel sauce.

POLISH CAULIFLOWER

Cook the cauliflower as above. Hard-boil and chop 1 egg. Take 2 oz / 50 g butter and brown this slowly in a saucepan, being careful not to burn it.

Sprinkle a few drops of lemon juice over the cauliflower, followed by the browned butter.

Chop some parsley and mix this with the chopped egg. Sprinkle this over the cauliflower and serve immediately.

I am told that the French think we serve everything in a white sauce, so this may be suitable for a French guest!

COURGETTES

Wash them and cut off the stalk and flower end. Slice them and if they are old and inclined to be bitter, blanch them by pouring boiling water over them. Bring back to the boil for a minute. Drain them and throw that water away.

In the saucepan gently fry ½ onion in butter until soft. Return the courgettes to the pan with the onion. Add a little water, and steam for about 5 minutes. Before serving, sprinkle some drops of lemon juice and some chopped parsley over them. Serve them in their own juice.

As a change, you may add 2 peeled and chopped tomatoes to the onion and the courgettes.

LEEKS

1 lb / 450 g for 4 people.

Remove the tough discoloured leaves. The green leaves contain iron so use them. Slit them lengthwise down the stalk. This makes it easier to wash out any earth.

Cut the leeks crossways into 1" / 2.5 cm lengths. Put them into boiling, salted water about 1" / 2.5 cm deep and boil for about 5 minutes. Drain them and reserve the water for the sauce below.

Melt 1 oz / 25 g butter in a saucepan and mix in 2 tblsp / 30 ml flour. With the milk and leek water, make up ½ pint / 300 ml. Add this slowly to the roux, whisking hard to remove lumps. Return to the heat and bring it to the boil, stirring constantly. Season to taste with salt, pepper and a dash of mace. Pour it over the leeks in a serving dish. This is particularly good with cold meat and baked potatoes.

POTATOES

New Potatoes need not be peeled. If wished, scrape them lightly with a knife before cooking and the peel will lift off. Cook in a little salted boiling water with a sprig of mint. Serve with melted butter and chopped parsley.

Old Potatoes are begun in cold salted water. When I married Peter I found that he was very particular about Irish potatoes. They should be floury and very well dried off after cooking.

SWEET POTATOES (South Africa)

For 4

1 lb / 450 g sweet potatoes
4 oz / 125 g butter
2 oz / 50 g brown sugar
1 stick of cinnamon, broken up

Peel the potatoes and cut into flat slices. Butter a flat casserole which has a lid and layer the potatoes in this with some of the butter. Dot the rest of the butter over the potatoes. Sprinkle the brown sugar over the top and add the cinnamon pieces. Season with some salt. Put the lid on and bake at 350°F / 180°C / gas 4 for about 1 hour. Remove the lid for the last 15 minutes so that the potatoes may brown a little.

PEAS

Allow about 4 oz / 125 g per person of shelled peas, or double this for peas in the pod. If you are using fresh peas, keep the pods for soup (see Index).

Put the peas with 1 tsp / 5 ml sugar into a little boiling water with a big piece of mint on top. Cover the pan and simmer for 5 to 10 minutes. When done, drain them, keeping the water to make soup. Serve them with a knob of butter.

Old peas: Line a saucepan with lettuce leaves. On top of them put some chopped onion and a knob of butter. Add the peas, a sprig of mint, salt and sugar. Cover the peas with some more lettuce and add a little boiling water. Cover the pan tightly and simmer for 30 minutes.

Sugar or Mangetout Peas: String them and boil in the pod in a little salted water for about 10 minutes.

SPINACH

4 oz / 125 g spinach per person.

If it is spinach beet with a long stalk, cut off the stalk and save this for Poor Man's Asparagus (see Index).

Wash the spinach in lots of cold water. Chop it up roughly and put in a big saucepan with a good tight lid. Do not add any more water as it makes its own juice. Bring it slowly to the boil and simmer for about 15 minutes.

Just before serving, stir in salt, pepper and a little nutmeg if liked.

CREAMED SPINACH
1 tblsp / 15 ml each of flour and
    butter
4 fl oz / 125 ml milk

If you have a food processor, put the cooked spinach into it. Cover and turn it on briefly. Add the flour, butter and milk and mix together. When blended, return it to the pan, bring it back to the boil and season to taste with salt, pepper and nutmeg.

Without a processor, make a thick white sauce with the flour, butter and milk. Push the spinach and its juice through a sieve and then add it to the white sauce. Bring back to the boil. Season to taste with salt, pepper and nutmeg.

SQUASH, GEM

Wash the squash and prick them well so that they do not burst. Put them in boiling, salted water for about 20 minutes.

When they are tender, drain them, cut them in half and take out the seeds. They may be served with a little butter in each.

For a party, fill them with cooked peas, mushrooms, tyrolean carrots, etc., according to choice.

SQUASH, YELLOW BUTTERNUT

Peel and de-seed the squash. Cook slowly in salted water. When soft, drain off the water. Mash the squash. Stir in an egg yolk mixed with evaporated milk or cream. Add a dab of butter and season with plenty of salt, pepper and a little mace.

Alternatively, peel and de-seed the squash as before. Cook, then cut up into chunks and place in a casserole. Sprinkle over the squash some sugar, salt and pepper. Spread on a knob of butter. Cover and bake in an oven at 350°F / 180°C / gas 4 for up to 30 minutes. Pumpkin may be treated in the same way or made into Pumpkin Pie (see Index).

TURNIP

Alec Miller was my brother's farm grieve. One day a visiting agricultural expert was inspecting the cattle. He asked Alec how he fed his animals in winter. Alec showed him the turnip cutter. 'But turnips are just water!' the expert said. 'Aye, but it's gey guid water!' replied Alec. So . . .

Either the small white turnips, or the large yellow swedes. Cut the peel and the leaves off the turnip. The leaves of the small white turnips may be chopped and cooked as spinach.

Cut the turnip into squares and put them in a saucepan with salt, lots of fresh ground pepper and a knob of butter. Put about 1" / 2.5 cm water in the bottom of the pan and steam gently for 20 to 30 minutes. Ideally the water should just boil dry. The butter will then start to sizzle, preventing the turnip from burning.

Take them off the heat, mash them and add 2 tblsp / 30 ml cream for 4 people to give extra richness. Serve sprinkled with chopped parsley.

SWEETS, DESSERTS AND PUDDINGS

In Scotland and Ireland we seem to use the word 'puddings' to describe the next course, while in America pudding means only steamed pudding. In restaurants it is always the 'dessert' trolley which is brought round. And 'sweets' is an increasingly common description, in direct contrast, I suppose, to 'savoury'.

Technically, dessert is fresh fruit. This certainly has stuck in my mind since one of the few really formal banquets which I have been to. The Duke of Hamilton, as Lord High Commissioner, represented the Queen at Holyroodhouse in Edinburgh in 1953. He invited my brother to be an aide-de-camp. My mother stood in as lady-in-waiting for two nights. I was simply a guest for those nights.

That evening there was a banquet for 90. We all assembled in our evening dresses and long white gloves. Everyone's jewels were out of the bank. As the Duke and Duchess entered, the room rippled with bows and curtseys. When some of the guests had been formally presented, we formed up for dinner. The Major Domo announced, 'The Lord High Commissioner will take into dinner the . . .' He stepped forward and offered his arm to his chosen guest, and so on down the line.

It came to my turn. 'The Earl Haig will take into dinner the Lady Fiona Graham.' He stepped forward and offered me his arm. As we proceeded up the length of the room I almost tripped over my feet. My partner steadied me with a smile and I arrived safely at my place.

Grace was said. I undid the buttons of my gloves and tucked them up. Soon I was deep in fascinating conversation with my companions. At one point I looked up to see that the whole table was waiting for me to finish eating before the next course could be served. My healthy appetite failed, and the clearing began.

Finally, after five courses, we came to the dessert – fresh fruit. Fruit plates were brought in, on each a lace mat and a small glass fingerbowl of water. On either side of the bowl was a knife, fork and spoon. I lifted off the bowl and its mat, putting it on the table to my left. My knife, fork and spoon I placed in front of me.

Then the fruit was passed. I carefully chose something I could manage to eat elegantly with my knife and fork – a peach. Afterwards I dipped my fingers in the fingerbowl, dried them on my napkin and put my hand back in my glove.

The Duchess rose and we ladies retired to the (with)drawing-room where we were served coffee while guests were presented to Her Grace. The men then rejoined us after their port. Finally our elders retired to bed and the party began. My brother produced his pipes and we made a night of dancing.

Next day, a tea party. Two ladies were coming to present a gift to the Duchess for the palace. An equerry came flying past my room. 'Where are the maids of honour? Someone must pour tea!'

'I don't know,' I said, coming out of my room. 'There's only me.'

'You'll do,' he said.

So down I went to be seated behind the high silver urn and the silver teapot to make conversation with these ladies until the Duchess returned from her engagements.

After dinner next evening I changed and caught the night train to London. My case was most beautifully packed for me by the maid, with everything folded in new tissue paper.

I didn't lose a glass slipper, only a diamond earring. I heard later that it had been found but by that time I was on my way to Africa and then to America, not returning to Scotland for many years.

BAKED CUSTARD

For 4

4 medium eggs
1 pint / 600 ml milk
4 tblsp / 60 ml white granulated sugar
1 tsp / 5 ml vanilla

Beat the eggs slightly to mix them. Bring the milk, sugar and vanilla to the boil in a saucepan and pour this over the eggs.

Grease a 1½ pint / 1 litre mould with butter. Pour in the custard. Put the mould in a roasting tin with water halfway up the sides. Bake in the oven at 300°F / 150°C / gas 2 for about 1 hour, refilling with water as needed. Do not let the custard boil or it will not be smooth. It is ready when a skewer inserted comes out clean.

CARAMEL CUSTARD

3 oz / 75 g white granulated
    sugar
2 fl oz / 50 ml water
basic custard mixture, as
    previous recipe

Put the sugar and water in a heavy frying pan and place on a low heat until it melts and turns brown – do not stir, though it may be moved from side to side to ensure even melting.

Take a 1½ pint / 1 litre metal mould and pour in the boiling caramel, turning the mould until the bottom and sides are covered. Run the outside of the mould under cold water until you hear the caramel cracking. Add the custard mixture and bake as previous recipe. To serve, turn it out onto a plate large enough to allow for the caramel which will melt and run.

CARAMEL SNOWBALL

For 4

Caramel
4 oz / 125 g castor sugar
2 fl oz / 50 ml water

Snowball
4 egg whites
3 tblsp / 75 ml castor sugar
½ tsp / 3 ml vanilla

Sauce
4 yolks of eggs
2 tsp / 10 ml castor sugar
6 fl oz / 175 ml milk
6 fl oz / 175 ml double cream

Caramel Put the castor sugar and water in a heavy frying pan. Bring it slowly to the boil until the sugar melts and then boil hard until it turns brown. Pour half of this caramel into a large round metal tin, tilting it to cover the bottom and sides.

Into the remaining caramel add another 2 fl oz / 50 ml of water and leave it to dissolve.

Snowball Beat the egg whites to a stiff froth. Gradually beat in the sugar and vanilla and put this into the tin lined with caramel, ¾ full to allow room to rise. Put the tin into a big pan with water halfway up. Bake for 20 to 25 minutes – not longer or it will go flat – in a hot oven at 400°F / 200°C / gas 6. Let it stand for a few minutes after taking from the oven before turning out onto a large dish.

Sauce Mix together the egg yolks, sugar, remaining caramel and the milk. Stir in a double boiler until it thickens to a custard. Strain when cold and add the cream. Pour around the base of the snowball.

CRÈME BRULÉE

For 4

1 tblsp / 15 ml cornflour
1 tblsp / 15 ml milk
1 pint / 600 ml double cream
4 egg yolks
2 oz / 50 g castor sugar
8 oz / 225 g brown sugar

Mix together the cornflour and milk in a bowl. Bring the cream to the boil and pour it over the cornflour. Whisk the egg yolks and add them and the castor sugar to the cream.

Put this bowl over gently boiling water and stir constantly until the egg yolks are cooked and the cream thickens. Pour into a casserole and leave overnight or at least for 6 hours. The next day you may *either*:

(1.) Melt the brown sugar with ½ oz / 15 g butter and pour

it over the custard to cover. Put it back in the fridge for half an hour until cold and brittle.

or

(2.) Crumble the brown sugar thickly over the cream custard and put under a medium grill until the sugar is melted. Refrigerate again for half an hour.

The trick is that the cream custard should be really cold and thick so that the caramel or sugar does not sink through it when it is poured on or placed under the grill.

This pudding may be varied by putting your choice of fruit – either sliced oranges, bananas, stewed plums or gooseberries – in the bottom of the glass dish before pouring the custard over them and continuing as before.

CARAMEL MOUSSE

For 6

4 oz / 125 g white granulated sugar
¼ pint / 150 ml water
1 tblsp or 1 pkt / 15 ml gelatine
3 medium eggs, separated
4 fl oz / 125 ml milk
4 fl oz / 125 ml whipping cream
4 fl oz / 125 ml natural yoghurt

A light sweet though it seems rich. It is delicious served with an acid fruit such as stewed gooseberries. Start preparing it the day before.

This mousse is made in 3 stages:

(1.) First caramelise the sugar by spreading it over the base of a heavy pan. Put it on a low heat and allow the sugar to become liquid without stirring it. Turn the heat up a little and let the liquid turn a nice brown (the colour of tea). Watch it carefully or it will burn.

Remove from the heat, let it cool a little and then add the water. It may fizz up and the caramel at first will harden. It may then be melted by stirring it over a very gentle heat.

(2.) Mix the gelatine with 2 tblsp / 30 ml water. Take half the liquid caramel and dissolve the gelatine in it, but do not allow it to boil. Put it aside to cool. Whip the egg whites and pour this gelatine/caramel mixture into them before it sets.

Take a 2 pint / 1 litre mould. Rinse it out in cold water and pile the caramelised egg whites into it. Put this in the fridge and leave for at least 6 hours, but better overnight.

(3.) Put the egg yolks with the milk in a basin over boiling water and stir continuously until it thickens (if it looks like curdling, remove the basin from the heat immediately and set it in cold water). Stir the remaining caramel into this custard and set it aside to cool. When cold, whip the cream and fold it into the custard together with the yoghurt.

To serve: take the mould, dip it briefly into hot water and turn the mousse out onto a large deep platter. Spoon the caramel cream carefully around it and bring it to the table.

I had a part in cooking for hundreds of the Germans who came to the Caux conferences in the post-war years. Along with the miners, with whom I had stayed, the industrialists, the politicians and the housewives, came Princess Margaret of Hesse, granddaughter of Queen Victoria and an old friend of Frank Buchman, who carried major responsibility for the conferences.

The Princess had suffered greatly in the war and was ill and confined to a wheelchair. She needed much care, so Dr Buchman asked me to be among those who would bring her meals to her room. I think that he also felt that it would do no harm for some of us arrogant younger ones to learn to pay proper respect to our elders.

One day the Duchess of Aosta, her cousin and also a royal princess, came to visit. I had laid the table in their room and was bringing in a tray with three crystal glasses of tomato juice when, unexpectedly, I found Princess Margaret and the Duchess already in the room.

She called me over to introduce me to the Duchess. In my confusion I could find no place to put down the tray. The Duchess extended her hand, I tried to curtsey, and of course the glasses shot off the tray and tomato juice splashed to the four corners of the room. They very sweetly retired and allowed me to gather myself and to clean it up before continuing with the meal. My family still tease me that I am likely to panic in a crisis!

This recipe for Zabaglione was a great favourite with the Princess.

ZABAGLIONE

For 4

3 egg yolks
3 tblsp / 45 ml sherry or marsala
1½ oz / 35 g castor sugar
¼ pint / 125 ml double cream
1 egg white

Whisk the egg yolks, sherry or marsala, and the sugar in a bowl over gently boiling water until lemon-coloured and thick enough to hold the traces of the whisk. Remove from the heat and chill.

Whip the cream until just thick and the egg white until

stiff. Combine them with the egg mixture.

Pour into individual glasses and serve with fine biscuits or sponge fingers.

GREAT-GRANDMOTHER'S SWEET

From my mother's family in Morven.

1 tsp / 5 ml cornflour
2 oz / 50 g granulated sugar
1 pint / 600 ml light cream
the juice and grated rind of 1 lemon
8 oz / 225 g macaroons or sponge fingers

Mix the cornflour with the sugar and a little cold cream.

Bring the rest of the cream to the boil and, when boiling, stir it into the sugar and cornflour mixture. Set this aside to cool and then add the lemon juice and rind.

Put the macaroons or sponge fingers in a dish and pour the cream over. You may decorate this with crystallized lemons or some of the grated rind.

For 6

QUEEN OF PUDDINGS

A bread pudding covered with jam and meringue.

1 pint / 600 ml milk
4 oz / 125 g soft white breadcrumbs
2 large eggs, separated
4 oz / 125 g granulated white sugar
1 tsp / 5 ml vanilla
pinch of salt
1½ tblsp / 25 ml melted butter
raspberry jam

Bring the milk to the boil. Pour it over the breadcrumbs and set aside for half an hour.

Beat the egg yolks with 1 oz / 25 g of the sugar. Add the vanilla, butter and salt and mix with the milk and crumbs.

Pour this into a buttered casserole and bake in the oven at 350°F / 180°C / gas 4 for half an hour until set. Take the pudding out and spread the top liberally with a juicy, home-made jam – raspberry, strawberry or blackcurrant. Reduce the oven temperature to 300°F / 150°C / gas 2.

Whisk the egg whites until they peak. Beat in half the remaining sugar. Then fold in by hand all but a spoonful of the rest of the sugar.

Pile the meringue over the pudding, covering it well. Sprinkle the remaining spoonful of sugar on top and bake in the cooler oven for half an hour. The top will rise, turning brown and crisp, while the inside of the meringue remains soft.

Serve with milk or cream.

For 4

CRÊPES OR PANCAKES (A basic recipe)

These are traditionally served on Shrove Tuesday to use up all the fat in the house before the Lenten fast begins next day. Many villages have pancake-tossing competitions. We used to toss them at home and, surprisingly, not as many landed on the floor as one might have expected.

These can be used as a sweet dish or with savoury fillings.

4 oz / 125 g plain flour
a pinch of salt
2 medium eggs
½ pint / 300 ml milk
2 oz / 50 g melted butter

Sift the flour and salt into a bowl. Make a well in the flour and drop the eggs and half the milk into it.

With a wooden spoon start beating the liquid in the centre. The flour will gradually be incorporated. When all is mixed in, beat the batter for 100 strokes to make it really smooth. Add the remaining milk and set it aside to rest for an hour.

Melt all the butter slowly in the pan and pour it off into the batter, beating it in. (It is a help to have a special pan for pancakes about 7" / 18cm diameter as an ordinary frying pan may tend to stick.) There will still be a coating of butter left in the pan. When this is hot, take a small ladle and put in just enough batter to cover the surface when you tilt the pan. When the pancake is browned on the one side, toss or turn it over for a further moment and keep it warm as you cook the rest of the batter mixture.

For Shrove Tuesday, roll each pancake up and sprinkle white sugar over it. Serve with quarters of lemon and cream.

ICELANDIC PANCAKES

For 4

4 fl oz / 125 ml whipping cream
jam of your choice

Cook one basic pancake recipe. Put a spoonful of jam and of whipped cream in each pancake before rolling it up. Sprinkle with sugar and serve at once.

CRÊPES ST JACQUES

Put a filling of fresh fruit salad and ice cream into each pancake and fold. Warm some brandy in a ladle and set it alight before pouring it over the pancakes. Bring it flaming to the table.

BUCHTELN

For 8

A German recipe for light yeast bread filled with jam.

¼ pint / 150 ml milk
2 oz / 50 g butter
2 tblsp / 30 ml sugar

Bring the milk to the boil. Take it off the heat and melt the butter in it. Add the sugar and dissolve it. Set aside until it is lukewarm. Sprinkle the yeast onto it and allow it to

½ oz / 12 g fresh yeast *or* 2 tsp /
 10 ml dried yeast
7 oz / 200 g flour
 2 small eggs

filling
4 oz / 125 g melted butter
raspberry or strawberry jam

'sponge', i.e. froth up.

Sift the flour. Make a well in the centre and add the yeast/milk mixture and the eggs. Knead it by hand for 10 to 15 minutes, or by machine for 5 minutes. Cover the bowl with a plastic bag and blanket and leave in a warm place – e.g. airing cupboard – for an hour or two until doubled in bulk.

For the filling, brush a deep cake tin with some of the butter.

Take the dough, punch it down and knead again for 5 minutes.

Dip your hands in the melted butter, break off portions of the dough and pat out flat in the palm of one hand with the fingers of the other. Put a small spoonful of jam in the centre and fold the dough over it, making sure it is completely covered.

Place it with the folded side down in the baking tin. Dip your hands in the butter as you take each portion of dough, filling them and placing close alongside each other. It is important that there are no holes in the dough through which the jam can escape.

Brush the dough with the remaining butter and set the tin aside to rise again in a warm place until doubled in bulk – this will take about an hour.

Heat the oven to 400°F / 200°C / gas 6 and put in your Buchteln. After 10 minutes turn the heat down to 350°F / 180°C / gas 4 and cook for about a further 30 minutes. Test it by knocking the bottom and if it sounds hollow it is cooked. Dust with icing sugar and serve with cream or a foaming sauce (see Index).

For 8

4 fl oz /125 ml orange juice
1 tblsp / 15 ml rum *or* 1 tsp /
 5 ml rum essence
4 oz / 125 g sugar
8 fl oz / 225 ml cream

RUM BABA

The dough for Buchteln is used for this.

After the first rising punch down the dough and put it into a buttered ring mould. Set it to rise again and then bake in a hot oven, turning the heat down after 10 minutes . . . It may take less time as it is a ring. When baked – test it in the same way – turn it out of its mould. Place it on a serving dish and, while it is hot, soak it with a syrup made of the orange juice, rum and sugar.

Fill the centre of your ring with a fresh fruit salad. Whip the cream and just before serving the baba, pipe a decorative ring around the bottom edge. Serve the remaining cream separately.

MERINGUE

Makes 48 small meringues

4 oz / 125 g castor sugar
2 egg whites

Oil 2 baking trays and shake a spoonful of flour around each.

First beat the egg whites until they stand up in peaks. Then, a spoonful at a time, beat in half the sugar, beating each addition. With a metal spoon, fold in the rest of the sugar.

Either take 2 teaspoons and put the meringue onto the baking trays, scraping it off one spoon with the back of the other.

Or put the mixture into a forcing bag with a wide star nozzle and pipe out 'kisses' onto the baking trays. Lightly dust each meringue with sugar.

Put the trays in the oven (250°F / 130°C / gas ½) and bake for 1 hour. Ovens vary in heat so keep an eye on them and if they are browning turn the oven down. If not cooking, turn it up. After 1 hour, turn the oven off but leave the meringues in to dry for some hours.

Whip ¼ pint / 150 ml cream and add 2 tblsp / 30 ml vanilla sugar. I find this best done by hand. If it is whipped too much it turns to butter. Fold the vanilla sugar into the cream. Sandwich the cream between two meringues.

Note: For vanilla sugar, put a vanilla bean upright in a tall jar and fill with sugar. Keep for 2 weeks and use as needed. Or mix ½ tsp / 3 ml vanilla essence with 2 tblsp / 30 ml sugar.

VACHERIN

For 8

A meringue gâteau filled with fresh fruit which has been folded into sweetened whipped cream.

3 egg whites
6 oz / 175 g castor sugar
fruit (strawberries, raspberries, blackberries or peaches – with lemon juice to stop them browning)
½ pint / 225 ml whipping cream

Oil 3 baking trays lightly. Line the bottoms with non-stick silicone paper cut to fit. Oil and flour the paper as for the previous recipe. Mark a circle in each tin by dropping a large 6" / 15 cm saucer upside-down at one end of each of the tins in turn, not too close to the edge. Pick it up carefully with a knife and you will see a circle left in the flour.

Put a wide star nozzle into a large piping bag. It helps when filling the bag to stand it in a tall glass with a cuff turned down to keep it open. When preparations are completed, start making the meringue.

Beat the egg whites until they peak. Beat in slowly, a spoonful at a time, half the sugar. Fold in the rest of the sugar with a metal spoon.

Fill the piping bag with the meringue. Pipe around the edge of the first marked circle and fill in with concentric circles inside it. Pipe a second circle on top of the outside edge to raise it higher. With the second and third circles only pipe a ring around the outside. Do not fill in.

In the spaces on the trays, pipe 6 or 8 V-shapes 4" / 10 cm high and 12 or more 'kisses'. Refill the bag as needed.

Bake very slowly in the oven at 250°F / 130°C / gas ½ for about 2 hours. Watch carefully that the meringue does not brown.

Assemble the vacherin as follows: loosen all the meringues from the paper. Take another egg white and with 2 oz / 50 g castor sugar make another meringue mixture as before. Put the filled-in circle back on the tray. Pipe a thin ring of new meringue around the top edge and place one ring on top. Repeat with the last ring. Take the V-shapes and, with the new meringue, stick them around the side, point upwards. Stick the 'kisses' similarly on top of the upper ring.

Return the meringue to the oven for 15 to 20 minutes before turning the oven off. Leave it in the oven to dry overnight.

For the filling, use the fruit of your choice with sugar. Whip ½ pint / 225 ml cream. Just before serving lift most of the fruit from the juice it will have made with the sugar, mix it with the whipped cream and carefully fill your meringue. Serve the rest of the fruit and juice in a sauceboat.

Note: The meringue needs to be made at least the day before. If you have an airtight tin it can be made further in advance.

For 6

CROQUEMBOUCHE

A baked dish of shortcrust pastry, with cream puffs in a pyramid on top held in place with caramel sugar.

Prepare half the recipe for shortcrust pastry (see Index). Roll it out to a circle 7" / 17 cm in diameter. Prick all over to release air bubbles when cooking and bake at 400°F / 200°C / gas 6 for about 10 minutes.

Make 1 recipe of cream puffs (see choux pastry in Index). Use 2 teaspoons to set out small puffs on a greased baking tray. After the shortcrust pastry is cooked, turn the oven up to 425°F / 210°C / gas 7 and bake the puffs for about 15 minutes, until puffed and brown. Put them on a wire rack to cool. Cut a hinged lid in each puff, removing any soft pastry inside.

Put 3 oz / 75 g sugar into a heavy frying pan on gentle heat to melt the sugar. When melted turn the heat up until the sugar is brown. Meanwhile, whip ½ pint / 300 ml cream and sweeten it with the sugar and vanilla to taste.

Dip the base of each puff, one by one, in the caramel and stick them onto the pastry in a single layer, filling the circle. Open the lid of each puff and slip in a spoon of cream before continuing in the same way with the second layer until you have built up the pyramid. If the caramel becomes solid, re-heat.

Sift icing-sugar over the pyramid and serve with chocolate sauce.

Note: Take care with boiling sugar as it can cause a bad burn.

CHARLOTTE MALAKOFF

For 8

3 fl oz / 75 ml orange liqueur
6 fl oz / 150 ml water
24 to 30 lady fingers (a light, crisp sponge finger)

Almond Cream
½ lb / 225 g unsalted butter
½ lb / 225 g castor sugar
6 oz / 150 g chocolate
2 fl oz / 5 ml strong coffee
2 fl oz / 50 ml orange liqueur
¼ tsp / 1 ml almond essence
9 fl oz / 250 ml ground almonds
16 fl oz / 450 ml whipping cream

Line the bottom of a dry 2 quarts / 2 litre mould with waxed paper. Mix together the water and liqueur in a flat dish. (Orange juice, sharpened with lemon, may be used instead of the liqueur.) Dip each lady finger quickly into the liquid and arrange upright around the inside of the mould, touching each other with the rounded end at the bottom and the flat side inwards. If they are too tall cut them to the correct height. Reserve any remaining lady fingers and pieces.

Cream the butter and sugar well until light.

Melt the chocolate in the heated coffee. Mix into it the orange liqueur and almond essence. Gradually beat this into the butter and sugar mixture. Mix in the ground almonds.

Whip the chilled cream only until the beater leaves light traces in it or it will not freeze smoothly. Fold the cream into the almond mixture and carefully turn one third of it into the mould inside the lady fingers.

Dip some of the remaining lady fingers and pieces into the liqueur and put a layer over the almond cream. Add a second layer of almond cream and of lady fingers, followed by a third layer topped with lady fingers.

Cover with waxed paper. Put a plate on top with a weight on it. Freeze it overnight.

To serve, dip the mould briefly in hot water and run a knife around the inside. Turn out the mould onto a chilled serving dish. Decorate with grated chocolate or chocolate caraque (see Index).

For 6 to 8

1 lb / 450 g cottage cheese
6 oz / 175 g cream cheese
1 tblsp / 15 ml lemon juice
3 tblsp / 45 ml bitter orange
   Dundee marmalade
2 tblsp / 30 ml sugar
2 tblsp / 30 ml whisky

CALEDONIAN CREAM

Press the cottage cheese through a sieve and beat it together with the cream cheese until smooth. Beat in all the other ingredients. Put into a covered dish and freeze.

I enjoy these well-laced puddings. They sometimes remind me of an old friend of ours, Judge Claassen, in South Africa.

On one occasion he was attending a formal legal dinner. It was all beautifully presented, with separate wines for each course. As it happened he did not drink, so as each new wine was served he graciously declined.

His fellow judges ribbed him unmercifully which he took in good humour. Then the dessert was handed round – a trifle, well laced with sherry to which he helped himself with gusto.

'Aha!' said his friends, 'now we have you. What about your not drinking?'

'Oh,' replied Judge Claassen, 'I am just being true to the old legal maxim: "De Minimis Non Curat Lex".'

For those of us whose Latin may be a little rusty, 'The law does not concern itself with trifles'.

FRUIT DISHES

BAKED STUFFED APPLES

For 4

4 cooking apples (Bramleys are
good)
1 banana
4 oz / 125 g brown sugar
2 oz / 50 g dates
1 oz / 25 g butter
4 tblsp / 60 ml golden or maple
syrup
½ pint / 300 ml water
juice of 1 lemon
4 glacé cherries

Core the apples and cut a slit in the peel around the middle.
Place them in an ovenproof dish.

Cut the banana into chunks and push one piece into the
hole in each apple. Then add some brown sugar. Chop the
dates and push them into the holes, finishing the stuffing
with more sugar and banana.

Put a dab of butter on top of each apple. Dribble the syrup
over the apples, pour the water and the lemon juice into the
dish and bake in the oven at 350°F / 180°C / gas 4 for half
an hour until the apples are fluffy. Decorate with the cherries
and serve with pouring cream.

GRATED APPLES

For 4

4 crisp apples
1 tblsp / 15 ml lemon juice
4 fl oz / 125 ml natural yoghurt
4 fl oz / 125 ml sweetened
condensed milk

Grate the apples, with their skin, into the lemon juice.

Combine the yoghurt and condensed milk and mix them
with the apple and lemon juice.

This may be decorated with thin slices of an unpeeled red
apple, for colour.

APPLE CRUMBLE

For 6 to 8

6 cooking apples
4 oz / 125 g sugar
1 tsp / 5 ml cinnamon
2 tsp / 10 ml lemon juice

The topping
8 oz / 225 g plain flour
4 oz / 125 g soft brown sugar
4 oz / 125 g granulated white
sugar

Butter a large flat casserole. Peel and core the apples and
slice them into the casserole. Sprinkle sugar and cinnamon
between the layers, ending with a layer of apple. Pile them
high, as they shrink in cooking. Sprinkle over the lemon
juice.

For the topping, mix together the flour, sugars and
cinnamon. Crumble the butter lightly into the mixture with
your fingers until it resembles breadcrumbs. Sprinkle this
thickly over the apples piling it well up in the centre. Bake in
the oven at 350°F / 180°C / gas 4 for half an hour or until a

1½ tsp / 7 ml cinnamon
8 oz / 225 g butter

little browned and crisp on top.

RHUBARB CRUMBLE
Layer the fruit with sugar and ginger (instead of cinnamon), ending with a layer of rhubarb. The crumble can equally well be made with stoned fresh cherries, plums, apricots etc., varying spices to suit your fruit.

DANISH APPLE CAKE

For 4

1½ lb / 700 g apples
1 lemon
2 cloves
2 oz / 50 g butter
sugar
3 oz / 75 g fresh white
   breadcrumbs
4 fl oz / 125 ml whipping cream
redcurrant jelly

Apple sauce: Cut up and core the apples. Put them in a saucepan with a strip of lemon peel, the cloves and a knob of butter. Cover them and simmer until pulpy.

Put them through a moulin-légume or coarse sieve. The cloves and apple skin will remain behind and you will have a lovely apple sauce. Flavour it to taste with grated lemon rind, lemon juice and sugar.

The cake: Gently fry the breadcrumbs in the rest of the butter until crisp and brown. Add 2 oz / 50 g of sugar.

In a glass dish layer the apple sauce and breadcrumbs alternately, finishing with the crumbs.

Whip the cream. Put it in a piping bag with not too wide a nozzle and pipe lines across the top, first in one direction and then in the other, to make a lattice-work pattern. With a teaspoon drop blobs of jelly in the squares.

Keep the apple cake cold until ready to serve.

When I make this cake I always think of Tove Cooper from Denmark. She and her Scottish husband, Jim, who was a doctor, lived with us for a year in Ireland when the children were babies. Jim was a fine pianist. When I said that Catherine, aged 3, could not sing in tune, he said, 'Nonsense. I'll teach her.' So off they would go to practise and, from that moment, Catherine never looked back.

APPLE MERINGUE

For 4

1 pint / 600 ml apple sauce (see
   previous recipe
6 oz / 175 g granulated white
   sugar
1 lemon, grated rind and juice
2 medium eggs, separated

Flavour the apple sauce to taste with a little of the sugar, the lemon rind and juice.

Stir the egg yolks into the sauce and put it in a casserole.

Whip the egg whites until they peak. Beat into them by degrees half the remaining sugar. Fold all but a spoonful of the rest of the sugar.

Pile the meringue over the apple to cover it. Dust it with the spoonful of sugar and bake in the oven at 300°F / 150°C / gas 2 for 40 minutes.

I have given a low temperature to cook this meringue as the outside then gets more crisp though not so brown.

TOFFEE APPLE FRITTERS

Susan, Duchess of Montrose.

For 4

4 large cooking apples
the juice and grated rind of 1
  lemon

syrup
2 oz / 50 g granulated white
  sugar
¼ pint / 150 ml water
2 tblsp / 30 ml runny honey

The batter
3 oz / 70 g self-raising flour
a pinch of salt
2 tblsp / 30 ml granulated white
  sugar
2 eggs, separated
¼ pint / 150 ml water

Heat the syrup ingredients slowly until the sugar melts and then boil for 5 minutes.

Peel the apples and cut them into segments. Pour the lemon juice and rind over them.

Pour the apples into the cooked syrup, but do not re-heat or the apples will go mushy. Leave this for 1 hour, turning from time to time.

To make the batter, sift the flour and salt together. Add the sugar. Make a well in the centre and into this pour the egg yolks and water and mix into a batter. Beat the whites stiffly and add them.

Lift the apples from the syrup, drain for a moment and coat them in the batter. Deep fry them in hot fat until puffed and golden. Drain them on kitchen paper.

Place them on a platter, dust with castor sugar, and serve at once. The remaining syrup may be served separately plus a jug of cream.

Note: You can use bananas instead of apples for this recipe.

COMPÔTE D'ORANGES À LA NORMANDE

For 6

2 lb / 1 kg apples
3 big oranges
4 oz / 125 g sugar
2 tblsp / 30 ml rum

Cut the apples into quarters. Core them but do not peel. Put them in a saucepan with just a little water. Bring to the boil and simmer for about 10 minutes. Pass them through a moulin-légume or sieve. The skin will stay behind and you will have a delicious compôte of apples (or compost, as my younger daughter irreverently called it).

Add the zest of 1 orange. (To do this, rub the orange all over with 1 or 2 sugar lumps. The flavour adheres to the sugar. Or grate the orange skin finely.) Add the rest of the

For 8

1 lb / 450 g raspberries
8 fl oz / 225 ml double cream
1 egg white
4 crushed macaroons
1 oz / 25 g castor sugar

RASPBERRY FOOL

Set aside some of the raspberries for decoration. Crush the remainder.

Whip the cream, but not too stiffly. Whip the egg white stiffly and fold it into the cream. Now fold in the crushed raspberries, macaroons and sugar.

Serve in individual glasses or a glass bowl. Decorate with the reserved raspberries.

Note: As it is made with whipped egg white it should be quickly served. Gooseberry Fool may be made the same way.

For 6

2 oz / 50 g castor sugar
2 tblsp / 30 ml cornflour
2 eggs, separated
juice of 4 oranges and 3 lemons,
    made up to 18 fl oz / 500 ml
    with water

ORANGE PUDDING

Put the sugar, cornflour and egg yolks in a heavy saucepan. Add some of the juice, stirring hard to remove any lumps. Then add the rest of the juice. Bring slowly to the boil.

Take if off the heat and leave it to cool, turning it occasionally so that a skin does not form.

Beat the egg whites until stiff but not dry, and fold them into the orange cream with a metal spoon.

Turn this into a bowl and keep in the fridge until ready to serve.

This was a favourite with my daughters when they were young.

For 4

ORANGE RICE

An unusual rice pudding.

6 tblsp / 90 ml short-grain or
    pudding rice
1 pint / 600 ml milk
4 tblsp / 60 ml sifted icing sugar
3 oranges
1 lemon
4 fl oz / 125 ml whipped cream

Put the rice on to boil in boiling water for 3 minutes. Drain the rice and add it to the milk which you have simmering in another saucepan. Simmer for about 30 minutes, uncovered, stirring frequently until all the milk is absorbed by the rice.

Remove it from the heat and stir in the sugar. Leave until cool before adding the grated rind and juice of 2 of the oranges and the juice of the lemon.

Whip the cream and fold it into the orange rice.

Cut the peel, including all the pith, off the third orange. Cut out the orange segments and decorate the top of the orange rice with them.

PEARS ALIMINA

6 pears (1 per person)

Alimina sauce
1 tblsp / 15 ml castor sugar
1 tsp / 5 ml cornflour
¼ pint / 150 ml milk
2 egg yolks
4 fl oz / 125 ml orange juice
finely grated orange rind

If the pears are fresh – and that is best – poach them with a stick of cinnamon in a light syrup of one part sugar to one part water. If they are tinned, drain off the syrup.

Mix the sugar and cornflour with a little milk taken from the measure. Put the rest of the milk on to boil.

Meanwhile, lightly beat the egg yolks into the sugar and cornflour mixture. Pour the boiling milk over this while stirring.

Have a pan of boiling water ready and place the bowl with the custard over this, stirring constantly until it thickens. Remove from the heat and add the orange juice. Pour this custard over the drained pears. Set the bowl aside to chill.

Decorate with zest of orange by taking a very fine shaving off the skin of an orange and cutting this into fine slices.

PRUNE WHIP

For 4

1 lb / 450 g prunes
4 fl oz / 125 ml orange juice
grated rind of 1 orange and 1
   lemon
2 egg whites
4 fl oz / 125 ml whipped cream
sugar to taste

Soak the prunes overnight in cold tea. Cook them, strain, remove the stones and chop finely. Add the orange juice and the orange and lemon rind. Also a little lemon juice if you like a sharper taste.

Whip the egg whites and fold them in. Whip the cream and fold it in. Taste for sweetness (adding sugar, if desired) and serve up.

STRAWBERRY GÂTEAU

For 8

1 lb / 450 g strawberries
4 tblsp / 60 ml Grand Marnier *or*
   2 tblsp / 30 ml lemon juice
2 oz / 50 g castor sugar
8 fl oz / 225 ml double cream
2 egg whites
1 sponge flan case – buy one or
   use the Victoria Sponge recipe
   (see Index)

Wash and slice the strawberries, reserving a few of the best for decoration. Cover them with either the Grand Marnier or lemon juice. Sprinkle them with the sugar and leave in a cold place for an hour.

Whip the cream. Whisk the egg whites and fold them into the cream together with the strawberries and the juice. Pile them into the flan case.

Decorate with the reserved strawberries and serve at once.

SUMMER PUDDING

This was a speciality of my mother-in-law, Hilda Hannon. Before my daughter Catherine was married Hilda came to stay with us. One day I returned home to find that she and Peter had set to and made over a dozen of the puddings and frozen them for the wedding. Traditionally they are made in pudding basins, but for the wedding we used tinfoil loaf pans.

Put blackcurrants or raspberries – or, perhaps best, a mixture of both – into a heavy-based saucepan with some sugar and slowly bring to the boil. Turn it off and taste for sweetness, adding more sugar if desired.

Cut the crusts off a white thin-sliced pan loaf of bread. Dip the slices into a bowl of the fruit juice and line the bottom and sides of the pudding basin or loaf tin with these. Ladle in layers of fruit alternately with bread, finishing with a layer of the soaked bread on top.

Put a weight on top and set aside to cool, and then put into the fridge for 24 hours. At this point it may, if you wish, be frozen. It certainly is economical of effort to make more than one at a time.

To serve, turn it out and decorate with lots of whipped cream.

FRESH FRUIT SALAD

oranges
grapes
apples
pineapple, tinned or fresh

Do not use strawberries, raspberries or other red berry fruits as they stain the other fruit and you lose colour contrast.

I find that the best technique for peeling oranges is to take them in one hand and with a small sharp knife cut away the skin as if peeling an apple. Over a bowl cut out each segment of the orange by cutting into the centre on one side of a membrane and then on the other, letting the segment drop out into the bowl. At the end you are left with a handful of membrane. Squeeze this as dry as possible for the juice.

If using fresh pineapple, cut off the top and bottom. Place it on a board or a tray to catch any juice. Cut the skin off and remove the eyes. Place the cut-up skin and eyes in a saucepan, add a little water, cover and bring it slowly to the boil. Then strain off the juice. Sweeten to taste and sharpen with lemon juice. Use as much of this juice in the salad as you need. The pineapple is then sliced and cut up.

For the grapes, cut them in half and remove the pips. If you wish to take off the skins, use a teaspoon and scoop out the flesh from the skin.

For apples, choose crisp fruit with a good skin colour. Do not peel them, but cut them in quarters and then across the quarters into a bowl, sprinkling them with lemon juice as you go to keep them from browning.

Mix the fruit and keep refrigerated until needed.

EXOTIC FRUIT SALAD

½ pineapple per person
1 orange per person
1 passion fruit per person
1 banana per person

Cut the pineapples in half lengthways, keeping on the leaves. Scoop out the flesh without piercing the skin. Cut into pieces, put in a bowl and sprinkle with castor sugar.

Prepare the oranges as above. Add to the pineapple. Cut the passion fruit in half and scoop out the inside, adding it.

Just before serving, slice the bananas and add them. Mix the salad and fill each half pineapple. Serve with a fine biscuit and pouring cream or ice-cream.

LEMON PUDDING

For 4

2 oz / 50 g butter
8 oz / 225 g granulated white
   sugar
2 eggs, separated
grated rind and juice of 2 lemons
2 tblsp / 30 ml plain flour
8 fl oz / 225 ml milk

Cream the butter and sugar together until light. Beat in the egg yolks. Add the lemon rind and juice. Add the milk alternately with the flour. It will look curdled.

Beat the egg whites to a peak and fold them into the lemon batter.

Pour the batter into a buttered soufflé dish and bake in the oven at 350°F / 180°C / gas 4 for about 40 minutes. It should be puffed and browned on top but runny inside. Serve with cream.

ORANGE SOUFFLÉS

For 6

6 oranges
1 tblsp / 15 ml cornflour
3 tblsp / 45 ml icing sugar
2 eggs, separated
1 tblsp / 15 ml lemon juice
1 oz / 25 g chopped, toasted
   almonds

Cut the top off each orange. Scrape out all the flesh without piercing the skin. Pass the flesh through a sieve.

In a small saucepan put the cornflour, icing sugar and egg yolks. Add the sieved orange juice, stirring with a wooden spoon. Bring it gently to the boil, stirring continuously until it has thickened.

Remove from the heat and add the lemon juice and the almonds. Leave aside to cool.

20 minutes before serving have the oven heated to 425°F / 210°C / gas 7. Beat the egg whites until stiff but not dry and fold them into the orange mixture. Fill each orange with the mixture and bake for 10 minutes until the soufflés have risen. Serve at once or the soufflés will fall.

PINEAPPLE UPSIDE-DOWN CAKE

For 6

1 small tin pineapple rings
glacé cherries
2 oz / 50 g butter
6 oz / 175 g soft brown sugar
2 tblsp / 30 ml water
Victoria Sponge mixture

Butter a 8" / 20 cm cake tin. Put as many rings of pineapple in the tin as will fit flat. Put a glacé cherry in the centre of each ring.

Put the butter, sugar and water into a saucepan and bring slowly to the boil, being sure the sugar is dissolved before it boils. Pour this gently over the pineapple in the cake tin.

Prepare the mixture for a Victoria Sponge cake (see Index) and pour this over the pineapple and syrup, being sure it is evenly covered. Bake in the oven at 350°F / 180°C / gas 4 for 30 minutes until done. Test with a skewer.

When cooked, turn the cake out onto a warm plate. Serve with whipped cream.

PEAR UPSIDE-DOWN CAKE
The method for this is the same as for the pineapple cake above except that you use a Chocolate Victoria Sponge, made by substituting 1 oz / 25 g of the flour with 1 oz / 25 g cocoa.

Use tinned pear halves and the glacé cherries. Substitute pear juice for the water in the syrup.

PEACH SHORTCAKE

For 8

8 oz / 225 g sifted plain flour
½ tsp / 3 ml salt
3 tsp / 15 ml baking powder
1 tblsp / 15 ml castor sugar
4 oz / 125 g butter or margarine
1 egg, beaten
3 fl oz / 75 ml milk

filling
16 fresh peaches
2 oz / 50 g sugar
2 tblsp / 30 ml lemon juice

To make the shortcake, first sift the flour, salt and baking powder into a bowl. Add the sugar and then rub in the butter with your fingertips until the mixture is like fine breadcrumbs. Add the beaten egg and enough of the milk to make a workable dough. (This is basically a scone dough.)

Turn it out onto a floured board and knead it lightly into a ball. Roll it out approximately ½" / 1 cm thick.

For individual shortcakes, cut out the dough with a large scone-cutter and bake in the oven at 350°F / 180°C / gas 4 for 12 minutes on a baking sheet. You can, if you wish, make one big shortcake.

When the cakes are cooked, cut them in half while still hot

2 oz / 50 g butter
8 fl oz / 225 ml whipping cream

and leave them to cool.

For the filling, peel the peaches and slice them into a bowl, sprinkling with sugar and lemon juice as you layer them.

Spread each half of shortcake with butter. Pile on a good layer of peaches. Put the top back on each shortcake. Put a dollop of whipped cream on each. Serve with any extra peaches.

This can equally well be made with strawberries or raspberries.

For 6

For the base

8 oz / 225 g digestive biscuits or ginger snaps
¼ tsp / 1 ml cinnamon
2 tblsp / 30 ml granulated white sugar
4 oz / 50 g melted butter

For the cheesecake

1 tblsp / 15 ml gelatine
1 tblsp / 15 ml lemon juice
4 oz / 125 g sugar
a pinch of salt
1 egg, separated
4 fl oz / 125 ml milk
1 tsp / 5 ml grated lemon rind
12 oz / 325 g creamed cottage cheese
4 fl oz / 125 ml whipping cream
½ tsp / 2 ml vanilla

LEMON CHEESECAKE

Crumb the biscuits in a blender or by crushing with a rolling-pin – put them in a paper bag to do this.

Mix together the crumbed biscuits, cinnamon, sugar and butter and press well into the bottom of an open dish. Bake at 350°F / 180°C / gas 4 for 10 minutes.

Soak the gelatine in the lemon juice and put aside.

Mix together three-quarters of the sugar, the salt, egg yolk and milk in the top of a double boiler. Cook this over boiling water, stirring all the time until it is thick enough to coat the back of a spoon. Add the lemon/gelatine mixture and the rind. Stir until dissolved and set aside to cool.

Press the cottage cheese through a sieve and beat it until smooth. Stir it into the gelatine mixture before it sets.

Beat the egg white until stiff but not dry. Gradually add the rest of the sugar and continue beating until the white is really stiff. Fold this into the gelatine mixture and then fold in the whipped cream mixed with the vanilla.

Turn this out onto the crumb base and chill until firm before serving.

CHOCOLATE DISHES

I have in my recipe book an original letter written sixty years ago from Banchory in Scotland to my grandmother when she was visiting my parents in Rhodesia. It reads:

Your Grace,

Christina has asked me to send Your Grace one or two chocolate sweet recipes. I feel that Your Grace would like your own chocolate mousse recipe, so the following is as near as I can remember it.

CHOCOLATE MOUSSE

4 oz / 125 g chocolate
4 eggs, separated

Melt the chocolate in very little water. If watched carefully the water can be poured off.

Beat the yolks of the eggs until quite stiff. Then add the melted chocolate. Beat the egg whites until they are stiff and fold lightly into the chocolate mixture. Pour into a shallow dish. Allow to stand for 2 hours in a cool place before serving.

CHOCOLATE CANOUGA

the weight of 2 eggs each in butter, castor sugar and chocolate
1 heaped tblsp flour
6 eggs, separated

Melt the chocolate with a little water over a low heat. If the chocolate is grated first it will melt more easily.

Then add in turn the butter, sugar, flour and the egg yolks. Whip the egg whites well and add them too. Mix lightly but well and pour into a well-buttered plain mould. Simmer very gently in a pan of water for 2½ hours.

This dish is best made the day before and kept overnight in a cool place. Serve covered with whipped cream.

COLD CHOCOLATE SOUFFLÉ

5 oz / 150 g chocolate
1 oz / 25 g gelatine
5 eggs, separated
1 cupful of milk
5 fl oz / 150 ml whipping cream

Take a soufflé dish and surround it with an oiled paper standing about 2" / 5cm above the top.

Melt the chocolate in a little water. Dissolve the gelatine in a little water. Whisk the egg yolks until quite stiff. Add the milk to the yolks and then the melted chocolate and the gelatine. Set aside until just beginning to stiffen.

Meanwhile, whip the egg whites. In a separate bowl, whip the cream. When the chocolate mixture is starting to become stiff add the whipped cream to it, keeping back a little to decorate the top. Then lightly fold in the beaten egg whites.

Pour the mixture into the prepared soufflé dish and leave to set in a cool place. Decorate the top with the reserved cream and chopped nuts, if desired.

CHOCOLATE ROLL

the weight of 2 eggs each in
    butter, castor sugar and flour
2 eggs
2 oz / 50 g chocolate, melted
½ tsp / 3 ml baking powder
pinch of salt

Cream the butter and sugar together. Beat in each of the eggs separately. Add the melted chocolate and the flour sifted with the baking powder and salt.

Take a biscuit tray. Line it with greaseproof paper, well buttered and dusted with flour. Pour the mixture into this and bake in the oven at 350°F / 180°C / gas 4 for about 10 to 15 minutes. When ready, turn out and roll up in a dampened towel or greaseproof paper. When cool, unroll, spread with whipped cream, roll again and sprinkle with castor sugar.

The letter ends with the words: 'I trust Your Grace will find something useful among these recipes. They would all be improved by being put on ice, which would, perhaps, be necessary in the heat.

I am, Your Grace,
Yours respectfully
C. MacLeod

For 8

EDWARDIAN CHOCOLATE SOUFFLÉ

The next recipe is from my maternal grandmother, Evelyne Sellar.

3 eggs, separated
3 oz / 75 g good chocolate
1 tblsp / 15 ml icing-sugar
8 fl oz / 225 g evaporated milk
1½ tblsp / 22 ml gelatine
a squeeze of lemon juice
1 tblsp / 15 ml rum
2 oz / 50 g granulated white
   sugar
2 oz / 50 g slivered almonds
6 fl oz / 175 ml whipping cream
1 tsp / 5 ml vanilla essence

Prepare a 2 pint / 1½ litre soufflé dish. Tie a band of greaseproof paper, folded double, round the outside of the dish, coming 2" / 5 cm above the top. Oil the inside of the paper standing above the dish.

Take 2 bowls. Put the egg whites into one, and the yolks into the other. To the yolks add the chocolate broken in pieces, the icing-sugar and the evaporated milk. Set this bowl over a pan of boiling water and stir continuously until the chocolate melts and it all thickens enough to coat the back of a spoon.

Remove from the heat and sprinkle the gelatine over the hot custard, stirring until it is dissolved. If it does not dissolve adequately, put the bowl back over the hot water and stir until it does. Add a squeeze of lemon juice and the rum. Put this aside to cool, but do not let it set.

For the caramel almonds: If you have a stone slab, oil it. Otherwise, take some ice cubes and crush them onto a tray. Place an oiled metal tray over the ice so that it gets cold.

Sprinkle the sugar into a heavy frying pan. Let this melt over a low heat, before turning the heat up to brown the sugar. Watch carefully that it does not burn. When a nice brown colour, add the slivered almonds. Stir the almonds around and turn them out immediately onto the cold tray.

When the caramel almonds are cold and hardened, crush them with a pestle or heavy rolling-pin. Add half of this to the chocolate custard. Beat the cream and then the egg whites separately and fold them and the vanilla in to the chocolate mixture.

Pour this mixture into the soufflé dish and set it aside until set for at least 6 hours, but better overnight.

Just before you are ready to serve, take the paper off the outside and press the remaining caramel almonds all round the sides above the dish.

My grandmother's note says, 'Put lilac in the centre and green coconut sprinkled around it.' However, that decoration can be left to the individual's taste and imagination! (To make green coconut, simply mix a few drops of green food colouring with the desiccated coconut.)

ICE-CREAMS

VANILLA ICE-CREAM

For 4 to 6

4 egg yolks
2 oz / 50 g castor sugar
8 fl oz / 225 ml double cream
2 tsp / 10 ml vanilla essence
2 egg whites

Whisk the egg yolks and sugar in a bowl over a saucepan of hot water until thick enough to hold the shape of the whisk. Remove from the heat and beat until the mixture is cold.

Whip the cream not too stiffly and fold it into the egg mixture, together with the vanilla.

Beat the egg whites until stiff and fold them in.

Pour the mixture into a plastic box with a lid. Cover it and leave in the freezer until set. It is delicious as it is or as a base for other flavours.

To make *fruit ice-cream:* when the egg yolk and sugar mixture is cooked and cold, stir in 1 pint / 600 ml of fruit purée of your choice (strawberries, raspberries, black-currants, blackberries) on which you have sprinkled 3 oz / 75 g icing-sugar. Then continue with the cream and egg whites.

ICE-CREAM SPECIAL (Granpa's Special)

For 4 to 6

4 egg yolks
1½ oz / 37 g castor sugar
½ pint / 225 ml double cream
1 tblsp / 15 ml brandy
2 egg whites
2 tsp / 10 ml lemon juice
1 tsp / 5 ml vanilla essence

Whisk the egg yolks and sugar in a bowl over a pan of hot water until thick enough to hold the shape of the whisk. Remove from the heat and continue beating until the mixture is cold.

Whip the cream not too stiffly and fold it into the mixture together with the brandy, vanilla essence and lemon juice to taste.

Whisk the egg whites until stiff and fold them into the mixture.

Pour into a charlotte tin or individual moulds. Cover with foil and leave in the freezer until set.

To serve, turn the ice-cream out and decorate with grated chocolate or chocolate caraque (see Index).

For 4 to 6

4 egg yolks
1½ oz / 37 g castor sugar
4 oz / 125 g dark chocolate
¼ pint / 150 ml double cream
1 tsp / 5 ml rum essence
2 egg whites

CHOCOLATE ICE-CREAM

Whisk the egg yolks and sugar over a pan of hot water until thick enough to hold the shape of the whisk. Remove from the heat and whisk until cold.

Meanwhile, put the chocolate in a bowl over hot, not boiling, water until melted. Then whisk it into the cooled egg yolk mixture.

Whip the cream and fold it in together with the rum essence. Whip the egg whites and fold them in.

Put the mixture in a covered dish in the deep freeze and leave until set. Turn it out and decorate with whipped cream and walnuts.

For 4

2 eggs, separated
6 oz / 175 g granulated white
    sugar
4 mangoes
1 lemon
8 fl oz / 225 ml whipping cream

MANGO ICE-CREAM

Beat the egg yolks and 2 oz / 50 g of the sugar together until stiff and lemon-coloured.

Peel the mangoes and purée the flesh. Add the juice of the lemon to the mango. Fold it into the egg yolk mixture.

Whip the cream not too stiff and fold it into the egg yolk mixture. Freeze it in a metal container for 30 minutes. Just before you take it out, beat the egg whites until stiff and beat in the remaining sugar. Take the mango cream out of the freezer, beat until smooth and mix it well with the egg whites. Re-freeze.

For 8

½ pint / 300 ml thick custard
    made with:
½ pint / 300 ml milk
1 tblsp / 15 ml cornflour
2 egg yolks
1 oz / 25 g castor sugar

Banana mixture
½ pint / 300 ml whipping cream
4 large bananas (overripe ones
    give the best flavour)
4 oz / 125 g castor sugar
1 tblsp / 15 ml lemon juice
2 egg whites
pinch of salt

BANANA ICE-CREAM

Mix together a little of the milk with the cornflour, sugar and egg yolks. Bring the rest of the milk to the boil and pour it over the egg yolk mixture. Put it back in the pan and stir it over a low heat until thickened and coming to the first boil. Set it aside to cool in a basin of iced water.

Beat the cream until thick but not too stiff. Combine it with the cooled custard. Mash the bananas with the sugar. Add the lemon juice and fold in the custard cream.

Beat the egg whites with the salt until stiff and fold them in to the mixture. Pour into a chilled ice-cream container, cover, and put in the freezer.

This freezes very hard so take it out of the freezer and put it into the fridge at least an hour before serving.

For 6

1 Victoria Sponge round
1 pint / 600 ml ice-cream
4 egg whites
8 oz / 225 g castor sugar

Raspberry sauce
1 pint / 600 ml fresh raspberries
8 oz / 225 g castor sugar

BAKED ALASKA

Bake the Victoria Sponge ahead of time (see Index). Prepare the ice-cream, if home-made, and press it into a pudding basin to mould it. Keep it in the freezer until needed. Layer the raspberries in a serving bowl with their sugar and keep them in the fridge.

Place the cake on a wooden board. Turn the ice-cream out of its mould onto the cake.

Whisk the egg whites until stiff. Beat in half the sugar and fold in the remainder.

Completely mask the cake and ice-cream with this meringue, leaving it rough with peaks.

Bake in the oven at 450°F / 220°C / gas 8 for 4 minutes until the meringue just begins to turn brown. Take the board out and put it on a tray or platter to serve at once. Serve the raspberry sauce separately.

GELATINE PUDDINGS

Every day, after breakfast, my grandmother would go to the kitchen to consult with the cook about the day's menus – which leftovers needed to be used up, what produce had come in from the garden, for we grew most of our own vegetables and fruit, and what meat, fish or game was ready. My brother still has her menu books at home.

When entertaining, or even looking after the family, I have found a menu book for the days ahead an incentive to produce meals with greater variety. It also enables me to plan ahead for shopping without last-minute panics.

One day when I was staying with my grandmother she asked me to come to the kitchen with her – it was the cook's day off – to make a treacle sponge. It is a very simple pudding. She said that it was a favourite of my grandfather.

TREACLE SPONGE

For 4

1 tblsp / 15 ml gelatine
8 fl oz / 225 ml water
3 tblsp / 45 ml treacle
4 oz / 125 g sugar
1 tsp / 5 ml ground ginger
3 egg whites

Soak the gelatine in a spoonful of the water. Heat the rest of the water and pour it onto the gelatine, stirring it until dissolved. Add the treacle, sugar and ginger.

When it has cooled, beat it together with the egg white until foaming and beginning to set.

Have ready a wetted mould. Pour in the mixture and leave to set for about 6 hours before turning out.

Serve with a custard made from the egg yolks (see Index).

LEMON PARFAIT

For 6

2 tsp / 10 ml gelatine
1½ tblsp / 22 ml cold water
2 tblsp / 30 ml boiling water
4 oz / 125 g granulated white
   sugar

Combine the gelatine with the cold water. Leave for 5 minutes. Then pour the boiling water over this and stir until the gelatine is dissolved. If the mixture is still not clear, place it in a double boiler over boiling water and stir until it clears.

4 tblsp / 60 ml lemon juice
grated rind of 2 lemons
¾ pint / 450 ml vanilla ice-
cream

Add the sugar, lemon juice and then 1 tblsp / 15 ml of the lemon rind, reserving the rest as garnish. Put all this into the bowl of a mixing machine and leave in a cold place until it begins to thicken and set. Then place the bowl on the machine and beat in the ice-cream by degrees.

Have a glass bowl ready and pour in the mixture immediately. It will set almost at once.

Sprinkle the remaining lemon rind over the top and decorate with mint leaves if desired.

ORANGE AND GRAPEFRUIT JELLY

For 4

3 oranges
2 grapefruit
4 tblsp / 60 ml granulated white
sugar
1 tblsp / 15 ml gelatine
¼ pint / 150 ml hot water
¼ pint / 150 ml whipping cream

Prepare the oranges and grapefruit, removing the pith and membrane.

Strain the juice from the fruit segments into a measuring jug. Add the sugar to the juice, stirring to dissolve it and make it up to ¾ pint / 450 ml, adding water and more orange juice if necessary.

Dissolve the gelatine in the hot water and add to the juice. Set it aside to cool and thicken. Just before it sets, stir in the fruit and pour it into a glass bowl. Decorate with the whipped cream.

SEAWEED JELLY

For 4

When we first went to South Africa with our young children we were introduced to this lovely jelly which became a great favourite.

It first requires a day at the beach to find your seaweed. In South Africa it is usually purple-coloured flat fronds up to 1 foot / 30 cm long and ½" / 1 cm wide, crinkly at the edges, attached to the great long thongs which are washed up on the shore. Collect as much as you can find. When it is dried it will keep for years.

Take it home, wash it in fresh water and lay it out in the sun to dry for several days or a week, turning it from time to time. It will bleach whiteish in colour. It may now be stored away in a bag and used, handful by handful, as wanted.

Here in Northern Europe carrageen seaweed can be used – often available at health shops.

1 handful of seaweed
2 pints / 1¼ litres water

Boil the seaweed in the water for about 20 minutes. Strain the seaweed off through a fine sieve.

8 oz / 225 g sugar
the juice of 4 lemons
½ glass white wine, if desired

To the water add the sugar, lemon juice and wine, if used. Taste the liquid to check the flavour. (It will change colour when the lemon juice is added.)

Pour the liquid into a bowl and leave to set. (The seaweed contains its own setting agent.) Serve from the bowl. It cannot be turned out.

For 4

1 packet pineapple jelly
4 bananas
2 tsp / 10 ml lemon juice
¼ pint / 150 ml whipping cream
2 tblsp / 30 ml flaked almonds,
  toasted

PINEAPPLE AND BANANA BLEND

Make the pineapple jelly as directed on the packet. Divide it between 4 glasses and leave until nearly set. Cut up 1 banana and stir a few slices into each glass.

When the jelly has set, mash the 3 remaining bananas with the lemon juice and sugar to taste. Place them in heaps on the jelly in the glasses. Pile on the whipped cream and scatter the toasted almonds over the top as decoration.

For 6

1 pint / 600 ml fresh
  strawberries
8 oz / 225 g castor sugar
1 tblsp / 15 ml gelatine
2 tblsp / 30 ml cold water
4 tblsp / 60 ml boiling water
1 tblsp / 15 ml lemon juice
8 fl oz / 225 ml whipping cream

STRAWBERRY BAVARIAN CREAM

Cut up most of the strawberries, reserving some for decoration. Pour the sugar over the cut-up berries and leave aside for an hour to draw the juice.

Soak the gelatine in the cold water and then dissolve it with the boiling water. Add the lemon juice. In another bowl whip the cream.

Add the gelatine to the strawberry mixture and, when beginning to set, add the cream. (I have found that it sets very quickly which is why I whip the cream before adding the gelatine to the strawberries.) Pour it into a bowl and decorate with the reserved strawberries.

For 6

2 tsp / 10 ml gelatine
4 fl oz / 125 ml hot water
3 eggs, separated
4 oz / 100 g castor sugar
2 tsp / 10 ml coffee essence
1 tsp / 5 ml vanilla essence
½ pint / 250 ml whipping cream

COFFEE BAVAROISE

Sprinkle the gelatine over really hot – not boiling – water and stir until dissolved. Allow to cool.

Meanwhile, beat the egg yolks with the sugar until they are thick and creamy. Add the dissolved gelatine to them, with the coffee and vanilla essence.

Beat the egg whites until stiff but not dry. Beat half the cream and fold this and the beaten egg whites into the coffee gelatine mixture. Leave to set. (It will take an hour.)

Serve with the remaining whipped cream, sweetened to taste and flavoured with ½ tsp / 3 ml rum essence, if liked.

For 6

¼ pint / 150 ml milk
8 oz / 225 g dark chocolate, broken up
1 tsp / 5 ml coffee powder
3 eggs, separated
4 oz / 125 g castor sugar
1 tblsp / 15 ml gelatine
¼ pint / 150 ml hot water
½ pint / 300 ml whipping cream

MOCHA MOUSSE

Bring the milk to the boil. Take it off the heat and add the chopped chocolate and the instant coffee powder.

Beat the egg yolks and sugar together in a bowl and pour the chocolate and milk mixture over them, beating all the time to prevent curdling. Place this bowl over a pan of gently boiling water and stir until it thickens like custard. Set aside to cool.

Dissolve the gelatine in the hot water. Allow this to cool. Whisk the egg whites stiffly and stir in the gelatine.

Whisk the cream softly. Reserve some for decorating the top of the mousse. Stir the remainder into the cooled chocolate mixture, followed by the gelatine mixture before it sets. Pour into a glass bowl and decorate with a layer of the whipped cream and grated chocolate or chocolate caraque (see Index).

STEAM PUDDINGS

ON STEAMING
This method may be used for both sweet and savoury puddings. The ingredients are put into a pudding basin filled three-quarters full to allow for expansion. The basin is covered with a butter paper and then a cloth tied below the rim with string, leaving an end long enough to tie across the top as a handle to lift the basin.

Stand the basin in a larger pot on a trivet or upturned plate so it is not resting on the bottom. Pour boiling water down the side of the pot to come halfway up the basin. If it is an aluminium pot, add 1 tblsp / 15 ml vinegar to prevent discoloration. Put the lid on.

Bring the pot to the boil, turn the heat down and leave to simmer for the recommended time. If the cooking is long, refill from time to time with boiling water.

CANARY PUDDING

For 4

weigh 2 eggs and then take the same weight each of:
butter or margarine
sugar
self-raising flour
1 tsp / 5 ml vanilla essence
2 spoonfuls of golden or corn syrup

Cream the butter and sugar together. Beat the eggs and gradually beat them into the creamed butter and sugar. Sift the flour and fold it into the mixture. Then add the vanilla essence.

Put 2 spoonfuls of syrup in the bottom of a buttered 1 lb / 450 g pudding basin. Pour the batter in on top. Cover the basin and steam as described above for 1½ hours.

Turn the pudding out onto a hot plate and serve with cream or with warmed golden syrup, flavoured with orange.

To make a MARMALADE PUDDING, put marmalade in the bottom of the basin instead of syrup. To make a CHOCOLATE PUDDING, substitute 1 oz / 25 g cocoa for the same measure of flour. Put some chocolate sauce (see Index) in the bottom instead of syrup and serve with more of the same sauce or with cream.

STEAMED CHOCOLATE SOUFFLÉ

A lovely light dish.

For 6

½ pint / 300 ml milk
4 oz / 125 g grated chocolate
5 oz / 150 g crumbed sponge
    fingers *or* breadcrumbs
3 eggs, separated
2 oz / 50 g castor sugar

chocolate sauce
½ pint / 300 ml milk
2 oz / 50 g chocolate

Warm the milk in a saucepan, but do not boil. Stir into it the grated chocolate and the crumbs. Stir it over a low heat without boiling until the chocolate dissolves. Pour it into a dish containing the beaten egg yolks and set aside to cool.

When cold, mix in the castor sugar. Whisk the whites until stiff and fold them in.

Pour the chocolate mixture into a well-buttered 2 pint / 1.2 litre pudding basin. Cover and steam for 1½ hours.

To serve, turn the steamed soufflé onto a hot plate. Serve with whipped cream or a chocolate sauce made by melting the chocolate in the heated milk. Add sugar and vanilla to taste.

GUARDS PUDDING (Brodick Castle)

For 4

2 oz / 50 g butter
3 oz / 75 g soft breadcrumbs
3 eggs, separated
3 tblsp / 45 ml strawberry or
    raspberry jam

Melt the butter gently. Take it off the heat and stir in the crumbs. Beat the egg yolks and add them, together with the jam. Beat the whites until stiff but not dry and fold them in. Turn the mixture into a buttered pudding basin. Cover and steam for 1½ hours.

CLOOTIE DUMPLING (A Scottish dish)

This is a pudding boiled in a cloth.

For 6

6 oz / 175 g flour
½ tsp / 3 ml baking soda
½ tsp / 3 ml ground cinnamon
½ tsp / 3 ml ground cloves
2 oz / 50 g suet or butter
2 oz / 50 g brown sugar
2 oz / 50 g white sugar
2 oz / 50 g currants
4 oz / 125 g raisins
½ pint / 300 ml sour milk or
    buttermilk

Sift the flour, soda, cinnamon and cloves together. If you are using butter, rub it into the flour mixture with your fingers until like breadcrumbs. If suet, chop it finely and add it to the flour.

Mix the sugars together with the dried fruit and add them to the mixture. Then stir in the sour milk or buttermilk.

Have ready a large square cloth. Scald it and wring it out. Dredge the inside of the cloth with flour. Lay it over a pudding basin and put all the mixture into it. Draw the cloth together evenly, leaving room for the pudding to swell. Tie it tightly with string with a bow knot.

Lift the dumpling in its cloth out of the basin and put it into a large saucepan of boiling water. Simmer for 2 hours, adding more boiling water if needed.

Lift it out onto a colander to drain. Untie the cloth and turn the dumpling out onto a hot ashet. Dust it with castor sugar and serve with a hot lemon or custard sauce.

FIG PUDDING

For 6

8 oz / 225 g suet, finely chopped
8 oz / 225 g sugar
8 oz / 225 g soft breadcrumbs
1 tsp / 5 ml mixed spice
12 oz / 375 g figs, finely chopped
4 eggs, well beaten
2 tblsp / 30 ml brandy

Mix the suet, sugar, breadcrumbs and spice. Add the figs. Add the eggs beaten with the brandy. Put into a buttered 2 pint / 1.2 litre pudding basin and steam for 2 hours. Turn out and serve with custard or cream.

CHRISTMAS PUDDING

Christmas puddings should be made not later than November. In our home there has always been the excitement of everyone in the household coming into the kitchen and making their own wish as they had their stir of the pudding before it was cooked. This recipe – my grandmother's note says it comes from the Duke of Connaught – makes 1 large or 2 small puddings.

8 oz / 225 g soft breadcrumbs
½ tblsp / 8 ml ground nutmeg
8 oz / 225 g finely chopped suet
8 oz / 225 g demerara sugar
8 oz / 225 g sultanas
8 oz / 225 g raisins
4 oz / 125 g currants
4 eggs
2 tblsp / 30 ml brandy
the grated rind and juice of 1 lemon

Mix together the breadcrumbs and nutmeg. Add the suet, sugar and dried fruit and mix well. Beat the eggs a little and stir them in together with the brandy and the juice and rind of the lemon.

Put the mixture in 1 large or 2 small basins. Cover and steam the smaller puddings for 5 hours, the large one for 8 hours. Put them aside to keep for a month or more. (See instructions at the end of the following recipe.)

On Christmas Day, steam for 2 more hours before turning out. Have ready some charms wrapped in greaseproof paper – a bachelor's button, a ring, a silver coin, etc. Slip these into slits in the pudding.

Serve with a sprig of holly and a large spoon of heated brandy poured over the top and set alight.

BRANDY BUTTER
4 oz / 125 g butter
4 oz / 125 g castor sugar
2 tblsp / 30 ml brandy (or to taste)

Cream the butter and sugar together until light and fluffy. Beat in the brandy. Pile in a serving dish and keep cool.

CHRISTMAS PUDDINGS
(a multiple recipe)

I often make a number of puddings at a time to give as presents or to keep for later use. This slightly richer and darker recipe is enough for 5, 6 or 7 puddings of various sizes.

1 lb / 450 g beef suet, finely chopped

8 oz / 225 g fresh white breadcrumbs

8 oz / 225 g flour

8 oz / 225 g soft brown sugar

8 oz / 225 g granulated sugar

1 nutmeg, grated

1 tsp / 5 ml mixed spice

a pinch of salt

1 lb / 450 g currants

1 lb / 450 g raisins

1 lb / 450 g sultanas

8 oz / 225 g mixed peel

1 lb / 450 g carrots, grated

4 oz / 125 g almonds, peeled and chopped

juice and grated rind of 2 lemons

8 eggs, well beaten

¼ pint / 150 ml milk

¼ pint / 150 ml brandy

2 oz / 50 g melted butter

Mix together the suet, breadcrumbs, flour, sugars, nutmeg, spice and salt.

In a large basin – I have an old-fashioned wash-hand basin – mix together the dried fruit, mixed peel, carrots, almonds and grated lemon rind. To this add the flour and breadcrumb mixture and combine them well.

In a separate bowl beat the eggs. To them add the milk, brandy and lemon juice. Melt the butter and stir it in. Now add this to the dried fruit mixture and stir. At this point everyone's help is needed. The total mixture makes about 8 lb / 3½ kg.

Have buttered pudding basins ready. You can use the old-fashioned china ones, or tinfoil ones with lids. Fill them three-quarters full to leave room for expansion. Cover them and steam as directed earlier – small puddings for 5 hours, larger ones for 8 hours, replenishing the boiling water as needed.

When cooked, cover the puddings which are in china basins with fresh butter paper and a clean cloth, ready for their final cooking. Store them in a single layer in a cool open place. On the day, prepare and serve as in the previous recipe.

PASTRY

SHORTCRUST PASTRY

10 oz / 275 g plain flour
½ tsp / 2 ml salt
4 oz / 125 g lard or white fat
4 oz / 125 g butter or margarine
4 fl oz / 125 ml cold water,
    approximately

This will make the base or top for two 8" / 20 cm pie dishes.

Sieve the flour and salt into a bowl. Take the fat and butter from the fridge and grate it into the flour. It may now either be cut in, with a knife in each hand working against each other like a pair of scissors until it resembles breadcrumbs, or it may be rubbed in by hand. With the fingers of one hand lift the flour and fat and rub it as it falls, repeating again and again until it resembles fine breadcrumbs. This incorporates as much air as possible and ensures that your pastry is light. If you squash the mixture in your palm, the heat of your hand will melt it and make your pastry heavy – the less pastry is handled, the better.

Finally, make a well in the centre of the mixture and add the water all at once. Cut it in with a round-ended knife and then gather the mixture into a ball. Cover it and set it aside to rest for at least half an hour so that it does not shrink as it cooks. Flour varies and some may need a little more water.

To bake an empty pastry shell, roll the pastry out. Pick it up on the rolling-pin and drop it carefully into the tin. Lift the edges and ease the pastry to fit the bottom without stretching. Pick the tin up and trim the edges. Flute them with your finger and thumb. Prick the base all over with a fork. Put some greaseproof paper on top of the pastry and a layer of dried beans kept for this purpose. These provide enough weight to prevent the pastry bubbling.

Bake in a hot oven (425°F / 210°C / gas 7) for 10 minutes. Remove the beans and paper and finish off the cooking for a further 5 minutes. Cooking quickly in a hot oven makes the pastry crisp.

If you are going to cook the pie filling and the pastry together – i.e. for quiche, a fruit pie or steak and kidney pie – do not prick the pastry shell, but brush it with egg white. This stops the pastry going soggy. Fill with your chosen filling.

SWEET PASTRY

This makes a shortbread-type base or cover for many fruit pies.

8 oz / 225 g flour
a pinch of salt
5 oz / 150 g butter
1 oz / 25 g sugar
2 tsp / 10 ml grated lemon rind
3 tblsp / 45 ml double cream
1 egg yolk

Sift the flour and salt together in a large mixing bowl. Make a well in the middle. Into this put the butter, sugar, lemon rind, cream and egg yolk.

With the fingers of one hand, mix this all together, gradually drawing in the flour until it is all incorporated. Gather the dough into a ball and set aside for at least 1 hour.

To bake 'blind' (empty), roll out the pastry, fit into the dish and prick before baking. Cook in the oven at 375°F / 190°C / gas 5 for about 20 minutes.

PUFF PASTRY

This is difficult but I think it tastes much better than the ready-made bought variety. Puff pastry is good for vol-au-vent cases, sausage rolls, steak and kidney pie or pastry biscuits sandwiched with jam and cream.

TIPS
(1.) Work in a cool kitchen. Keep hands, board, rolling-pin and pastry as cool as possible.
(2.) Have the butter well chilled, firm but not so hard that it breaks through the dough. The layers of butter between the layers of dough give the puff and lightness.
(3.) In between each rolling the dough is rested for half an hour. If it gets too soft and warm, put it in the fridge. It is the resting between rollings that also helps give the pastry its lightness.
(4.) When the pastry is shaped, chill well before baking. Unbaked puff pastry will keep for several days in the fridge, or several weeks in the freezer.

8 oz / 225 g butter
8 oz / 225 g flour
½ tsp / 3 ml salt
4 fl oz / 125 ml iced water

Reserve 1 oz / 25 g of the butter. Work the remainder of the butter with the back of a wooden spoon until as pliable as putty. Put it between sheets of waxed paper and roll it out into a rectangle 8″ × 6″ × ½″ (20 cm × 15 cm × 1 cm) thick. Chill this thoroughly in the fridge for 1 hour.

Sift the flour and salt into a mixing bowl and rub in the remaining 1 oz / 25 g butter until it resembles coarse meal.

Gradually add the iced water, tossing with a fork, and then gather it into a ball. Turn it out onto a lightly floured surface and knead until smooth and elastic – about 5 minutes. Cover it with a bowl and let it rest for 10 minutes. Again roll out the dough on a lightly floured surface until it measures approximately 15″ × 9″ (38 cm × 23 cm).

Take the butter from the fridge. Peel off the top sheet of paper and invert it onto one half of the dough. Peel off the second sheet of paper and fold the other half of dough to cover the butter. The edges should meet. Seal the edges together by pressing with the side of your hand. Cover the dough with wax paper and chill for half an hour.

Unwrap and roll out the dough on a lightly floured surface from the short end in one direction. Fold it in three, seal the edges again, give the dough a quarter turn and roll out again from the short end in one direction. Fold it once more in three, sealing the edges. Cover and let it rest in the fridge for half an hour. Repeat this rolling and resting twice more. Chill again for an hour and it is now ready for use.

To cook small pastries, brush a baking tray with water, cut out your shapes and bake in a hot oven (450°F / 230°C / gas 8) for about 10 minutes. For large pies, such as steak and kidney, follow the recipe for any different timing needed.

Note: Place all pie dishes on a baking sheet before putting them in the oven. This will save cleaning the oven if the pie bubbles over.

CHOUX PASTRY

This recipe makes 6 large or 9 medium puffs. Cream puffs may be used for many things, not only puddings or sweets. They may have savoury fillings as for Bouchées.

A teaspoon of the dough will make tiny puffs which, filled with a savoury filling, go well with drinks. They, of course, take less time to cook.

2 oz / 50 g butter
4 fl oz / 100 ml water
2 oz / 50 g flour
2 eggs

Put the butter in the water and bring to the boil. Add all the flour at once and stir hard until it comes away from the side of the pan. Remove the pan from the heat. This is most important as otherwise the eggs will cook too soon and the puffs will not rise. Crack the eggs and beat them in one at a time, beating well after each egg.

Butter a baking tray and set the cream puffs out in spoonfuls with plenty of room around them as they spread and puff. Bake in the oven at 375°F / 190°C / gas 5 for about half an hour. If in doubt, remove one and see if it stands up.

They may be served with a filling of ice-cream or whipped cream. Dust the top with icing-sugar and serve with hot chocolate sauce.

Eclairs are made with the same recipe, but piped out in long fingers. Ice the top with glacé coffee icing and fill with créme chantilly (see Index).

PASTRY DISHES

DEEP-DISH APPLE AND BLACKBERRY PIE

One of our treats as children was to go blackberry picking with our friends, the Bannermans, on the hills above Loch Lomond.

Wonderful autumn weather: the curlews – or whaup as we knew them – calling to each other; the call of the grouse, 'Go back, go back', as they darted from under our feet; the larks soaring up, singing their hearts out. We competed to fill the big baskets. I don't know how, but my mother always found the most and the biggest berries.

Then a picnic lunch – thermoses of hot soup, and salmon sandwiches made with our own salmon from the loch, eaten with purple-stained fingers. Our arms and legs were scratched but the only real drawback was the midges! Then home with our heaped baskets to an orgy of jam and jelly-making – and Blackberry and Apple Pie.

Make 1 recipe of shortcrust pastry. This is a large pie.
2 lb / 900 g apples, cored, peeled and sliced
12 oz / 350 g sugar
2 tblsp / 30 ml flour
1 lb / 450 g blackberries sorted and cleaned
juice and grated rind of 1 lemon

Put a china pastry funnel or an upturned egg-cup in the centre of a large pie dish to hold up the pastry and stop it becoming soggy. Layer the apple slices in the dish and sprinkle them with half the sugar mixed with flour. Add the blackberries and the rest of the sugar. Mound the fruit well up as it shrinks in cooking.

Roll out the pastry a little bigger than you need. Brush the edges of the dish with water. Cut strips of pastry and lay them along the edges, sticking them together with water.

Brush the edges again with water, pick up the pastry on the rolling pin and unroll it over the pie. Trim the edges, holding the pie up in one hand and cutting the excess away with the knife pointing away from the centre of the dish. In this way you keep a nice fat edge to the pastry. Knock up the pastry edge with the back of your knife, held parallel to the edge. Then with your thumb gently on the top, and with the knife perpendicular, cut flutes into the pastry all round. Cut slits in the pastry top to let the steam escape.

Bake the pie at 425°F / 210°C / gas 7 for 15 minutes. Then turn the oven down to 350°F / 180°C / gas 4 and bake for about a further half-hour. If the pastry is browning too quickly, cover with brown paper.

Dust the top of the pie with castor sugar and serve with cream.

GOOSEBERRY PIE

For 6

Make 1 recipe of shortcrust pastry
1½ pints / 900 ml gooseberries
1 tblsp / 15 ml plain flour
8 oz / 225 g granulated white sugar *or* 8 fl oz / 225 ml elderflower syrup (see Index)

Put the gooseberries, flour and sugar or elderflower syrup into a 2 pint / 1.2 litre pie dish, cover and proceed as for Deep-Dish Apple Pie. Bake at 425°F / 210°C / gas 7.

OPEN APPLE TART

For 6 to 8

Make 1 recipe of sweet pastry
4 oz / 125 g ground almonds
1½ lb / 700 g eating apples (Cox's or Granny Smith)
4 oz / 125 g granulated white sugar
2 tblsp / 30 ml melted butter
4 oz / 125 g redcurrant *or* apple jelly *or* apricot jam
4 fl oz / 125 ml whipping cream

Roll out the pastry to fit a 10" / 25 cm pie dish. Sprinkle the ground almonds over the pastry. Put 1 layer of sliced apple over the almonds. Peel, core and halve the remaining apples. Slice these halves, retaining the shape, and put them onto the pie, rounded side-up. Scatter half the sugar over the top.

Brush the apples with half the melted butter. Bake in the oven at 400°F / 200°C / gas 5 for 15 minutes until half-cooked. Then sprinkle on the rest of the sugar and brush again with the remaining butter. Turn the oven heat down to 350°F / 180°C / gas 4 and bake for a further 15 minutes or until done.

Meanwhile, gently melt the jelly or sieved apricot jam and brush the pie with this when you take it finally from the oven. Set aside to cool. Before serving, whip the cream stiffly and pipe it around the edge of the pie.

AMERICAN APPLE PIE

For 6

1 recipe shortcrust pastry to fit a 9" / 23 cm pie dish
1 egg white
1½ lb / 700 g cooking apples
1 tblsp / 15 ml plain flour

Roll out half the pastry to fit the bottom of the pie dish. Brush it with the egg white.

Peel, core and slice the apples. Pour the lemon juice over them and mix them with the flour, cloves, sugar, cinnamon and lemon rind. Pile them into the pie shell.

½ tsp / 2 ml cloves
4 oz / 125 g light brown sugar
½ tsp / 3 ml cinnamon
juice and grated rind 1 lemon

Roll out the remaining pastry. Brush the edges of the shell with water and pick up the new pastry on the rolling-pin and place it over the pie, trimming the edges. Press together and flute them. Brush the top with egg white, and sprinkle with a little sugar.

Cut slits for the steam to escape and bake at 425°F / 210°C / gas 7 for 10 minutes before reducing the heat to 350°F / 180°C / gas 4 for half an hour.

For 6

Make 1 recipe for sweetcrust
   pastry
1½ pint / 900 ml blackcurrants
¼ pint / 150 ml cold water
a sprig of mint
8 oz / 225 g granulated white
   sugar
3 tblsp / 45 ml cornflour
4 fl oz / 125 ml whipping cream

BLACKCURRANT TART

Roll out the pastry to fill a 9" / 23 cm pie dish and bake it blind as in the recipe. Leave aside until cold.

Put the blackcurrants, water and mint in a saucepan and bring to the boil. Add the sugar and stir slowly until dissolved. Bring it back to the boil and thicken with the cornflour mixed to a paste with a little cold water. Remove the sprig of mint and leave the blackcurrants to cool.

Pour the fruit into the baked pastry case and decorate with whipped cream.

For 8

Pastry
4 oz / 125 g plain flour
¼ tsp / 1 ml salt
¼ tsp / 1 ml baking powder
4 oz / 125 g white fat

Filling
8 oz / 225 g butter
8 oz / 225 g granulated white
   sugar
6 medium egg yolks
6 medium egg whites
6 oz / 175 g icing-sugar
1 tsp / 5 ml vanilla essence
1 tsp / 5 ml lemon juice

CHESS PIE (a 3-tiered, filled pie)

Make the pastry by sifting the flour, baking powder and salt together. Crumble the fat into this flour mixture with your fingertips. Add enough cold water – about 5 tblsp / 75 ml – to mix to a firm dough. Divide this into three and roll out to fill three 8" / 20 cm pie tins.

For the filling, cream the butter and sugar. Beat the egg yolks until cream-coloured. Then beat them slowly into the creamed butter and sugar. Beat 3 of the egg whites and fold them in. Divide the mixture between the 3 pies and bake in the oven at 400°F / 200°C / gas 6 for about 10 minutes.

Meanwhile, beat the other 3 egg whites with the icing-sugar to make a meringue. Flavour with the vanilla and lemon juice and leave in the fridge to stiffen while the pies cool.

Loosen the pie shells in their tins but leave them until cold before taking them out.

To serve, spread the meringue over each of the pies. Stack them one on top of each other and cut as you would a cake.

For 8

1 recipe for shortcrust pastry
1 tblsp / 15 ml gelatine
4 tblsp / 60 ml cold water
4 medium eggs, separated
¼ tsp / 1 ml salt
4 fl oz / 125 ml hot water
6 oz / 175 g granulated white
    sugar
3 tblsp / 45 ml rum *or* 1 tsp /
    5 ml rum essence, to taste
1 tsp / 5 ml nutmeg
8 fl oz / 225 ml whipping cream

EGGNOG PIE

Bake two 8″ / 20 cm pie shells, unfilled, as directed, at 425°F / 210°C / gas 7.

Soak the gelatine in the cold water and set it aside.

Mix together in the top of a double boiler the egg yolks, salt, hot water and 4 oz / 125 g of the sugar. Cook over boiling water, stirring constantly, until thick enough to coat the back of a spoon. If you overcook it or stop stirring, it may curdle. If this happens, put the saucepan immediately into cold water and whisk hard.

When this custard mixture is cooked, add the soaked gelatine together with the rum and nutmeg and stir until dissolved. Set this aside to cool until quite thick.

Beat the egg whites until stiff. Beat in the remaining sugar and fold into the custard mixture. Pour this immediately into the cold pie shell and leave until set. Before serving, whip the cream and spread it over the pie. Shake a dusting of nutmeg over the top.

This recipe was given to me by Kate Cross.

For 6

½ the recipe for shortcrust
    pastry
2 tsp / 10 ml gelatine
2 tblsp / 30 ml lemon juice (cold
    water for lemon pie)
2 medium eggs, separated
a pinch of salt
oranges or lemons to make
    1 tblsp / 15 ml grated rind
    and 3 fl oz / 75 ml juice
3 oz / 75 g granulated white
    sugar
4 fl oz / 125 ml whipping cream

ORANGE OR LEMON CHIFFON PIE

This recipe derives from the previous one but is half the size.

Bake an 8″ / 20 cm pie shell as directed.

Soak the gelatine in the lemon juice. Put the egg yolks, salt, juice and rind and 2 oz / 50 g of the sugar in the top of a double boiler over boiling water. Cook until thick.

Remove from the heat and add the gelatine, stirring until dissolved. Leave it aside to cool and thicken, but not set. When ready, whip the egg whites until stiff, beat in the remaining sugar and fold all this into the custard mixture. Pour this immediately into the pie shell and leave to set.

Just before serving, whip the cream, spread it over the pie and grate some more rind over it.

At the height of the race integration crisis in the United States I was among those invited to bring the musical play, *The Crowning Experience*, to Atlanta, Georgia. The play was based on the life of Mary McLeod Bethune who was born of slave parents. As a pioneer for her people, she rose to become an advisor to the President.

The Crowning Experience was the first to play in that theatre in Atlanta to a fully integrated audience. Muriel Smith, the

,MURIEL SMITH SINGS "SWEET POTATO PIE".

great mezzo soprano, gave up a contract in Hollywood voluntarily to take the lead role.

I was in the chorus line of the last act of the show. One day I had been sweeping out a very dusty cupboard and arrived at the theatre with my eyes streaming from a violent attack of hay fever. The nurse gave me an anti-histamine tablet which stopped the streaming but sent me to sleep. I arrived on stage barely able to keep my eyes open. Muriel Smith, a good friend, spotted me immediately and if you have ever had a furious opera singer – she had played Carmen at Covent Garden – singing full blast at you from two feet away, I can tell you it is an experience you will never forget.

A brother and sister in Atlanta, Guy and Franny Woolford, opened their gracious old family home to us for entertaining. I offered to help and many were the parties we had there. I remember Daisy Bates, head of the National Association for the Advancement of Coloured People in Little Rock, Arkansas, coming for lunch. She was in bitter confrontation with Governor Faubus over admitting black children to white schools. Rajmohan Gandhi joined the lunch party and the discussion ranged over how people and their attitudes could change. In the following months the children were admitted to the schools and, later, a picture of Mrs Bates shaking hands with the Governor was chosen by the national press as a photo of the year.

One of the show stoppers in *The Crowning Experience* was the song 'Sweet Potato Pie', about the dish which Mary McLeod

Bethune had baked and sold to raise funds for her first school. After the show many in the audience would stay and talk, and we often served them with the pie. So over those five months we must have baked hundreds of this next recipe.

For 6

1 shortcrust pastry recipe to make a 9" / 23 cm shell
12 oz / 350 g hot mashed sweet potato
3 large eggs, lightly beaten
3 oz / 75 g soft brown sugar
½ tsp / 2 ml salt
¼ tsp / 1½ ml cinnamon
¼ tsp / 1 ml all-spice
¼ tsp / 1 ml ginger
4 fl oz / 125 ml milk
2 fl oz / 50 ml brandy
2 tblsp / 30 ml melted butter

SWEET POTATO PIE

Boil, drain and mash the sweet potato. Set it aside to cool.

Prepare the uncooked pastry shell. Brush the base with a little egg white.

Beat the eggs lightly. Add them to the sweet potato with the sugar, salt, spices, milk, brandy and melted butter.

Pour this into the pie shell and bake it in the hot oven – 425°F / 210°C / gas 7 – for 10 minutes. Then reduce the oven to 350°F / 180°C / gas 4 and bake for a further 25 to 30 minutes. Test with a skewer or knife.

For 8

enough shortcrust pastry to make two 8" / 20 cm shells
12 fl oz / 350 ml pumpkin purée
1 tblsp / 15 ml gelatine
4 tblsp / 60 ml cold water
8 oz / 225 g granulated white sugar
3 large eggs, separated
½ tsp / 2 ml nutmeg
½ tsp / 3 ml ginger
½ tsp / 3 ml cinnamon
½ tsp / 2 ml salt
3 fl oz / 75 ml milk
4 fl oz / 125 ml double cream

PUMPKIN CHIFFON PIE

Bake the 2 pastry shells.

Peel and skin a 1 lb / 450 g pumpkin. Cut it into strips and place in a greased casserole. Dot it with a little butter and bake for about 45 minutes at 350°F / 180°C / gas 4. Purée the cooked pumpkin through a coarse sieve or in a food processor.

Put the gelatine to soak in the cold water and set aside.

In a china bowl add half the sugar to the egg yolks and beat until light and creamy-coloured. Add the pumpkin purée, the spices and salt.

Bring the milk to the boil and add it to the mixture. Place the mixture over a pan of boiling water and cook, stirring all the time until it thickens and the egg yolks are cooked.

Remove the bowl from the heat and add the gelatine mixture. Stir until dissolved and allow to cool but not set.

Beat the egg whites until stiff and beat in the remaining sugar. Fold this into the pumpkin mixture with a metal spoon and fill the cooked pie shells. Leave aside until cold and set. Before serving, whip the cream and spread a thin layer over the pies.

For 6

half a recipe for sweet pastry
1 × 14 oz / 397 g tin sweetened
 condensed milk
4 fl oz / 125 ml lemon juice
the grated rind of 1 lemon
2 medium eggs, separated
4 oz / 125 g granulated white
 sugar

LEMON MERINGUE PIE

Lightly bake the sweet pastry in a 9″ / 23 cm shell.

Mix together the condensed milk, lemon juice and rind, and the egg yolks. Pour this into the pie shell.

Beat the egg whites and beat in half the sugar. Fold in most of the remainder, reserving a little. Cover the lemon mixture with this meringue, sprinkling the reserved sugar on top.

Bake in the oven at 380°F / 190°C / gas 5 for 10 minutes.

For 6

3 oz / 75 g hazelnuts
4 oz / 125 g butter
2 oz / 50 g castor sugar
5 oz / 150 g plain flour
12 fresh peaches, sliced and
 sprinkled with 2 oz / 50 g
 sugar
8 fl oz / 225 ml whipping cream

TONILLES AUX PÊCHES

A French recipe for peaches in a hazelnut pastry.

Spread the nuts on a tray and toast them in the oven at 350°F / 180°C / gas 4 until brown but not burnt – about 15 minutes. Grind them finely in a coffee grinder or with a rolling pin. Keep the oven on.

Cream the butter and sugar. Add the flour and nuts and knead into a ball. Divide this into 3 balls and roll out each ball into a round 8″ / 20 cm diameter. Place the rounds on flat buttered baking sheets and bake for about 15 minutes.

Remove the rounds from the oven and, while still hot, cut each round into 6. Leave on the sheets to cool.

Peel and slice the peaches. Sprinkle the sugar over them. Whip the cream. Just before serving, drain the peaches and fold them into the cream. Sandwich this between the layers of pastry, making 6 individual servings. Dust with icing-sugar and serve as soon as possible. Any extra peaches and juice may be served separately.

Note: Strawberries may be used instead of peaches.

For 8

1 recipe for sweet pastry
6 tblsp / 90 ml water
6 tblsp / 90 ml redcurrant jelly
 (see Index)
1 tblsp / 15 ml cornflour
1 lb / 450 g fresh raspberries or
 strawberries, halved
whipping cream to serve

RASPBERRY OR STRAWBERRY TARTS

Push the pastry into two 8″ / 20 cm cake tins and bake until just beginning to turn colour, but not brown. While hot, cut each shell into 4 sections and leave aside to cool.

Heat the water and jelly together until the jelly is dissolved. Bring it to the boil and add the cornflour mixed with a little cold water, stirring constantly until cooked.

Arrange the raspberry or strawberry halves on the pastry sections. Cover each tart with the jelly glaze. Let it set and decorate with whipped cream.

HONEY AND HAZELNUT TARTLETS

For 4 to 6

half a recipe for sweet pastry
4 oz / 125 g lightly roasted
    hazelnuts
3 tblsp / 45 ml honey, warmed
¼ pint / 125 ml double cream
icing-sugar

Roll the pastry out and line 12 or more patty pans. Bake for about 10 minutes at 400°F / 200°C / gas 7. Cool the tarts and then remove them from the tin.

Chop the roasted nuts finely by hand or in a processor. Combine them with the warmed honey. Whip the cream and fold it in. Chill the mixture and just before serving fill the tarts. Dust with icing-sugar.

MELK TERT (South Africa)

1 recipe shortcrust pastry
8 fl oz / 225 ml milk
½ stick of cinnamon
1 oz / 25 g butter
1 tblsp / 15 ml plain flour
a pinch of salt
4 medium eggs, separated
5 tblsp / 75 ml granulated white
    sugar
½ tsp / 3 ml powdered
    cinnamon

Lightly bake the pastry to make two 8" / 23 cm shells.

Bring the milk slowly to the boil with the cinnamon stick and the butter.

Mix the flour and salt with a little cold milk to make a thin paste. Take the milk off the heat and strain it over the flour paste, whisking thoroughly. Remove the cinnamon stick. Return the mixture to the heat and bring it back to the boil, stirring constantly. Turn the heat down and simmer very gently until thickened.

Beat the 4 egg yolks and 4 tblsp / 60 ml of the sugar until thick and creamy and pour over them the milk and flour mixture, stirring them together.

Beat the whites until stiff and fold them into the mixture with a metal spoon. Pour this into the pie shells and bake for 15 minutes in the oven at 425°F / 210°C / gas 8. Then turn the heat down to 350°F / 180°C / gas 4 for a further 15 minutes. They should look risen and golden. Take them out of the oven and sprinkle over them the remaining 1 tblsp / 15 ml sugar mixed with the powdered cinnamon.

The recipe for Melk Tert comes from Mrs Joey Daneel, wife of the oldest living Springbok rugby player, Ds George Daneel. As I came to know her I discovered that Mrs Daneel's father had been one of the Boers besieging Ladysmith at the time my grandfather was trapped inside with the British army.

I learnt many things from the Daneels and other senior Afrikaners who became very dear friends during our 15 years as a family in South Africa.

I also discovered that, along with the black/white issue which we all know about, another relationship ran very deep in South Africa – that between the English-speaker and the Afrikaner. Some of this I tried to sum up in a letter which was published both in the *Cape Times* and in the Afrikaans daily *Die Burger* as part of a debate on these issues. It read:

Thursday, April 5, 1984

My grandfather fought in the Boer War, on the British side. He was in the siege of Ladysmith. For myself, though I grew up in Britain, I am raising my family in South Africa.

What interests me now is not how to forget the past, but how to heal it.

We of British stock find it hard to face that an enduring reality still shaping today's events is the strong feelings which others hold against us.

My husband comes from Northern Ireland. Our British reaction to that tragedy is to shake our heads and say, 'If only they could be more reasonable, like us'.

We shirk the pain of our history where, for centuries, we fought to impose our will on another people, and then uprooted the original inhabitants who opposed our rule and supplanted them with settlers who would serve our purpose.

In Britain itself those of us who did not suffer the unemployment in the 1930s tend to gloss over those terrible conditions which still lie behind much of the class bitterness today.

Here in South Africa many Afrikaners have felt that, for more than a century, we tried to destroy their identity. We may have convinced ourselves that we knew best for them, but they have seen it as a pursuit of our own self-interest.

Many of those hurts still have to be healed. I remember at a friend's house admiring an occasional table. I was told that it had belonged to my hostess's great uncle who, at the age of 17, had been exiled from South Africa to Ceylon at the end of the Boer War.

Again I think of a visitor to our home telling us with tremendous feeling of her aunt who died in one of our British concentration camps. I could not argue about what they felt. I could only acknowledge its truth and ask forgiveness for what happened in the name of my people.

If we in South Africa are to move forward together,

we English-speakers must acknowledge that we have been a major part of what has been wrong.

I am not advocating a breast-beating exercise. I do say that we need to listen; and not just to the other person's words, but to try to understand what lies behind the words.

If we can so live that we answer the hurts and bitterness in others, then perhaps we shall find the right road ahead.

In the following days I had a number of surprising responses to the letter, both in person and in the press.

MINCE PIES

I always make a tinful of these before Christmas so that they are available at any time and I don't have to spend too much time in the kitchen. The mincemeat should be prepared a month ahead to allow it to season.

12 oz / 350 g raisins
8 oz / 225 g sultanas
12 oz / 350 g currants
8 oz / 225 g prepared suet
1 lb / 450 g apples
8 oz / 225 g mixed peel, chopped
8 oz / 225 g almonds, peeled and chopped
12 oz / 350 g brown sugar
the juice and grated rind of 2 lemons
a wine-glass of brandy or rum

Mix the dried fruit together with the suet. Peel and grate the apples and add them, the mixed peel and the almonds. Add the sugar, lemon juice and rind and the brandy or rum. Stir everything together and then store it in jars for at least a month.

Make a batch of shortcrust pastry and set the dough aside to rest for half an hour. One pastry recipe will make about 24 pies.

Roll it out quite thinly. With a large fluted cutter cut out rounds to fit your patty pans. Put a teaspoon of the mincemeat into the centre of each pie. With a smaller fluted cutter cut out lids to fit each pie. Brush the edges with water and press the lid gently to join the base.

Cut a cross in the centre of each pie. Brush them lightly with milk, dust them with castor sugar and bake them at 400°F / 200°C / gas 6 for about 15 minutes, until just turning brown at the edges.

The pies are best served hot, but they may be cooled or frozen to be used when you wish.

Note: If you do not want to use suet, melted butter can replace it.

SWEET SAUCES

BRANDY BUTTER

4 oz / 125 g butter
4 oz / 125 g castor sugar
2 tblsp / 30 ml brandy (or to
  taste)

Cream the butter and sugar together until light and creamy. Beat in the brandy. Pile into a glass bowl and chill until needed. Serve with Christmas Pudding.

BUTTERSCOTCH SAUCE

6 oz / 175 g soft brown sugar
2 good tblsp / 40 ml golden
  syrup
2 fl oz / 50 ml whipping cream
1½ oz / 35 g butter

Combine all the ingredients in a saucepan. Heat until boiling and boil for 3 minutes.

On an electric stove, once it is boiling, you can turn the heat off while leaving the saucepan on the hot plate. The residual heat will cook it adequately.

CHOCOLATE SAUCE

5 tblsp / 75 ml boiling water
8 oz / 225 g granulated white
  sugar
5 tblsp / 75 ml cocoa
½ oz / 15 g butter
2 good tblsp / 40 ml golden
  syrup
a pinch of salt
½ tsp / 3 ml vanilla essence

Add the boiling water to the sugar and cocoa. Add the remaining ingredients and simmer for 5 minutes – no more.

Note: It is worth making the full quantity as it will keep. Re-heat by standing it in a jug in boiling water.

CRÈME CHANTILLY

8 fl oz / 225 ml double cream
2 oz / 50 g castor sugar
1 tsp / 5 ml vanilla essence

Whip the cream until the whisk leaves traces in it. Fold in the sugar and vanilla.

CRÈME PETIT SUISSE

4 oz / 125 g cream cheese
2 or 3 tblsp / 30 to 40 ml icing-
 sugar
4 fl oz / 125 ml yoghurt

Beat these all together until really creamy. It can be used as a substitute for whipped cream.

VANILLA CUSTARD

1 tblsp / 15 ml cornflour
1 pint / 600 ml milk
2 egg yolks
4 tblsp / 60 ml granulated white
 sugar
1 tsp / 5 ml vanilla essence

Mix the cornflour with a little of the milk. Beat the egg yolks into this.

Bring the rest of the milk to the boil. When boiling, pour it over the egg yolk mixture, stirring constantly.

Pour it back into the saucepan and, while stirring all the time, bring the custard carefully to the first boil when it will thicken. Take it off the heat immediately and stir in the sugar and vanilla and a pinch of salt. Pour it into a serving jug.

If you want it cold, sprinkle a little sugar over the surface. This will prevent a skin forming.

FOAMING CUSTARD SAUCE

1 recipe for vanilla custard
2 tblsp / 30 ml granulated white
 sugar
2 egg whites

Make the vanilla custard, adding the extra sugar. Beat the egg whites until stiff and fold them into the cooled custard. This is delicious with bananas cut into it.

FOAMY SAUCE

2 medium eggs, separated
4 oz / 125 g icing-sugar
sherry, vanilla or lemon for
 flavouring

Beat the egg yolks over boiling water until light-coloured and stiff. Add the icing-sugar and flavouring.

Beat the egg whites until stiff. Combine them with the egg yolks and serve at once.

This may be used with steam puddings.

FRUIT SAUCE

1 tblsp / 15 ml cornflour
½ pint / 300 ml water
2 medium eggs, separated

Mix the cornflour with a little of the water. Add the egg yolks. Bring the rest of the water to the boil and pour it over the cornflour and egg-yolk mixture. Return it to the saucepan and

233

8 oz / 225 g granulated white sugar

the grated rind and juice of 1 lemon and 1 orange

bring it to the first boil. Take it off the heat and stir in the sugar until dissolved. Add the juice and grated rind of the orange and lemon. Beat the egg whites until stiff and fold them in.

RASPBERRY OR STRAWBERRY SAUCE

1 lb / 500 g raspberries or strawberries

4 oz / 125 g castor sugar

2 tblsp / 30 ml redcurrant jelly (see Index) dissolved in an equal amount of hot water

Prepare the fruit, cutting the strawberries, if used, into quarters. Cover with the sugar and let it soak in. Pour the dissolved jelly over the fruit and sugar mixture. Leave aside for an hour until the juice is fully drawn from the fruit. This is good with Baked Alaska.

LEMON SAUCE

4 oz / 125 g granulated white sugar

1 tblsp / 15 ml cornflour

4 fl oz / 125 ml water

1 oz / 25 g butter

½ tsp / 3 ml lemon rind

a pinch of salt

1½ tblsp / 25 ml lemon juice

Combine the sugar, cornflour and water in a saucepan and heat, stirring constantly, until boiling. Remove from the heat and beat in the remaining ingredients. Serve with a canary sponge steam pudding.

When I was growing up there was a ritual to the tea-table. In Scotland, tea was always laid in the dining-room while, in England, it was served in the drawing-room.

The hostess would be seated behind her silver teapot set on a polished wood or silver tray. The table was laid with a lace cloth.

As children we had to help ourselves first to the very finely cut brown or white bread. Only then could we come to the cucumber or egg sandwiches. In Scotland we always had fresh home-made scones and pancakes, with butter and a jar of home-made jam. Next would be a selection of biscuits and, perhaps, slices of gingerbread loaf with butter. To finish there was sponge cake and a plain fruit cake.

One may ask how our figures survived, but I suppose that, in those days of unheated houses, one had to eat to keep warm. Nowadays one is happy with a mug of tea in the kitchen!

CAKES

Note: For cakes and biscuits, where I have specified only *flour*, this is *plain flour*.

BASIC 3-EGG CAKE

½ lb / 225 g flour
2 tsp / 10 ml baking powder
½ tsp / 2 ml salt
6 oz / 170 g butter or margarine
10 oz / 275 g castor sugar
3 eggs, separated
4 fl oz / 125 ml milk
1 tsp / 5 ml vanilla

Prepare two 8″ / 20 cm cake tins. Butter them and line the base with fitted butter paper. Dust with flour.

Sift the flour, baking powder and salt into one bowl. In another, cream the butter and sugar until light. Add the egg yolks one by one, beating each one in well. Then add the flour and milk alternately, stirring in gently and making sure each addition is mixed in well before adding the next.

Beat the egg whites until stiff but not dry. Fold them into the cake mixture with a metal spoon, adding the vanilla. Put the mixture into the tins, about half to three-quarters full, and bake in the oven at 350°F / 180°C / gas 4 for about 20 minutes or until done.

CHERRY CAKE
Make the 3-egg cake as above, but before folding in the egg whites, take 1 cup of cherries – maraschino or glacé as you prefer – cut them in half, dip them in flour and shake off the excess. Stir them into the mixture and then continue as before, beating the egg whites, folding them in and baking as above. To decorate, use a white boiled icing.

MOCHA WALNUT CAKE
Make a 3-egg cake, substituting for the milk 4 fl oz / 125 ml strong coffee (2 tblsp instant coffee in hot water). Add 1 cup of broken walnuts to the mixture before folding in the egg whites. Decorate with a coffee butter icing and walnut halves.

CHOCOLATE CAKE
Substitute 2 oz / 65 g cocoa powder for an equivalent amount of the flour, and add an extra egg as cocoa is very drying. This

235

is delicious iced with Fluffy Icing (see Icing Recipes).

ORANGE CAKE

Instead of the milk use fresh orange juice plus the juice of a lemon to make up the 4 fl oz / 125 ml. Omit the vanilla.

Before squeezing the oranges and the lemon, grate the rinds and beat this in together with the butter and sugar.

Decorate with orange butter icing flavoured with some extra orange and lemon juice and grated rind.

SWISS ROLL

2 oz / 50 g castor sugar
3 medium eggs
3 oz / 75 g flour
½ tsp / 3 ml baking powder
2 oz / 50 g jam, warmed

Heat the oven to 400°F / 200°C / gas 6. Line a Swiss roll or biscuit tin with paper. Grease and flour this well.

Beat together the sugar and eggs until thick and creamy. Sift together the flour and baking powder, and then sift them into the egg mixture, folding them in with a metal spoon. Pour the mixture into the prepared tin and level it into the corners. Bake in the heated oven for 8 to 10 minutes, until springy to the touch.

Meanwhile, prepare a clean damp tea-towel and place it on the table. Sprinkle it with castor sugar. When the cake is cooked, remove it from the oven, invert it onto the tea-towel and tear off the paper on which it has cooked. Trim the edges with a sharp knife.

Spread the cake with the jam you have warmed, and roll it up from the long side. Fold the tea-towel around it until it is cold to allow the cake to set.

SPONGE CAKE

3 medium eggs, separated
6 oz / 175 g castor sugar
2 fl oz / 50 ml boiling water
6 oz / 175 g cake or plain flour
½ tsp / 2 ml salt
½ tsp / 2 ml baking powder
½ tsp / 2 ml of either vanilla,
  almond or lemon essence

Heat the oven to 325°F / 170°C / gas 3. Prepare 2 cake tins by greasing them and then lining with butter paper, cut to fit the bottom of the tin. Sift some icing-sugar into the tins and shake around so that the insides are covered, tipping out the excess.

Put the egg yolks, sugar and the boiling water all together in a basin and beat hard for 5 to 10 minutes (easier if you have a cake mixer) until the mixture is pale, light and fluffy.

Combine and sift the flour, salt and baking powder. Repeat this 3 or 4 times to incorporate as much air as possible. Now fold the dry ingredients gently into the egg mixture. If you have a machine, sift the dry ingredients while the machine is beating the eggs and then fold them in by hand when the beating is finished.

Next, beat the egg whites and fold them in to the mixture together with the vanilla. Divide the mixture between the prepared cake tins and place in the heated oven for about 40 minutes or until cooked – when you touch it the cake springs back. If overcooked, the cake shrinks and becomes dry. If undercooked, it will fall.

Sandwich the cakes together with whipped cream.

To vary the flavour you can do one of the following:
(1.) Add 2 tblsp / 30 ml instant coffee to the boiling water before mixing it with the egg.
(2.) Substitute 1 oz / 25 g cocoa for 1 oz / 25 g of the flour.
(3.) Add grated lemon rind to the mixture and flavour with ½ tsp / 2 ml lemon essence instead of the vanilla.

VICTORIA SPONGE

6 oz / 175 g butter
6 oz / 175 g castor sugar
3 medium eggs
6 oz / 175 g self-raising flour
(the weight of the butter, sugar and flour each to equal the weight of the eggs)

This is a drier sponge, especially suitable for puddings.

Heat the oven to 350°F / 180°C / gas 4. Prepare 2 sandwich tins, size 8″ / 20 cm diameter, as for the previous sponge recipe.

Cream the butter and sugar well together. Beat the eggs and add them to the butter mixture while beating in. Sift the flour 2 or 3 times and fold in very gently.

Pour the mixture into the prepared tins and place them in the heated oven for about half an hour. If in doubt whether it is cooked, pierce it with a fine skewer. If done, the skewer will come out clean.

COFFEE SPONGE
Add 3 tsp / 15 ml instant powdered coffee.

CHOCOLATE SPONGE
Substitute 1 oz / 25 g cocoa for an equal amount of flour.

MOIST CHOCOLATE CAKE

8 oz / 225 g castor sugar
4 fl oz / 110 ml sour milk
2 oz / 50 g cocoa
8 oz / 225 g sifted plain flour
1 tsp / 5 ml baking soda
¼ tsp / 1 ml salt

Butter and line 2 cake tins. In a bowl, combine the first 3 ingredients – the sugar, sour milk and cocoa. In another bowl, sift the plain flour, baking soda and salt.

In a mixing bowl, by hand or machine, cream together the butter and the second lot of sugar. Separate the eggs and beat in the yolks, one at a time.

237

4 oz / 125 g butter
8 oz / 225 g castor sugar
3 eggs, separated
8 fl oz / 225 ml sour milk
1 tsp / 5 ml vanilla

By hand mix in alternately the flour mixture from the second bowl and the 8 fl oz of sour milk, making sure each addition is well mixed before the next is added. Then add the cocoa mixture from the first bowl.

Whip the egg whites until stiff but not dry and fold them and the vanilla in.

Pour the mixture into the prepared cake tins and bake at 350°F / 180°C / gas 4 for about 30 minutes until done.

Note: Buttermilk or yoghurt may be used in place of sour milk.

When we returned from South Africa to live in Ireland we came via the Caux conference in Switzerland. My 14-year-old daughter, Veronica, was feeling rather lost.

Before long a very dear Swiss friend of ours, Hildi Zeller, came across her and took her a walk up the mountain. Afterwards Veronica commented that she had never met anyone who cared so much.

Hildi was in charge of the baking kitchen at the conference centre. She invited Veronica to work with her, and being a whizz at cakes and biscuits, taught her much. Veronica loved being given a lot of responsibility and later, at home, she would demonstrate her new skills to us.

This cake is one of Hildi's specialities.

BLACK MIDNIGHT CAKE

6 oz / 175 g butter
10 oz / 275 g castor sugar
3 medium eggs
4 oz / 125 g cocoa
¾ pint / 450 ml water
8 oz / 225 g flour
½ tsp / 2 ml baking powder
1¼ tsp / 6 ml baking soda
1 tsp / 5 ml salt

Cream together the butter and sugar in a bowl. Beat in the eggs one at a time. In another bowl blend together the cocoa and water. In a third bowl sift the flour, baking powder, soda and salt. Stir the contents of these two bowls alternately into the first one.

Prepare two 9" / 23 cm cake tins and divide the mixture between them. Bake in the oven at 350°F / 180°C / gas 4 for about 30 minutes until done.

Turn out the cakes. When cold, ice with glossy chocolate icing (see Index).

SCHWARZWALDER TORTE

5 oz / 150 g butter

8 oz / 225 g castor sugar

4 large eggs, separated (with perhaps an extra 2 eggs)

2 oz / 50 g milk chocolate

2 oz / 50 g cocoa

2 tblsp / 30 ml instant coffee powder dissolved in 4 tblsp / 60 ml hot water

8 oz / 225 g ground almonds

1¾ oz / 45 g Zwiebuck or other rusk, grated

cream

1 scant tsp / 4 ml gelatine

1 tblsp / 15 ml hot milk

8 fl oz / 225 ml whipping cream

2 tblsp / 30 ml castor sugar

½ tsp / 3 ml vanilla

Beat together the butter and sugar. Beat in the egg yolks. In a separate bowl, melt together the chocolate, coffee and cocoa and in a third bowl mix together the almonds and rusk. To the first bowl alternately fold in the chocolate mixture and the almond mixture, adding the extra egg yolks if the mixture is very sticky.

Whip the egg whites (including the two extra ones if the yolks have been used) until stiff but not dry. Fold this into the mixture.

Pour into 3 greased cake tins and bake at 350°F / 180°C / gas 4 for half an hour, or until done. Watch it carefully as this is a delicate cake which must not be over- or undercooked. When just right it has a gorgeous texture.

While the cake is cooling, make the cream. Begin by melting the gelatine in the hot milk. Beat the cream lightly. Add the sugar and vanilla to the cream. Add a little cream to the gelatine before folding it into the rest of the mixture. The cream should be used quickly before it sets.

Cover each of the 3 cakes with the cream and stack them one on top of the other. Nowadays, black cherries are sometimes added between the layers. Decorate the cake with chocolate caraque (see Index).

DOBOZ TORTE (Hungarian)

2 medium eggs, separated

2½ oz / 65 g castor sugar

2 oz / 50 g self-raising flour, sifted

chopped almonds to decorate

Chocolate butter icing

4 oz / 125 g butter

4 oz / 125 g sifted icing-sugar

1 egg yolk

4 oz / 125 g dark chocolate

Caramel

4 oz / 125 g granulated white sugar

4 tblsp / 60 ml water

Heat the oven to 325°F / 165°C / gas 3. Grease and line a biscuit tin 15″ × 12″ / 30 cm × 38 cm.

Whisk the egg yolks and sugar to a pale creamy colour. Whisk the egg whites stiffly and fold them into the yolk mixture alternately with the flour. Spread this thinly in the prepared tin and bake for about 10 minutes.

Allow it to cool in the tin. Then divide the mixture into 4. Spread 3 portions with chocolate butter icing and sandwich them together. Pour caramel over the 4th portion and place it on top. Ice the sides of the cake with the remaining icing and press in chopped almonds.

To make the chocolate butter icing, cream the butter and sugar together. Beat in the egg yolk and the dark chocolate, melted.

For the caramel, put the sugar and water in a small heavy bottomed frying pan. Heat slowly until the sugar is dissolved. Then boil without stirring until it turns a nice brown. Do not allow it to burn. Pour it immediately over the reserved portion of the cake. If you wish you can mark it into slices before it cools.

When cold and set, place it on top of the other layers and decorate as described.

ORANGE CHIFFON CAKE

8 oz / 225 g plain flour
3 tsp / 15 ml baking powder
12 oz / 325 g granulated sugar
1 tsp / 5 ml salt
1 tblsp / 15 ml salad oil (not olive)
7 medium eggs, separated
3 tblsp / 45 ml grated orange rind
6 fl oz / 175 ml orange juice
½ tsp / 2 ml cream of tartar

Sift together the flour, baking powder, sugar and salt. Sift again. Beat together the salad oil, egg yolks, orange rind and juice until light. Add to the flour mixture, folding it in by hand until smooth. Beat together the egg whites and the cream of tartar until it stands up in peaks. Then fold into the flour and orange mixture.

Butter a large, deep cake tin, 10-11" / 25-28 cm in diameter, and line the base with a butter paper (I use a spring form cake tin). Dust it with flour.

Pour the mixture into the cake tin and bake at 325°F / 165°C / gas 3 for 55 minutes. Then turn the temperature up to 350°F / 180°C / gas 4 for a further 10 to 15 minutes. (Ovens vary in temperature, so be sure that it is not too hot to begin with.)

When cooked, the top should spring back when pressed with your forefinger. Or you can test it with a skewer: if it comes out clean the cake is ready.

Remove the cake from the oven and invert it over a rack. If it does not drop out, run a knife around the sides. To serve, either dust with icing-sugar or ice with an orange water icing.

BURNT SUGAR CHIFFON CAKE

6 oz / 175 g granulated sugar
8 fl oz / 225 ml water
8 oz / 225 g plain flour
3 tsp / 15 ml baking powder
2 oz / 50 g castor sugar
1 tsp / 5 ml salt
4 fl oz / 125 ml salad oil (not olive)
5 eggs, separated
2 tsp / 10 ml cream of tartar

Heat the 6 oz of sugar in a heavy pan. Keep the heat low until the sugar has melted. Then turn it up until the sugar has caramelised to a nice brown. Watch it carefully but do not stir. Take it off the heat and add the water. Stir to dissolve the caramel.

Sift together the flour, baking powder, sugar and salt twice over in a large mixing bowl. Make a well in the centre and add 6 tblsp / 90 ml of the caramel water, the salad oil and the egg yolks. Beat these together, gradually incorporating the flour.

Beat together the egg whites and the cream of tartar until stiff and fold them into the rest of the ingredients.

Butter a large, deep cake tin, 10-11" / 25-28 cm in diameter, and line the base with a butter paper. Dust it with flour. Pour the mixture into this. Bake at 325°F / 165°C / gas 3 for 55 minutes. Then turn the oven up to 350°F / 180°C / gas 4 for about 10 more minutes. Test as described previously.

Turn upside down onto a wire rack and leave for a while before removing from the tin. When cool, ice with fudge icing (see Index).

MRS CREASON'S JAM CAKE

This recipe was given to me by my hostess in Kentucky.

8 oz / 225 g butter/margarine
1 lb / 450 g castor sugar
5 medium eggs, well beaten
12 oz / 325 g flour
¼ tsp / 1 ml salt
½ tsp / 3 ml cinnamon
½ tsp / 3 ml all-spice or nutmeg
1 tsp / 5 ml baking soda
8 fl oz / 225 ml buttermilk
6 oz / 175 g nuts, finely chopped
6 oz / 175 g chopped dates
8 oz / 225 g strawberry jam

Butter three 9" / 23 cm cake tins, lining the bottoms with buttered greaseproof paper.

Cream the butter and sugar together. Beat in the eggs. In a separate bowl sift the flour, salt and spices together, twice over.

Dissolve the soda in a little of the milk and then alternately add the flour and the rest of the milk. Pour the mixture over the nuts and dates and fold them in. Lastly add the jam. Pour into the prepared cake tins and bake in the oven at 350°F / 180°C / gas 4 for 40 minutes.

Spread each layer with fudge icing (see Index) and sandwich them together.

CHOCOLATE BISCUIT CAKE

We were entertained on my mother's birthday in the home of another Swiss friend, Madame Odier, in Geneva. She had made this cake for us and I asked her for the recipe.

8 oz / 225 g digestive biscuits
8 oz / 225 g butter
4 oz / 125 g coconut
8 oz / 225 g chocolate
2 tblsp / 30 ml cocoa
1 tsp / 5 ml rum essence
1 egg, beaten

Crumb the biscuits in a food processor or with a rolling-pin. Melt the butter and combine it with the crumbs and coconut.

Melt the chocolate in a pan over hot, not boiling water. Stir in the cocoa and the rum essence and then beat in the egg. This makes the mixture quite stiff. Remove from the heat.

Take a loaf tin – 7" × 4" / 18 cm × 10 cm, approx. Line this with greased butter paper. Put in alternate layers of the chocolate and the biscuit mixture, starting and ending with chocolate. Set in the fridge to harden.

To serve, loosen the sides of the tin with a knife, invert it, and a short, sharp bang should release it. Peel off the butter paper and place the cake on a platter.

ROCK CAKES

8 oz / 225 g self-raising flour
a pinch of salt
3 oz / 75 g sugar
3 oz / 75 g butter or margarine
4 oz / 125 g mixed dried fruit –
    currants, raisins, peel
grated rind of 1 lemon
1 egg
a little milk for mixing

Sift the flour and salt. Add the sugar. Rub in the butter until the mixture resembles fine breadcrumbs. Add the fruit and rind and mix well. Beat the egg. Make a well in the mixture. Pour in the egg and sufficient milk to make a stiff dough.

Put the mixture out in small heaps on a greased baking tray. Do not smooth them as they should be stiff and spiky. Bake them at 350°F / 180°C / gas 4 for 15 to 20 minutes until turning light brown at the ends of the spikes. Cool them on a rack.

WEDDING CAKES

Our wedding in 1966 was at the height of the Rhodesian Unilateral Declaration of Independence controversy in which my father was much involved. As Minister of Agriculture, and later of Defence and Foreign Affairs in Ian Smith's cabinet, he was a signatory of the Declaration. Because he was also a member of the House of Lords he was a particular focus of attention. His British passport had been withdrawn and there was no question of being able to come to the wedding in Scotland. The press were out in force, always making the most of any controversy and scenting a story here. Even at the reception reporters were hovering at our shoulders. My father's sense of humour came to the rescue. His cable to us read:

> Fully support your bilateral declaration of inter-dependence.

'The Duke's Joke' was the headline in the next day's papers.

FRUIT CAKE FOR WEDDINGS AND CHRISTMAS

I have used this recipe, on a large scale, for Catherine's and Veronica's weddings and, more regularly, for our Christmas cakes. It is set out in 3 columns for different sizes of cake. This should be cooked up to 3 months in advance, so that it has time to mature. This cake should be stored wrapped in brown paper on an open shelf – not in a tin. The icing of a wedding cake needs to begin at least a month ahead.

THE PREPARATION OF THE TINS
This needs care. First brush the tins with melted butter. Cut a double band of greaseproof paper to go right round the inside of the tin. It should be the height of the tin plus 3" /

7.5 cm. Fold up the bottom inch / 2.5 cm, and cut slits in this, 1" / 2.5 cm apart. Push this band into the tin. The slits will spread out around the bottom.

Next, cut a double round of greaseproof paper to fit inside the bottom of the tin. Brush melted butter all over the paper inside the tin. Tie a double band of brown paper round the outside of the tin the same height as the grease-proof paper.

Quantities are on the next page. They are for round tins, measuring the diameter. A square tin should be 1" / 2.5 cm smaller than the round for the measure of ingredients.

(1.) First column for 2 tins, 1 × 11" / 28 cm and 1 × 8" / 20 cm.

(2.) Second column for 1 tin, 10" / 25 cm.

(3.) Third column for 1 tin, 6" / 15 cm.

These measurements can be taken as approximate. They depend a little on the height of your tin.

	(1.)	(2.)	(3.)
muscat raisins	28 oz / 800 g	14 oz / 400 g	7 oz / 200 g
seedless raisins	10 oz / 275 g	5 oz / 150 g	2½ oz / 60 g
sultanas	10 oz / 275 g	5 oz / 150 g	2½ oz / 60 g
currants	6 oz / 175 g	3 oz / 90 g	1½ oz / 45 g
candied mixed peel	12 oz / 350 g	6 oz / 175 g	3 oz / 90 g
dates	4 oz / 125 g	2 oz / 60g	1 oz / 30 g
glacé cherries	8 oz / 225 g	4 oz / 125 g	2 oz / 60 g
glacé pineapple	8 oz / 225 g	4 oz / 125 g	2 oz / 60 g
brandy	6 tblsp / 90 ml	3 tblsp / 45 ml	1½ tblsp / 25 ml
rum	6 tblsp / 90 ml	3 tblsp / 45 ml	1½ tblsp / 25 ml
butter	12 oz / 350 g	6 oz / 175 g	3 oz / 90 g
soft brown sugar	8 oz / 225 g	4 oz / 125 g	2 oz / 60 g
granulated white sugar	1 lb / 450 g	8 oz / 225 g	4 oz / 125 g
eggs, large	10	5	2
molasses	2 tblsp / 30 ml	1 tblsp / 15 ml	2 tsp / 10 ml
self raising flour	12 oz / 350 g	6 oz / 175 g	3 oz / 90 g
baking powder	1 tsp / 5 ml	½ tsp / 3 ml	¼ tsp / 1½ ml
nutmeg	½ tblsp / 8 ml	1 tsp / 4 ml	½ tsp / 3 ml
mace	1 tsp / 5 ml	½ tsp / 4 ml	¼ tsp / 2 ml
salt	½ tsp / 3 ml	¼ tsp / 1 ml	a pinch
blanched almonds	8 oz / 225 g	4 oz / 125 g	2 oz / 60 g
walnuts	8 oz / 225 g	4 oz / 125 g	2 oz / 60 g
rosewater (from the chemist)	1 tblsp / 15 ml	½ tblsp / 7 ml	¼ tblsp / 3 ml
brandy or rum for the cooked cake	9 tblsp / 135 ml	4½ tblsp / 70 ml	2¼ tblsp / 35 ml

COOKING INSTRUCTIONS

Put into a bowl the 8 fruits listed, chopping the dates and cutting the glacé pineapple into pieces. Pour over them the brandy and rum which are listed just below the fruit. Cover and leave this overnight to soak.

Next day, take half the flour and mix it with the fruit, adding the nuts. This flour prevents the fruit falling to the bottom of the cake while cooking.

Cream together the butter and sugars until light. Beat the eggs in, one at a time. Add the molasses.

In another bowl sift together the remaining flour, the salt, baking powder, nutmeg and mace. Fold this into the butter and egg mixture. Add the rosewater.

Add all this to the fruit mixture.

Put the mixture into the prepared tins, smoothing it out and then mounding it around the edges to leave a slight hollow in the centre. This will rise with cooking and should ensure a flat top.

Put the cake in the oven preheated to 325°F / 160°C / gas 3 seated on some folded brown paper or newspaper. After 1 hour's cooking, reduce the heat to 300°F / 150°C / gas 3. Be careful the cake does not brown too quickly (ovens vary a little). If it shows signs of this, cover the top with brown paper. The smaller cake takes approximately 5 hours. The larger one, 8 hours. Test with a skewer which should come out clean if it is done.

When completed, remove the tin from the oven. While the cake is still hot, prick it all over with a skewer and sprinkle with the brandy or rum which is specified at the bottom of the list of quantities.

When cold, take it out of the tin and wrap it in fresh, greaseproof paper to store for at least a week before icing.

ICINGS

ALMOND ICING OR MARZIPAN

	(1.)	(2.)	(3.)	(4.)
round tin	6" / 15 cm	8" / 20 cm	10" / 25 cm	12" / 30 cm
square tin	5" / 12 cm	7" / 18 cm	9" / 23 cm	11" / 28 cm
ground almonds	6 oz / 175 g	12 oz / 350 g	20 oz / 575 g	28 oz / 800 g
castor sugar	3 oz / 80 g	6 oz / 175 g	10 oz / 275 g	14 oz / 400 g
icing-sugar	3 oz / 80 g	6 oz / 175 g	10 oz / 275 g	14 oz / 400 g
eggs	1 yolk	2 yolks	2 big eggs	3 big eggs
lemon juice	1 tsp / 5 ml	2 tsp / 10 ml	3 tsp / 15 ml	4 tsp / 20 ml
almond essence	¼ tsp / 1 ml	½ tsp / 2 ml	¾ tsp / 3 ml	1 tsp / 5 ml

Mix together the ground almonds and the sugars. Make a well in the centre and drop in the lightly beaten eggs, the almond essence and the lemon juice. Knead it into a ball. Do not knead it too long or it will become oily.

If you wish to keep it, put it into an airtight container.

To roll it out, lightly dust a board with cornflour.

For smaller cakes the marzipan may be rolled out in one piece. Brush the cake with sieved warm apricot jam or marmalade. Place the marzipan over the cake, letting it fall down over the sides. Roll round the sides with a bottle to smooth them out and roll over the top with a rolling-pin.

For larger cakes, cut a long strip to go round the side, and a separate piece for the top which should cover the top edges of the side marzipan. Roll the sides and top as before.

ROYAL ICING

The following are the quantities to match those for the almond icing:

	(1.)	(2.)	(3.)	(4.)
icing-sugar	1 lb / 450 g	1½ lb / 700 g	2¼ lb / 1 kg	3 lb / 1½ kg
egg whites	2	3	4	5
lemon juice	1 tsp / 5 ml	1½ tsp / 8 ml	2 tsp / 10 ml	3 tsp / 15 ml
glycerine (optional)	1 tsp / 5 ml	1½ tsp / 8 ml	2 tsp / 10 ml	3 tsp / 15 ml

The glycerine or liquid glucose may be used for a Christmas cake icing where you do not want it too hard. Omit it for a wedding cake where you want one layer to sit on top of another.

Lightly froth up the egg white. Sift the icing-sugar and stir it in by degrees, adding the lemon juice as it becomes stiff. If you find the icing very stiff, add more lemon juice. Keep the bowl with the icing in it covered with a damp cloth while working, otherwise it is liable to form a crust.

These quantities should give enough for 3 layers of icing, but no decoration, for a wedding cake. For a Christmas cake I use one thick layer.

Have a jug of hot water beside you while working. Put the icing onto the cake and spread it roughly over the top and sides. If you wish to smooth it, dip your spatula in the hot water in between each stroke, shaking off any excess water.

Decorating a wedding cake is a specialist business which I will not go into here. There are books on the subject, or classes for those who want to learn.

FLUFFY ICING

1 tsp / 5 ml cream of tartar
1 lb / 450 g castor sugar
1 tsp / 5 ml vanilla
3 egg whites
7 tblsp / 105 ml cold water

Put all the ingredients in a heat-proof bowl – not aluminium, as it would turn grey. Place it over boiling water and beat everything hard and continuously until it stands up in peaks.

Decorate the cake at once. This icing is particularly good with a rich chocolate cake.

Note: Orange or lemon juice, or coffee, may be substituted for the water.

BUTTER ICING

For a 2-layer cake

4 oz / 125 g butter
8 oz / 225 g icing-sugar
2 tblsp / 30 ml flavouring liquid
(liquid strong coffee *or* orange juice and grated rind *or* lemon juice and grated rind *or* milk and 1 tsp / 5 ml vanilla)

Cream the butter until really soft. Gradually beat in the icing-sugar alternately with the flavouring liquid. Add more of the liquid if you want it softer.

Ice the cake and decorate simply as wished.

BOILED ICING

10 oz / 275 g icing-sugar
4 fl oz / 125 ml water
2 medium egg whites
1 tsp / 5 ml lemon juice

Mix the icing-sugar and water in a saucepan, bring it to the boil and boil until it reaches the 'soft ball' stage – it forms a ball when dropped in a glass of cold water.

Beat the egg whites until stiff. When the syrup is ready, pour it slowly over the egg whites, beating them constantly. Add the lemon juice and continue beating for 15 minutes.

This is a white icing and may be used over almond icing.

BUTTER CREAM ICING

4 fl oz / 125 ml water
2 oz / 50 ml granulated white sugar
2 egg yolks
4 oz / 125 g butter

Put the water and sugar in a small saucepan and boil to a short thread (when the syrup is pinched between thumb and forefinger and they are opened, it will form a short thread).

Beat the egg yolks until white and creamy.

Remove the syrup from the heat and pour it in a steady stream onto the egg yolks while continuing to beat them until it is all very creamy.

Cut the butter into pieces and beat in with a little rum essence, if wished. This is particularly good as a filling for a layered cake or for a Swiss Roll.

Note: To make a CHOCOLATE CREAM, add 1 tblsp / 15 ml sifted cocoa to the creamed egg mixture before adding the syrup.

For a COFFEE CREAM, add 1 tblsp / 15 ml very strong coffee.

For a VANILLA CREAM, add 1 tsp / 5 ml vanilla essence.

MERINGUE CREAM ICING

2 egg whites
4 oz / 125 g castor sugar
4 oz / 125 g butter

Put the egg whites and sugar in a heat-proof bowl (not aluminium) and beat together over boiling water until the meringue keeps its shape.

Beat the butter until really creamy. When the meringue is ready, remove it from the heat and beat in the creamed butter a little at a time. Flavour as you wish with vanilla, chocolate, coffee, orange, etc. A lovely light icing and very useful if you have spare egg whites left from making custard or mayonnaise and so on.

CHOCOLATE BUTTER ICING

4 oz / 125 g butter
4 oz / 125 g sifted icing-sugar
1 egg yolk
4 oz / 125 g dark chocolate

Cream the butter and sugar together. Beat in the egg yolk and the dark chocolate, melted.

CARAMEL

4 oz / 125 g granulated sugar
4 tblsp / 60 ml water

Put the sugar and water in a small heavy-bottomed frying pan. Heat slowly until the sugar has dissolved. Then boil without stirring until it turns a nice brown.

LEMON FUDGE ICING

4 oz / 125 g butter or margarine
the grated rind of 1 lemon
8 oz / 225 g icing-sugar
2 tblsp / 30 ml milk

Put all the ingredients in a bowl over a saucepan of hot water and stir until smooth and glossy. Remove from the heat and leave until cold. Then beat well until the mixture is thick enough to spread. This is good to sandwich 2 sponge cakes.

LEMON ICING

8 oz / 225 g icing-sugar
the juice from 1 lemon

Sift the icing sugar. Mix in the lemon juice until the icing is thin enough to spread.

To create a feathered effect, reserve about 1 tblsp / 15 ml of the lemon icing. Add a few drops of lemon colouring and thicken it a little to piping consistency. Pipe lines across the cake. Then you can take a pointed knife or skewer and draw it gently across the lines, first in one direction and then the other.

WATER ICING

8 oz / 225 g icing-sugar
2 fl oz / 50 ml water

Sift the icing-sugar and mix in the water until it is of a spreading consistency. Flavour, if wished, with orange or lemon juice, etc.

BERTI'S CHOCOLATE ICING

One of my first tasks in the Caux kitchens was to crack and separate 200 eggs. What a mess! But I learnt how to pass an egg yolk back and forth between the two half shells – and if you don't succeed, to fish out the bits of yolk using the half eggshell as a spoon.

Berti Zeller was one in the kitchen who made sure that standards were maintained and food never institutionalised. This is one of her recipes which she taught me.

These quantities will fill and cover 2 double layer cakes, 8″ / 20 cm diameter.

1½ oz / 40 g butter
4 oz / 125 g chocolate
1 lb / 450 g icing-sugar
7 tblsp / 105 ml milk
¼ tsp / 1 ml salt
1 tsp / 5 ml vanilla

Melt the butter with the chocolate over hot water.

In another bowl blend the icing-sugar, milk, salt and vanilla. Add the chocolate and stir for a few moments until it just thickens enough to pour over the cakes. Do not touch it after pouring and it will set with a lovely glossy sheen.

GLOSSY CHOCOLATE ICING

4 oz / 125 g butter or margarine
9 tblsp / 135 ml cocoa
5 tblsp / 75 ml scalded milk
½ lb / 225 g icing-sugar
1 tsp / 5 ml vanilla
½ tsp / 3 ml salt

Melt the butter and cocoa together over low heat.

In another bowl stir the hot milk over the icing-sugar with the vanilla and salt, until completly dissolved. Add the chocolate mixture and beat until it becomes thickened, smooth and glossy. Pour it at once over the cake and decorate to taste with whole almonds, walnuts, etc.

Do not touch the icing once set or it will spoil the glossy finish.

FUDGE ICING

Good with Mrs Creason's Jam Cake.

6 oz / 175 g soft brown sugar
8 oz / 225 g granulated white sugar
6 fl oz / 175 ml milk
4 oz / 125 g butter
1 tblsp / 15 ml double cream

Mix the sugars and milk in a saucepan and cook over a gentle heat without stirring until the sugar melts. Then increase the heat and continue cooking until it forms a soft ball. (To test for a 'soft ball', drop about half a teaspoon of the boiling liquid into a glass of cold water. When it forms a soft ball, it is ready.)

Remove from the heat and beat, adding the butter and the cream little by little. It takes a lot of beating. As soon as it has thickened, pour it over the cake. Decorate at once and leave to set.

MOCHA FILLING

For chocolate shortbread or biscuits.

1 tblsp / 15 ml instant coffee
2 tblsp / 30 ml water
4 oz / 125 g chocolate
1 tblsp / 15 ml castor sugar

In a saucepan, dissolve the coffee in the water. Grate the chocolate into this and stir until melted. Cook very gently till of spreading consistency. Add sugar to taste.

TEA LOAVES

BARN BRACK

An Irish recipe of my Mother's.

7 oz / 700 g dried fruit (currants, raisins, mixed peel)
¾ pint / 450 ml warm tea
7 oz / 200 g soft brown sugar
10 oz / 275 g self-raising flour
1 egg, well beaten

Soak the fruit overnight, or until plump, in the tea.

Stir the sifted flour and sugar together. Make a hole in the centre and into this pour the fruit mixture and the beaten egg. Mix this well together, but do not beat it.

Grease a loaf tin and put greased paper into the bottom. Pour the batter into the prepared tin and bake in the oven at 325°F / 160°C / gas 3 for 1¾ hours, making sure the top does not get too brown. The oven heat may be turned lower if it does.

When cooked, take the loaf out of the oven and leave it in the tin to cool for 15 minutes before turning it out to finish cooling on a rack.

BANANA LOAF

3 oz / 75 g butter or margarine
5 oz / 150 g castor sugar
2 medium eggs
3 tblsp / 45 ml sour milk
8 oz / 225 g apples, peeled and grated
8 oz / 225 g overripe bananas, mashed
8 oz / 225 g plain flour, sifted
½ tsp / 3 ml baking soda
½ tsp / 2 ml salt
1 tsp / 5 ml baking powder

Cream together the butter and sugar. Beat in the eggs. Stir in the milk and fruit alternately with the sifted dry ingredients.

Pour the batter into a greased loaf tin which has greased paper on the bottom. Let it stand for 20 minutes before baking at 350°F / 180°C / gas 4 for about 40 minutes.

Serve sliced and spread with butter.

GINGER CAKE

8 oz / 225 g plain flour
1 tsp / 5 ml baking soda
2 tsp / 10 ml cream of tartar
1 tsp / 5 ml ginger, powdered
8 oz / 225 g demerara sugar
2 medium eggs
6 fl oz / 190 ml hot water (not boiling)
8 fl oz / 225 ml black treacle

Sift the flour, baking soda, cream of tartar and ginger together. Stir in the sugar, eggs, hot water and treacle – it will be very runny. Pour the mixture into a greased loaf tin which has a greased paper on the bottom.

Bake at 350°F / 180°C / gas 4 for 1 hour. It will be deliciously moist and gooey and may sink in the middle, but that is as it should be. Serve sliced and spread with butter.

Note: A little chopped crystallised ginger may be added to the mixture if wished.

THE DUKE'S GINGERBREAD

Miss Stewart was our postmistress in Balmaha by Loch Lomond. She lived at one end of her cottage with the post office at the other, and knew everything that happened in the village.

I was having tea with her one day and complimented her on her gingerbread. 'That was always your grandfather's favourite,' she said, and gave me this recipe.

4 oz / 125 g butter
2 oz / 50 g castor sugar
2 fl oz / 50 ml golden syrup
2 fl oz / 50 ml black treacle
6 oz / 175 g self-raising flour
½ tsp / 3 ml baking powder
½ tsp / 3 ml cinnamon
½ tsp / 3 ml ground ginger
½ tsp / 3 ml all-spice
a little nutmeg
a little milk
2 medium eggs

Cream the butter and sugar together. Add the syrup and treacle. Sift the flour, baking powder and spices. Mix the milk and eggs together and add to the butter alternately with the dry ingredients.

Pour the mixture into a greased loaf tin which has greased paper on the bottom, and bake in the oven at 300°F / 150°C / gas 2 for 1 hour. To serve, cut into slices and spread with butter.

BIRTHDAY CAKES

Birthdays and birthday cakes were always special in our household. When I was growing up birthday cakes were kept secret until revealed at the party. I have found that the children derived much more fun from helping to design and decorate their own cakes. While for an adult party restraint may be more sophisticated, for children imagination can run riot.

One year we made *A Hedgehog*. For this, bake the basic 3-egg vanilla cake. Take a pudding basin and cut pieces of cake to fit the inside. Make coffee butter icing and ice each piece as you put it in, to stick it all together.

Make a smaller mould in a cup for the head. Invert the two bowls onto a board covered with foil, placing the head next to the body. Cover the whole cake with the coffee icing and stick slivered almonds end-wise all over to represent quills. 2 raisins will make eyes and a big raisin the snout. The board may also be iced and covered with coconut coloured green to represent grass.

During the children's silk moth stage we made *A Caterpillar Cake*. For this, make 2 chocolate Swiss rolls and ice them with coffee/chocolate icing to look like a log. Place them on a board. Use a Victoria sponge recipe which will make about 36 cup cakes in patty pans. Ice them all over with green-coloured icing and stick them together in pairs, broad end to broad end. Arrange them in a line on the log to represent a caterpillar crawling over it with raisins for eyes. Again the board may be iced to represent grass.

A Crinoline Doll Cake was very successful. Bake the basic 3-egg cake, flavoured as you wish. Pack it in a pudding basin with butter icing, as for the Hedgehog cake. Turn it out and make a hole down the centre into which you place a 12" / 30 cm plastic doll up to her waist.

Make a butter icing and divide it in two. Colour it in 2 tones. Put the icing in a piping tube with a star rose fitting and ice the whole cake in rosettes for frills. Ice the doll's body as well. For this party the children came in fancy dress.

Another year, when we had been staying on a farm, Veronica insisted on a *Farmyard Cake*. Bake a square cake of the child's favourite kind. Take sponge fingers and cut off one end of each so that it sits flat. Dip the round end in melted chocolate and leave on greaseproof paper to cool.

Put the cake on a board and ice with butter icing. Again it can be green to represent grass. In one corner pipe your birthday wishes. Place the chocolate fingers round the edge to form a stockade, chocolate end up. Position the candles and put any plastic animals you wish inside the stockade.

One of our best cakes was *Cinderella's Pumpkin Coach*. Bake the basic 3-egg cake. Pack it into a large bowl, as described above. Turn it out onto a long board covered in tinfoil. Hollow it slightly on top and carve it into a pumpkin shape. Ice this with coffee icing.

Take some marzipan from a ½ lb / 225 g block, colour it green and roll it out to resemble a stalk and calyx. Position this in the hollow on the top of your pumpkin. Marzipan may be rolled out and cut into the shape of vine leaves, marking out the veins with a toothpick. Paint them with food colouring and position them on the cake.

For wheels for the coach, take 4 biscuits of 2 different sizes. Put them on a wire rack. Take some royal icing, coloured orange, and ice one side of the biscuits. When quite dry – keep the remaining icing moist by covering the bowl with a damp cloth – turn the biscuits over and ice the other side. Put a Smartie in the centre of each wheel for the hub, and silver balls for the spokes. Dip the rims in melted chocolate and leave aside to harden.

For the mice, colour the marzipan brown with cocoa. Mould 6 mice, or as many as you wish. Use liquorice string for their tails, almonds for mouth and ears, and currants for eyes.

To assemble the cake: attach the 4 wheels, large ones at the back, with a dab of icing. Place the mice along the board, 2 by 2, with cord for traces. Birthday candles are placed along the sides of the board, held in a rosette of icing.

GRANMA'S BIRTHDAY CAKE
(a white fruitcake)

This is a more traditional cake.

8 oz / 225 g currants
8 oz / 225 g sultanas
½ pint / 300 ml tea to soak the fruit
8 oz / 225 g butter
8 oz / 225 g castor sugar
3 large eggs
12 oz / 325 g plain flour
2 tsp / 10 ml baking powder
4 oz / 125 g mixed peel
1 tsp / 5 ml almond essence

Soak the currants and sultanas in the hot tea.

Cream together the butter and sugar. Beat in the eggs, one at a time. Sift together the flour and baking powder. Fold this into the butter and egg mixture. Drain the fruit from the tea and add it to the mixture together with the chopped mixed peel and the almond essence.

Pile the mixture into a deep, lined, greased cake tin 9" / 23 cm in diameter, smoothing it up to the sides as for a wedding cake. Bake in the oven at 325°F / 160°C / gas 3 for 3 hours, reducing the heat to 300°F / 150°C / gas 2 after the first hour. Check that it does not get too brown. Test as usual.

Let it cool in the tin. Remove and ice with almond icing and then with royal icing. Or it may be left plain.

BISCUITS

We have a picture in our family photo album of Catherine, aged nine, in her Brownie uniform presiding over a cake sale which she and her friends, with Veronica's help, organised in our garden at Fish Hoek in the Cape to raise funds for their troop. The Brownie Cornflake Cakes recipe (which comes next) were a feature of the afternoon. They were the first things which the girls learnt to make entirely on their own.

The Brownies and the Girl Guides have had an important part at different times in my life and I now find myself a Divisional Commissioner here in Northern Ireland. But I suppose it all began, strangely enough, at Buckingham Palace. My brother and I had come back from Rhodesia with my mother. It was just before my sixth birthday and we were living in London for a period. My great-aunt, Lady Helen Graham, was Lady-in-Waiting to Her Majesty the Queen, and I was invited to join the Brownie troop at the palace. I think they were concerned how to civilise this little savage from the bush of Africa. Officially I was just too young and, along with other instructions as to how to behave, I was told to keep quiet about my age.

I remember being hurried along a corridor by my aunt, a tall figure with wonderfully piled hair, a black ribbon around her neck and pointed shoes which did up with two straps. We bumped into Princess Elizabeth and I dropped my best curtsey.

Finally I was ushered into a big room with all the Brownies and introduced to Princess Margaret. I immediately disgraced myself. 'How old are you?' I asked.

'I'm seven,' came the answer.

'Well, I'm five and I'm bigger than you!' I am told I retorted.

I have a vivid memory of a children's party from that time: everyone in their party dresses. Finally the cakes came round the tea table where we sat with our nannies standing behind us. I spotted my favourite right at the far side of the plate. As I reached for it, my nanny's hand came down sharply on me in front of all my friends. 'Take what is in front of you!' she said.

Then there was a wonderful children's Christmas party given at the palace. My great-aunt took me to buy a dress for the occasion. My eye fell on a delicious white confection of lace and ribbons, but she chose for me instead a pink taffeta with a good hem and lots of tucks which could be let out. That dress was to last me for three years, even at the pace that I grew, and I have it still.

Finally the party. My great-aunt led me through the palace to the entrance of the room where we were greeted by Her Majesty, Queen Mary, Their Majesties the King and Queen, and then the two Princesses. We curtsied to each in turn and I was taken into this wonderland of 100 children, all in our best dresses – and there was one little girl wearing the very confection on which my eyes had fallen.

A puppet theatre had been arranged where we entered fairyland. Someone later asked me if I remembered the King. 'No,' I answered, 'I do not remember him as the King,

but as a very kind man who sat and talked to me in a corner and then led me to the puppetteers backstage who answered all my questions about how they worked.'

The party ended with the most wonderful fireworks – a chicken laying an egg, and other marvels.

Sadly my great-aunt died of cancer at the end of the war just after she had bought a house in Scotland very near to us. I still have a rosebud locket which she left me. She never married, for her fiancé had been killed in the Boer War. My father once told me that she was 40 years old before she even took a walk alone with a man.

Some years later, when I was eleven, it was a difficult time. My parents had separated and my mother was finding it hard to arrange the right education for me. I had fought with many governesses at home – no wonder, perhaps, for I had to share a room with them as my grandparents' home was full of doctors and evacuees who had been allocated to live with us.

Money was short. A great friend of my mother, Lady Stratheden, offered to have me stay with them and share her daughter's governess. This was a strange new life. I was given a room at the top of their big old house. I suppose it had been a maid's room, but it was marvellous for me to be on my own for the first time. I used to lie in bed at night dreaming how I would redecorate it. In the long summer evenings I would read until the light faded.

They kept polo ponies and when they found that I loved to ride I was put on a great big black horse, nearly 17 hands high. It was like being in a rocking chair. Then I graduated to the young polo ponies being trained. I was not allowed to jump them but, with the groom, we rode all over the countryside, sometimes fetching them down from the high pasture.

Fiona Campbell and I, as the two oldest children in the house, were allowed to join the grown-ups for dinner on Saturday nights. This should have been a treat, but I did not always like the menu and eat it I must. Artichoke soup! It was quite awful but somehow I swallowed it.

Breakfast was better. There was always game pie on the sideboard, and sometimes sausages with fried apple and potato, or eggs from the hens which Fiona kept to earn her pocket money. She paid me to help her feed them.

Even then I was always hungry as I was growing so fast. Sometimes, when feeding the hens, the leftover porridge would be thrown on top of their food, nice and clean. When no one was looking I would help myself to a few mouthfuls.

One of the most enjoyable events of the week was the Girl

Guide meeting. Lady Stratheden was a keen Guider and later became Chief Commissioner for the Commonwealth Guides. We all joined the local company. Walking back one day with some of the girls, they fell to discussing their wardrobes. I kept very quiet as first one boasted of her nine dresses, another claimed twelve, and yet another thirteen. Then they turned to me. 'How many do you have?'

In a very small voice I said, 'Two!' That was the end of that conversation.

By this time my mother was able to buy her own home, Camallt, nestling in the Fintry hills north of Glasgow, where she had her office as Secretary of the Scottish Gardens Scheme. I could buy my own pony with money which my father gave me from his demob pay on leaving the navy. I christened him Ruraidh (Red) and together we explored most of the hills nearby, somewhat to the dismay of the shepherds as Ruraidh, with his extra weight, would sometimes break their sheep bridges constructed of turf.

But what a wonderful freedom it was. It is disturbing to realise that now I would hardly dare to let a daughter of mine roam alone as I did.

But back to the Brownie cakes . . .

BROWNIE CORNFLAKE CAKES

Makes 18

2 tblsp / 30 ml granulated sugar
2 oz / 60 g butter or margarine
2 oz / 60 g cocoa
2 tblsp / 30 ml golden syrup
4 oz / 125 g cornflakes

Put the sugar, butter and cocoa in a saucepan. Add the golden syrup and melt these together over a low heat, but do not boil. Remove from the heat and stir in the cornflakes lightly until well coated. Pile them in spoonfuls into paper cup cases and leave to set – about 6 hours.

ICED CORNFLAKE BISCUITS

Makes 15

4 oz / 125 g butter or margarine
4 oz / 125 g castor sugar
6 oz / 175 g self-raising flour
2 tblsp / 30 ml golden syrup
3 tblsp / 45 ml boiling water
3 teacups of cornflakes

Cream the butter and sugar together. Stir the flour into the creamed mixture. Combine the syrup and the boiling water and add this to the mixture. Lastly, add the cornflakes.

Butter a square tin. Spread the mixture into it, pushing it into the corners. Preheat the oven to 425°F / 210°C / gas 7. When ready, put the tin into the hot oven but immediately lower the temperature to 325°F / 160°C / gas 3 and cook the biscuits for about half an hour.

Cut them into squares while hot, and then allow them to cool. When cold, ice with a butter icing (see Index).

COFFEE KISSES

Makes 16

3 oz / 75 g butter
6 oz / 175 g self-raising flour
2 oz / 50 g castor sugar
1 egg yolk
2 tblsp / 30 ml instant coffee dissolved in 2 tsp / 10 ml hot water

Rub the butter into the sifted flour. Add the sugar, then the egg yolk and finally the coffee mixture. Knead the dough well together. Divide the dough into about 20 small balls, rolling them in the palm of your hand.

Bake them in the oven at 380°F / 190°C / gas 5 on a greased sheet for 10 to 12 minutes.

Lift them onto a wire rack and, when cold, sandwich them together with a coffee butter icing (see Index). Dust with icing-sugar.

CHOCOLATE PINWHEELS

(A Swiss recipe)

Makes 30

4 oz / 125 g butter or margarine
4 oz / 125 g castor sugar
1 large egg
8 oz / 225 g plain flour
4 tsp / 20 ml cocoa

Cream the butter and sugar together. Beat the egg and add it. Stir in the sifted flour thoroughly. Divide the dough in half. Knead the cocoa into one half and roll it out into an oblong ¼" / 0.6 cm thick.

Roll out the plain dough to the same measurements. Brush it with a little milk. Place the chocolate dough on top of the plain. Be sure there are no air bubbles. Again brush with milk. Roll up the two doughs together from the long side.

Wrap this cylinder in greaseproof paper and chill in the fridge for at least half an hour. Then cut it into slices about ¼" / 0.6 cm thick, place these on a greased baking sheet and bake in the oven at 400°F / 200°C / gas 6 for 10 minutes.

Cool the pinwheels on a rack.

SCOTS SHORTBREAD

1 lb / 500 g butter
8 oz / 225 g granulated white sugar
1 lb / 500 g plain flour

Mix together the butter and sugar. Sieve the flour and knead the butter and sugar into it by hand until it forms a ball and leaves the side of the bowl clean.

Divide the dough in half and press each half out into a circle about ½" / 1½ cm thick. Place these on a greased baking sheet. Pinch all round the edges with finger and thumb and mark the top edges with the prongs of a fork. Prick the centre all over, dust with sugar and bake in the oven at 300°F / 150°C / gas 2 for 1½ hours. It should not be brown but should remain a pale biscuit colour. Take it out and leave to cool before removing to a rack.

The Scottish tradition is that shortbread should be broken, not cut with a knife.

Makes 2 dozen

8 oz / 225 g butter
4 oz / 100 g castor sugar
12 oz / 300 g plain flour

SHORTBREAD (2)

Cream the butter and sugar together. Sift the flour and knead it in. Divide into small balls and press them out with the prongs of a wetted fork onto a greased baking tray.

Bake in the oven at 350°F / 180°C / gas 4 for 15 minutes. Take them out and immediately sprinkle them with castor sugar, leaving them on a rack to cool.

CHOCOLATE SHORTBREAD
Substitute 4 oz / 100 g of cocoa for an equal amount of flour. If you want a lighter biscuit, use self-raising flour. Bake as before. Then dredge with castor sugar. Leave for a moment before putting on a rack.

CHOCOLATE LOGS
Make double or treble the chocolate shortbread recipe. Cut out the dough with a large biscuit cutter. Bake as above. Sandwich these rounds together on end to form a long roll with mocha cream, which is made by mixing 8 fl oz / 225 ml whipped double cream with a double recipe of mocha filling (see Index).

Makes 6 dozen

8 oz / 225 g butter or
   margarine
6 oz / 175 g golden syrup
10 oz / 275 g granulated white
   sugar
½ tsp / 3 ml baking soda
18 oz / 500 g plain flour
½ tsp / 3 ml cloves
2 tblsp / 30 ml ground ginger
1 tblsp / 15 ml cinnamon
2 medium eggs, beaten

GINGER BISCUITS

Melt the butter and syrup but do not boil. Stir in the sugar. Leave to cool and add the baking soda, stirring it in well to dissolve it.

Sift the flour, cloves and spices together and add to the sugar mixture alternately with the beaten egg. Knead it all together well. Roll into balls and place on a greased baking sheet. Press out with a fork, dipping it in water as needed.

Bake in the oven at 375°F / 190°C / gas 5 until light brown – about 10 minutes. Cool on a rack.

Makes a dozen

4 oz / 125 g butter or margarine
2 oz / 60 g castor sugar
1 small egg, beaten
8 oz / 225 g plain flour
¼ tsp / 1 ml baking soda
¼ tsp / 1 ml cream of tartar

EMPIRE BISCUITS

Cream the butter and sugar together. Add the beaten egg and the flour, baking soda and cream of tartar one after the other, stirring each addition in well before adding the next. It should make a stiff dough.

Roll the dough out onto a floured board until ¼" / 0.6 cm thick and cut into 24 rounds with a fluted cutter. Place on a greased baking sheet and bake in the oven at 350°F / 180°C / gas 4 to a pale colour – about 10 minutes.

Cool on a rack. When cold, ice half the biscuits with a white water icing (see Index) and spread redcurrant or blackberry jelly on the other half. Sandwich them together.

Makes 30

6 oz / 175 g plain flour
1½ tsp / 8 ml baking powder
½ tsp / 2 ml salt
4 oz / 125 g butter or margarine
8 oz / 225 g granulated white
 · sugar
1 medium egg
1 tblsp / 15 ml milk
½ tsp / 3 ml vanilla

AMERICAN SUGAR COOKIES

Sift the flour together with the baking soda and salt. Cream the butter and sugar together. Beat in the egg and then stir in the flour. Add the milk and vanilla. The dough should be just stiff enough to roll.

Chill the dough well in the fridge. Then roll it out on a lightly floured board about ⅓" / 0.8 cm thick. Cut with a fluted biscuit cutter and bake at 350°F / 180°C / gas 4 on an ungreased baking sheet for about 10 minutes. This is a basic recipe, the flavour of which can be varied.

BUTTERSCOTCH COOKIES
Substitute an equal weight of soft brown sugar for the white sugar.

SPICE COOKIES
When sifting the flour, add ¼ tsp / 1 ml each of cinnamon, all-spice and cloves.

CHOCOLATE CRISPS
Mix ½ tsp / 3 ml cinnamon to the flour when sifting. Add 2 oz / 50 g melted chocolate when creaming the butter and sugar.

PEANUT COOKIES
Reduce the quantity of butter to 1 oz / 25 g. Add 4 oz / 125 g peanut butter (the crunchy kind is the best). Cream this with the remaining butter and the sugar. Continue with the basic recipe but increase the milk to 5 tblsp / 75 ml.

ALMOND DROPS
Substitute almond essence for the vanilla.

AMERICAN BROWNIES

Makes 15

8 oz / 225 g butter
8 oz / 225 g granulated white
  sugar
4 medium eggs
4 oz / 125 g dark chocolate
6 oz / 175 g sifted plain flour
½ tsp / 3 g baking powder
¼ tsp / 1 ml salt
4 oz / 125 g chopped walnuts
1 tsp / 5 ml vanilla

Cream the butter and sugar together. Beat in the eggs one at a time.

Melt the chocolate over a pan of hot, not boiling, water. Stir it into the creamed mixture. Sift together the flour, baking powder and salt and stir this in with a wooden spoon. Add the walnuts and vanilla. It will be a runny mixture.

Pour the mixture into a greased oblong baking tin – mine is 7 × 10" / 18 × 27 cm – to a depth of about ¾" / 2 cm and bake at 350°F / 180°C / gas 4 for 20 minutes. Remove from the oven. When cold, cut into fingers and dust with icing-sugar. As the mixture cools it should fall a little and the crust will crinkle. The brownies should be moist and chewy.

If ever unable to find bitter chocolate, I have substituted cooking chocolate and 3 tblsp / 45 ml cocoa for the same amount of flour.

I learnt to cook these American recipes during the many months I spent at the Mackinac Island conference centre which I have described earlier.

I remember one time when the summer conference was in full swing. I was busy that day clearing up in the kitchen where I had been since early morning cooking lunch for the hundreds of delegates when in walked six Malaysian MPs. They had recently arrived and were being shown around.

I was introduced to them. Hot, tired and in need of a good tidy up myself, I apologised for the way I looked.

'Oh, don't apologise,' they said. 'We are much more interested to meet you like this than to see you on the platform,' and they invited me to join them for lunch the next day.

Over lunch they told me of their many bitter experiences and I found that they all came from a Marxist background. I remember saying to them, 'I haven't gone through anything like you have, but I do know a little about bitterness.'

I told them something of my family breaking up and the resentment I felt about being deprived, as I saw it, of many of the advantages which my friends had. And how, one day,

I had gone on my knees and said to God, 'I give you my hatred. Whatever anyone else has done, bitterness is wrong and needs to be forgiven.' I was able to tell them that, from that moment, I had felt a free person.

I do not know what happened in the future to those Members of Parliament, but I realised as I talked with them that any choices I made were much more than just a personal matter.

CRUNCHIES OR FLAPJACKS

Makes 3 dozen

8 oz / 225 g butter or margarine
5 oz / 150 g soft brown sugar
2 heaped tblsp / 40 ml golden syrup
16 oz / 450 g rolled oats
½ tsp / 2 ml salt
1 tblsp / 15 ml plain flour

Melt the butter, sugar and syrup gently in a large saucepan. Add the oats, salt, and flour, stirring until blended. Remove from the heat.

Press the mixture into 1 or 2 greased biscuit trays – according to what sizes you have – to a depth of about ¾" / 2 cm. Bake at 350°F / 180°C / gas 4 for about 15 minutes. (My tray is 9" × 13" / 23 cm × 33 cm.)

Remove from the oven and, with a sharp knife, cut the crunchies into squares or bars. Leave in the tray until cold so that they set well. You can vary this recipe by adding 4 oz / 125 g raisins to the oats when mixing with the flour.

ROLLED OAT BISCUITS

Makes 30

8 oz / 225 g butter
4 oz / 125 g sugar
6 oz / 175 g rolled oats
4 oz / 125 g plain flour

A favourite recipe of my mother.

Cream the butter and sugar together. Mix in the rolled oats and the flour. This dough may either be rolled out and cut with a biscuit cutter or – the method I prefer – small pieces broken off, rolled into balls and then squashed flat with your thumb.

Put them on greased trays well apart – they may spread out if rolled by the second method – and bake at 380°F / 190°C / gas 5 for 10 minutes. Let them cool a little before removing to a wire rack.

NUT BUTTER BALLS

Makes 18 to 24

4 oz / 125 g sifted plain flour
¼ tsp / 1 ml salt
2 oz / 50 g granulated white sugar

Sift the flour and the salt together. Add the sugar. Work in the butter and the finely chopped nuts. Add the vanilla. Break off small pieces of dough and roll into balls. Put the balls on a greased baking sheet and bake for 40 minutes in

12 oz / 375 g butter
8 oz / 225 g nuts, finely chopped
1 tsp / 5 ml vanilla essence

the oven at 280°F / 140°C / gas 1.

Take them out of the oven and roll them in icing-sugar while still hot before cooling them on a wire rack.

Makes 2 dozen

4 oz / 125 g molasses (black treacle)
4 oz / 125 g butter
4 oz / 125 g sifted plain flour
1 tblsp / 15 ml ginger
¼ tsp / 1 ml salt
3 tblsp / 45 ml brandy

BRANDY SNAPS

Heat the molasses until boiling. Add the butter and the sifted flour, ginger and salt, while stirring constantly over a low heat. Lastly, stir in the brandy and remove from the heat.

Drop ½ tsp / 3 ml of the mixture at a time onto greased baking trays, making sure they are 3" / 7.5 cm apart as they will spread. You can only bake a few at a time. Bake in the oven at 300°F / 150°C / gas 2 for about 12 minutes.

Take the tray out of the oven and cool the biscuits for 1 minute. Remove them from the tray with a spatula, rolling them immediately around the handles of wooden spoons. If they are removed too soon from the tray, they will break. If too late, they will not roll up.

Keep them in an airtight container. To serve, fill them with whipped cream.

Makes 2 dozen

4 oz / 125 g butter
4 oz / 125 g ground blanched almonds
4 oz / 125 g castor sugar
2 tblsp / 30 ml milk
1 tblsp / 15 ml plain flour

ALMOND WAFERS

Melt the butter in a saucepan. Have ready all the other ingredients and stir them into the melted butter until well blended.

Drop teaspoonfuls of the mixture, allowing 3" / 7.5 cm between them, onto greased and floured baking trays, 6 at a time. Bake at 300°F / 150°C / gas 2 for about 10 minutes. Remove and curl round the handles of wooden spoons or round a rolling-pin. When cold, store in an airtight container.

Makes 30

8 oz / 225 g ground almonds
10 oz / 310 g castor sugar
2 oz / 60 g plain flour
4 medium egg whites
½ tsp / 3 ml almond essence

CURLIE MURLIES (Scotland)

Mix the almonds with the sugar and flour. Beat the egg whites until stiff and fold in the almond mixture. Add the almond essence.

Roll out this paste on a floured board and cut into 6" / 15 cm long 'cigarettes'. They may then be twisted into corkscrews or folded into a heart-shape.

Bake at 350°F / 180°C / gas 4 on a buttered and floured tray for 10 minutes. Dredge them in castor sugar while still hot.

Makes 4 dozen

Syrup
4 fl oz / 125 ml water
¼ tsp / 1 ml powdered ginger
the juice of ¼ lemon
8 oz / 225 g granulated white
   sugar
a pinch of salt

The kooksusters
10 oz / 275 g plain flour
2½ tsp / 12 ml baking powder
½ tsp / 2 ml salt
1 medium egg
5 fl oz / 150 ml milk
½ tblsp / 7 ml melted butter

KOOKSUSTERS (South Africa)

Put all the syrup ingredients in a saucepan and heat gently to dissolve the sugar. Boil for 10 minutes to make a syrup. Chill.

Sift together the flour, baking powder and salt. Whisk the egg and add the milk and melted butter. Make a well in the centre of the flour and stir in the egg/milk mixture. Knead together until smooth and roll out to ¼" / 0.6 cm thickness. Cut into oblongs and cut each oblong into an E shape with elongated arms. Plait these arms, pinching the ends together.

Drop the kooksusters into a pan of deep hot oil and fry until golden brown. Then dip them immediately into the chilled syrup and put on a rack to drain. Keep the syrup cold by standing it in a pan of iced water.

I spent one winter in Sweden staying with Swedish friends in their home in a lovely park in Stockholm. It ran down to the Baltic Sea and we could ski and watch the ski-jumping there.

One morning I returned home after having to spend a long wait at a bus stop. My hostess took one look at me, brought me into the kitchen and stripped off my boots and socks, rubbing my feet and hands as hard as she could despite my protests. I had not realised how easy it is to get frostbite.

I learnt to tell when the temperature had fallen below −15°C because the snow squeaks when you walk on it.

Christmas is a magical time for the Swedes. It begins with Santa Lucia's Day, the saint who brought Christianity to Sweden – and had her eyes put out. Early on that morning a girl dressed in white with four lighted candles in a wreath in her hair will go round every room in the house. Her attendants will wake everyone up with a steaming hot drink and a biscuit as they sing Santa Lucia's carol.

The Christmas tree has no fancy decorations. It stands on a lovely tablecloth embroidered with gnomes, and is decorated with straw stars, home-made iced pepperkakor biscuits, apples and candles.

The Christmas feast is on Christmas Eve. Ham is eaten, followed by a creamy cold rice pudding in which one almond is hidden. Whoever gets the almond has to perform a party piece.

"SANTA LUCIA"

On Christmas Day everyone is awake early and sets off to church with a lantern through the dark morning, singing carols as they go. Then home again to a beautiful smorgasbord.

PEPPERKAKOR BISCUITS

5 oz / 150 g soft brown sugar
10 oz / 275 g molasses or treacle
1 heaped tsp / 6 ml ginger
1 tsp / 5 ml cloves
¾ tblsp / 10 ml baking soda
5½ oz / 160 g butter
1 medium egg
1 lb 6 oz / 650 g plain flour

Heat the sugar, molasses or treacle and spices to boiling point gently at first until the sugar is dissolved. Add the soda – it will froth up.

Pour the mixture onto the butter and stir until it melts. Add the egg and flour and knead the mixture hard to blend it thoroughly.

Chill the dough in the fridge. Then roll it out as thinly as possible. Cut it out with decorative cutters.

Bake the biscuits at 325°F / 160°C / gas 3 on a greased tray for about 10 minutes until done. Cool them and then decorate with royal icing (see Index) piped around each biscuit. Once the biscuits are iced, leave them to dry and harden completely. They can then be stored in an airtight tin for 2 to 3 weeks.

If you wish to hang them on the tree, have a bodkin or

fine skewer ready. As soon as you remove the tray from the oven, carefully poke a hole through the corner of each biscuit before it cools and hardens. When icing the biscuits, keep this hole clear, and thread Christmas string through it.

GINGERBREAD HOUSE

To make the gingerbread house, roll out the Pepperkakor dough from the previous recipe fairly thinly. Cut out the shapes drawn below as designated:

1 front
1 back
2 roof pieces
2 sides
2 chimney pots (front and back)
2 chimney-pot sides

Bake them in the oven as directed for Pepperkakor biscuits. When cooked, leave them on a wire rack to cool.
Assemble the house on the piece of wood or tray on which it will stay.

To join the pieces together, dip the edges in hot caramel (see Index) which you have made in a frying-pan. (This is not a job for children as caramel burns badly.)

First join the 4 walls of the house. Then join the front roof piece and, when the caramel has set, join the back roof piece, putting caramel along the roof peak.

Join the chimney-pot, putting the matching pairs opposite each other and, when the caramel has set, place it on the roof.

Decorate with royal icing, using a fine tube to follow the design and to cover up the caramel.

SKETCH OF COMPLETED HOUSE

Front & back panels

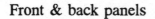

17.8cm

8.8cm

Roof pattern – 2 panels

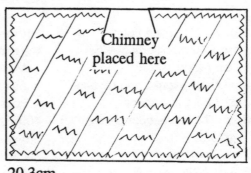

Chimney placed here

12.7cm

20.3cm

Side – 2 panels

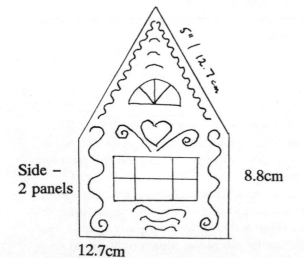

12.7cm

8.8cm

5" / 12.7cm

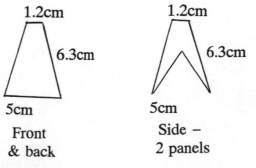

1.2cm

6.3cm

5cm

Front & back

1.2cm

6.3cm

5cm

Side – 2 panels

Chimney

SCONES AND BREAD

HOT CHEESE BISCUITS

4 oz / 125 g butter or margarine

8 oz / 225 g cheddar cheese, grated

4 oz / 125 g sifted plain flour

¼ tsp / 1 ml salt

¼ tsp / 1 ml dry mustard powder

¼ tsp / 1 ml paprika

Cream the butter and the grated cheese together. Sift together the flour, salt, mustard and paprika and mix into the butter and cheese. Shape into 1" / 2.5 cm balls. Place on a tray and freeze hard. Store in the freezer until required.

To use, bake on a greased tray at 350°F / 180°C / gas 4 for about 15 minutes until just beginning to brown at the edges.

CHEESE MUFFINS

8 oz / 225 g plain flour

2 tsp / 10 ml baking powder

½ tsp / 2 ml salt

a pinch of paprika and cayenne

2 oz / 60 g margarine

8 oz / 225 g cheddar cheese, grated

2 medium eggs

8 fl oz / 225 ml milk

Sift the flour, baking powder, salt and spices together. Rub the margarine in with your fingers. Mix in the grated cheese.

Make a well in the centre. Break in the eggs and add enough milk to make a sloppy consistency.

Pour into greased patty pans, about half full, and bake at 400°F / 200°C / gas 6 for about 15 minutes, until puffed and brown. Be careful not to open the oven too soon or they will fall. Serve hot and buttered.

Note: Buttermilk or yoghurt instead of the fresh milk makes extra good puffs.

OATCAKES

The first time that I made these was in the United States when some of us from Scotland decided to give a Hogmanay party on New Year's Eve with traditional food and reels for our American friends.

Another occasion which I will always remember was in South Africa when my father and his wife, Susan, came to stay with us. We happened to have already arranged a large tea party on the Sunday afternoon for about 30 guests.

When my father discovered this, he said, 'I'll make them oatcakes.' So he set to with expertise, and our visitors – Afrikaans professors, civil servants and coloured educationalists – enjoyed this Scottish speciality for the first time in their lives.

2 oz / 50 g dripping, bacon fat or lard
8 oz / 225 g pinhead oatmeal
½ tsp / 2 ml salt (less if using bacon fat)
½ tsp / 2 ml baking soda
7 fl oz / 195 ml boiling water

Rub the dripping into the oatmeal to which the salt and baking soda have been added. Pour on the absolutely boiling water.

Knead the dough to form a ball. Divide the ball in 2 and roll each out into a round 10″ / 25 cm in diameter on a surface spread with oatmeal. Cut each round into triangles.

Bake on a cool girdle (see below) or in a cool oven (280°F / 140°C / gas 1) for half an hour. They should dry out but not brown. They will curl up a little at the edges. Finish drying them out in front of the fire or in a very cool oven.

Note: You can use whey from making crowdie/cottage cheese. It would replace the water and fat. You would use 9 fl oz / 250 ml.

If you like the oatcakes slightly sweet, 1 tblsp / 15 ml sugar may be added.

The following recipes are for girdle (or griddle, as it is called in Ireland) scones. A girdle is a heavy flat iron sheet without edges. In the old days it had a hoop handle which was hung on a swee over the peat fire. Nowadays you can get them designed for the modern stove. You may also use a large heavy frying pan. The scones or pancakes are cooked on this, turning them over once. It is hot enough to start baking when flour sprinkled on it turns brown within a minute. They may also be baked in the oven at 350°F / 180°C / gas 4 for 15 minutes.

GIRDLE SCONES

1 lb / 450 g plain flour
1½ tsp / 7 ml cream of tartar
1 tsp / 5 ml salt
1½ tsp / 7 ml baking soda
2 oz / 50 g lard, white fat or margarine
½ pint / 300 ml sour milk or buttermilk

Combine and sift the dry ingredients. Rub in the fat lightly through the fingers to incorporate as much air as you can. Add all the milk at once to a hollow made in the centre. (If you have no sour milk, use fresh, plus an extra 1 tsp / 5 ml cream of tartar.) Mix this to a light elastic dough, working it as little as possible.

By hand, press out the dough onto a floured board into a round ½″ / 2.5 cm thick. Cut into triangles and place on the heated girdle a little apart. When the bottom half of the cut edge begins to look dry, turn the scones and leave until cooked. Do not have the girdle too hot or they will burn.

Note: I have used this as a basic recipe. If you wish the scones shorter, double the fat used to 4 oz / 125 g. The scones may also be baked in the oven 350°F / 180°C / gas 4 for about 20 minutes. In this case, after pressing out the dough, cut it into 2" / 5 cm squares or use a scone cutter. Roll together any scraps and re-cut.

Variations of this basic recipe follow below:

CHEESE SCONES
To the basic recipe, add 4 oz / 125 g cheddar cheese to the flour mixture before adding the sour milk. Roll out and bake as before. If you are using the oven, sprinkle a little grated cheese on top before baking for 15 to 20 minutes.

RAISIN SCONES
Add 4 oz / 125 g each of raisins and sugar to the flour mixture before adding the milk. Bake as described.

TREACLE SCONES
Add 4 oz / 125 g soft brown sugar to the basic flour mixture. Dissolve 4 tblsp / 60 ml treacle in the sour milk to make up to a total of ½ pint / 300 ml. Bake as described.

BROWN SCONES

4 oz / 125 g brown or
    wholewheat flour
4 oz / 125 g plain flour
4 tblsp / 60 ml brown sugar
a pinch of salt
1 tblsp / 15 ml baking powder
2 oz / 50 g butter or margarine
¼ pint / 150 ml milk

Mix the flours together with the sugar, salt and baking powder. Rub the butter into this with your fingers. Add the milk all at once and cut it in with a knife to make a light elastic dough.

Gather the dough into a ball. Press it out and cut with a scone cutter or knife.

Cook on a heated girdle, turning once as described, or in the oven at 350°F / 180°C / gas 4 for about 15 minutes.

WHEATEN LOAF

8 oz / 225 g plain flour

8 oz / 225 g wholemeal flour

2 tsp / 10 ml baking soda

2 tsp / 10 ml cream of tartar

1 tsp / 5 ml salt

1 oz / 25 g butter or white fat

½ pint / 300 ml sour milk or
buttermilk (some flours vary
slightly in their absorption so
you may need a little more)

Sift the flours together with the baking soda, cream of tartar and salt, throwing in the chaff left in the sieve. Rub in the fat.

Make a well in the centre and add the milk all at once. Gradually stir in the flour mixture and knead it together lightly on a floured board.

This may then be baked in a greased bread tin, or kneaded into a ball which you place on a greased baking sheet. Flatten it slightly and cut a cross right through with a knife. (Do not separate the 4 'farls'.)

Bake in the oven at 350°F / 180°C / gas 4 for about 30 minutes or until done.

DROP SCONES/PANCAKES

8 oz / 225 g plain flour

1 tsp / 5 ml salt

1½ tsp / 7 ml baking soda

1½ tsp / 7 ml cream of tartar

2 medium eggs

1 full tblsp / 25 ml golden syrup
butter

½ pint / 300 ml buttermilk, sour
milk or yoghurt

Sift together the flour, salt, baking soda and cream of tartar. Make a well and break in the eggs. Melt the butter and syrup together and add them and the milk, mixing quickly to a fairly soft batter. It does not matter if it is a little lumpy.

Grease a hot girdle or heavy frying pan – hotter than for the scones – and drop teaspoonfuls onto it. When bubbles appear on the surface, turn them over. Keep them on a clean tea-towel, covered with another.

Note: If you only have sweet milk, add an extra 1 tsp / 7 ml cream of tartar.

POP'S PANCAKES

Pop Saul was a great character whom I knew in America. He had many stories of the old cowboy days and of digging for gold. He could still throw a lariat with the best of them.

Sometimes for a treat he would invite us young ones for a pancake breakfast, served with coffee and lots of fresh butter, crisp bacon and maple syrup.

12 oz / 350 g flour, plain, brown
   or mixed
2 tblsp / 30 ml soft brown sugar
2 oz / 50 g mealie or cornmeal
2 tsp / 10 ml baking powder
1 tsp / 5 ml salt
1½ tsp / 7 ml baking soda
2 fl oz / 50 ml salad oil
4 medium eggs
1¼ pints / 750 ml sour milk,
   buttermilk or yoghurt

Sift together the dry ingredients. Mix together the oil, eggs and milk and pour them into a well in the dry ingredients, gradually incorporating them. It may be a little lumpy.

Cook the pancakes on a hot greased girdle, turning them once when they begin to bubble. Serve at once.

Note: If you have only sweet milk, sour it with 4 tblsp / 60 ml vinegar.

POTATO SCONES/CAKES

These were the cause of our first marital fight!

We had set up home in a flat made out of the converted ballroom at the back of Peter's parents' home in Ireland. We added to it ourselves by breaking a door through into an old hay loft and making a delightful little dining-room, full of character.

After a month of dust and dirt, we were tired and edgy. As we were driving back from Belfast one evening, Peter asked, 'What are we having for supper? Potato cakes would be lovely.'

'Fine,' I said as we drew up at a bakery, 'I'll get some potato scones.'

'You're in Ireland now,' said Peter. 'Here we call them potato cakes.'

'I'll get potato scones,' said I, and we were off! It confirms the point that it is these great, important issues that cause the best fights!

Anyway, here is the recipe which I used to enjoy, sitting round the fire of a winter's evening on getting home from school. The scones would be served hot and dripping with butter – and we were allowed to lick our fingers.

1 lb / 450 g potatoes
2 oz / 50 g butter
4 oz / 125 g plain flour
½ tsp / 2 ml salt
2 fl oz / 50 ml buttermilk, sour
   milk or yoghurt

Boil and drain the potatoes and mash them with the butter. Add the flour, salt and buttermilk and knead gently by hand into a soft and pliable dough.

Divide the dough in two. Roll each piece out on a well-floured board into a 12″ / 30 cm square, which you cut in 4 and then into triangles.

Bake on a hot girdle well dusted with flour, turning them once. They may puff up but will subside again. Spread with butter and roll up as soon as they are cooked. Keep them in a hot serving dish. Serve as soon as possible.

You can also roll the dough out more thickly. The fatter cakes (Peter is typing this) are then lovely, fried with rashers of bacon – part of the traditional Irish 'fry' which includes eggs, wheaten bread, sausages and tomatoes.

WHITE MILK BREAD

3 to 4 loaves

16 fl oz / 450 ml milk
2 oz / 50 g white fat
2 oz / 50 g granulated white
    sugar
16 fl oz / 450 ml water (from
    boiling potatoes, if possible)
2 oz / 50 g fresh yeast *or*
    2 packets dried yeast
3 lb / 1.4 kg plain flour
1 tblsp / 15 ml salt

Bring the milk to the boil. Remove from the heat and add the fat and sugar. Stir until the fat is melted and the sugar dissolved. Add the water.

Cool the milk to a lukewarm temperature and crumble in the fresh yeast. (If using dried yeast, follow the instructions on the packet.) Set this aside to 'sponge' – become frothy and puff up.

Sift half the flour and salt together. Make a well in this, pour in the yeast mixture, gradually stir in the flour and beat well. Knead in hard the remaining flour. The dough should be firm but not dry. Continue until it is elastic – about 15 minutes by hand, 5 minutes by machine.

Put the dough into a large greased bowl. Brush the top with melted butter, cover with a plastic bag and a blanket and set aside in a warm place to rise until double in bulk – about 2 hours.

Punch the dough down and knead it until it squeaks. Divide the dough and shape into loaves to half fill the baking tins. Allow the dough to rise to the top of the tin.

Bake for 20 minutes at 450°F / 230°C / gas 8, and then turn the oven down to 320°F / 160°C / gas 3 for a further 20 minutes. When cooked, the loaves should sound hollow when tapped on the bottom. Turn them out of the pans onto a wire rack to cool.

FRENCH BREAD

2 loaves

1 oz / 25 g fresh yeast *or*
    1 tblsp / 15 ml dried yeast
¾ pint / 450 ml warm water
1 tblsp / 15 ml granulated white
    sugar
2 tsp / 10 ml salt
18 oz / 500 g plain flour

Sprinkle the fresh yeast onto the warm water to dissolve it. If using dried yeast, follow the instructions on the packet. Add the sugar and salt and allow to 'sponge'. Then add all the flour at once. Knead it together. It is a stiff but dry dough. Continue kneading until the dough is really elastic. Cover it and set it aside to rise until double in bulk – at least 1 hour.

Punch the dough down and divide it in two. Shape into 2 long rolls. Place on a greased sheet. Cut 3 or 4 diagonal gashes in each loaf and set to rise again until doubled in size. Brush liberally with water and, if wished, sprinkle with sesame seeds.

Bake the loaves for 10 minutes at 425°F / 210°C / gas 7. Brush them again with water, turn the oven down to 325°F / 160°C / gas 3 and bake for about a further 40 minutes. During this period brush again with water. When cooked, cool quickly in a draught. This helps to ensure a good crust.

If you wish to make a cottage-shaped loaf with this recipe, after the first rising divide the dough into two, one part twice as big as the other. Knead the larger piece into a ball and place it on a greased baking sheet. Knead the remaining dough likewise and place it on top of the first.

With your forefinger press a hole through the centre of the top loaf down into the bottom. This hole keeps them joined together. Then set the loaf aside to rise until doubled in size. Brush with water and bake as above.

WHOLEMEAL BROWN BREAD

2 loaves

¾ pint / 450 ml milk
2 oz / 50 g white fat
4 oz / 125 g soft brown sugar
3 oz / 40 ml molasses or treacle
¾ pint / 450 ml cold water
1¼ oz / 30 g fresh yeast *or*
    4 tsp / 20 ml dried yeast *or*
    2 pkts 'easy blend' yeast
1 tblsp / 15 ml salt
8 oz / 225 g plain flour
2½ lb / 1150 g medium ground
    wholemeal flour

Bring the milk to the boil, add the fat and melt it, and then the sugar and dissolve it. Add the molasses or treacle. Add the cold water. When the liquid is lukewarm crumble in the fresh yeast – or add the dried – and leave to 'sponge'. With 'easy blend' yeast, follow packet instructions.

Sift the salt and the flours together, throwing in the bran left in the sieve. Add half the flour to the liquid mixture and beat it well. Knead in the remaining flour until the dough is elastic, adding a little more flour if the dough is too wet – it depends on the type of flour used. It should be firm but not dry.

Put it into a greased bowl, cover with a plastic bag and blanket and set to rise in a warm place until doubled in size. Punch down the dough and knead again. Divide the dough in half and place it in greased baking tins. Brush with melted butter and set to prove until the dough reaches the top of the tins – about half an hour.

Bake for 20 minutes at 425°F / 210°C / gas 7. Then turn the oven down to 320°F / 160°C / gas 3 for a further 20 minutes. When cooked, the loaves should sound hollow if tapped on the bottom. Take them out of the tins and place on a folded dish towel to cool.

2 dozen

1 oz / 25 g fresh yeast *or* 1 tblsp / 15 ml dried yeast

3 oz / 45 g granulated white sugar

8 fl oz / 225 ml scalded milk

4 oz / 125 g boiled potato

1 lb / 450 g plain flour

1 oz / 25 g butter or margarine

½ tsp / 3 ml mixed spice

¼ tsp / 1 ml saffron

½ tsp / 2 ml cinnamon

a pinch of salt

1 medium egg

4 oz / 125 g raisins or sultanas

a little leftover shortcrust pastry or a stiff paste of flour and water

HOT CROSS BUNS

If the yeast is fresh, cream it together with 1 oz / 25 g of the sugar. Cool the milk to lukewarm and add the yeast mixture. Stir to dissolve. (If the yeast is dried, follow the directions on the packet.)

Put the freshly cooked potato through a moulin-légume or a coarse sieve. Sift one-third of the flour into a bowl and add the potato, mixing it in lightly. Add the yeast and milk mixture, beating together until smooth. Set it aside in a warm place until it bubbles. Rub the butter into the remaining flour and add the spices, remaining sugar and salt.

When the yeast mixture is bubbling, beat the egg into it. Add the fruit and the flour mixture and knead the dough until elastic. Turn it into a large clean bowl, cover with a plastic bag and blanket and set aside in a warm place until double in size.

Punch the dough down and cut into 24 equal portions. Knead each into a smooth round ball and place on a greased baking tray. Set aside to prove for 30 minutes until well risen.

Meanwhile, roll out the pastry or flour and water dough. Cut it into thin strips. When the buns are ready, brush them lightly with water and make a cross with the strips on each. Bake in the oven at 400°F / 200°C / gas 6 for 20 minutes.

While hot, glaze the buns with sugar water made by dissolving 4 tblsp / 60 ml sugar in half a cup of warm water.

Makes 2 dozen

2 oz / 50 g sugar

2 oz / 50 g butter, margarine or white fat

2 tsp / 10 ml salt

¾ pint / 450 ml scalded milk

2 oz / 50 g fresh yeast *or* 2 tblsp / 30 ml dried yeast

1¼ lb / 600 g plain flour

4 oz / 125 g cooked potato, freshly mashed and sieved

SOFT DINNER ROLLS

Mix the sugar, fat and salt into the scalded milk and stir until dissolved. Cool to lukewarm. Crumble in the fresh yeast (if using dried yeast, follow the packet instructions).

Mix in the flour and potato to form a soft dough. Knead this until elastic and put it into a clean, greased bowl. Cover with a plastic bag and a blanket and leave to rise in a warm place until double in size – about 2 hours. Punch down the dough and knead until it squeaks. It may now be made into any shape of roll you choose.

Set the rolls to prove for half an hour and then bake them at 375°F / 190°C / gas 5 for about 15 minutes, until done. Turn out onto a clean dish towel and serve warm.

To shape the rolls:

Clover leaf: Break off some small pieces of dough and knead into small balls. Place 3 of these in each of greased patty pans.

Folded rolls: Take pieces of dough, roll each out flat and, on the palm of your hand which you have greased with butter, fold it in half and place on a greased baking sheet.

Plain rolls: Shape them into smooth rounds and brush with melted butter.

Prove them as described above.

SWEDISH CHRISTMAS BREAD

2 oz / 50 g granulated white sugar
2 oz / 50 g butter, margarine or white fat
2 tsp / 10 ml salt
¾ pint / 450 ml scalded milk
2 oz / 50 g fresh yeast *or*
  2 tblsp / 30 ml dried yeast
1¼ lb / 600 g plain flour
4 oz / 125 g cooked potato, freshly mashed and sieved
4 oz / 125 g softened butter
4 oz / 125 g brown sugar
8 oz / 250 g raisins

Follow the previous recipe to the first rising. Punch it down, knead it well and roll it out flat on a floured board to about ¼" / 0.6 cm thickness.

Spread the softened butter gently over the dough. Sprinkle on the brown sugar and the raisins. Roll the dough up from the long side. Place on a greased baking sheet in a circle, joining the two ends together. With a knife, cut gashes halfway through the roll, folding the edges out a little.

Set it to prove for half an hour and bake at 375°F / 190°C / gas 5 for about 25 minutes.

SPOON BREAD

Serves 6

12 fl oz / 325 ml milk
½ oz / 15 g melted butter
½ tsp / 3 ml salt
4 oz / 125 g cornmeal
8 fl oz / 225 ml sour milk or buttermilk
½ tsp / 3 ml baking powder
¼ tsp / 1½ ml baking soda
2 eggs, beaten

Put the milk, butter, salt and cornmeal in a double boiler and cook until thick. Take it off the heat.

Add the baking powder and soda to the buttermilk or sour milk. Stir it together and add to the cooked cornmeal. Add the well-beaten egg. The mixture will be fairly sloppy.

Pour into a well-greased casserole dish and bake at 350°F / 180°C / gas 4 for about half an hour. It will still be fairly soft. Serve at once. This is a good accompaniment for Southern Fried Chicken (see Index).

CONFECTIONERY

FUDGE

Mrs Inglis in Brodick on the Isle of Arran always had a box of this fudge when we came to call. When she died, her daughter, Mabel, passed this recipe on to me.

When our two girls were children I taught them to make this, and they became much more expert at it than I.

2 lb / 900 g granulated white sugar
4 oz / 125 g butter
8 fl oz / 225 ml milk
1 big tblsp / 40 ml golden syrup
1 tsp / 5 ml vanilla essence
1 × 14 oz / 397 g tin of sweetened condensed milk

Put all the ingredients into a saucepan and bring slowly to the boil, stirring all the time. Once the sugar has melted it may be boiled more quickly.

Boil it for about 15 minutes, stirring constantly so that it does not stick on the bottom. It should be turning a lovely brown shade. Keep stirring until it reaches the 'soft ball' stage. To test for this, drop a little of the boiling fudge into a glass of cold water. If it forms a soft ball, it is ready. If not, continue for another few moments and test again.

Take it off the heat, add 1 tsp / 5 ml vanilla, and beat hard with a wooden spoon for 3 to 4 minutes.

Turn it out into a buttered baking tray 9" × 13" / 23 cm × 33 cm. When it has cooled a little, mark it out into squares.

CHOCOLATE FUDGE
To the above recipe add 4 oz / 125 g grated dark chocolate when mixing all the other ingredients. Continue as above.

CHOCOLATE LEAVES

These can look very professional, but are really very easy to make. Make sure that you select leaves which are not poisonous. I often use rose leaves for cake decoration, while ivy leaves are a lovely garnish under ice-cream.

Melt a bar of good chocolate – dark or milk, to taste – over warm, not boiling water or the chocolate will harden.

Wash the leaves well. Set them out, underside up, on wax

paper. Coat them with the melted chocolate. Leave them to harden. Peel off and discard the leaf and you will find the stem and veins all beautifully marked.

CHOCOLATE CHERRIES

8 oz / 225 g marzipan
6 oz / 175 g glacé cherries
8 oz / 225 g plain chocolate

Roll out the marzipan quite thinly. Cut it into strips and wrap each cherry in the marzipan. Melt the chocolate in a china bowl over hot, not boiling water. Dip each marzipan cherry in the melted chocolate. Place them on greaseproof paper and leave them to harden.

CHOCOLATE CARAQUE

Melt a bar of good dark chocolate over warm water. Pour the melted chocolate thinly onto a marble slab or formica worktop. Leave it to cool.

With a sharp knife held obliquely to your worktop, slowly scrape up the chocolate into rolls. These may be stored until required for decorating cakes, desserts or ice-cream.

MILKSHAKES AND FRUIT DRINKS

COFFEE MILKSHAKE

For 8

5 tblsp / 75 ml instant coffee
5 tblsp / 75 ml granulated white
    sugar
6 tblsp / 90 ml water
1 lb / 450 g vanilla ice-cream
2 pints / 1.2 litres cold milk
4 fl oz / 125 ml whipping cream
2 tblsp / 30 ml instant chocolate
    powder
a pinch of cinnamon

In a liquidiser blend together the instant coffee powder, sugar, water, ice-cream and cold milk. Chill it as much as possible.

Whip the cream and stir in the instant chocolate and cinnamon. Pour the milkshake into 8 glasses and put a spoonful of the whipped cream mixture into each glass before serving.

BANANA EGGNOG

2 bananas (overripe ones are
    better)
2 ice cubes
1 egg
8 fl oz / 225 ml milk
2 tblsp / 30 ml granulated white
    sugar

Put everything in the blender and whizz it up until smooth and frothy. This was a favourite of the children when they returned home hungry from school in the mid-afternoon.

BANANA AND ORANGE MILKSHAKE

3 bananas
2 tblsp / 30 ml honey
2 tblsp / 30 ml orange juice
1 pint / 600 ml milk

Whizz everything in the blender until smooth. Dust the top with powdered chocolate.

MY MOTHER'S ELDERFLOWER CORDIAL

Pick as many elderflower heads as you wish when they are in bloom. Put them in a large china basin. Pour in enough cold water to cover them. Put a rack over the basin, cover with a towel and leave to steep for 48 hours.

Strain off the flowers through a scalded cloth and measure the liquid. To every 1 pint / 600 ml of liquid add 1 lb / 450 g granulated white sugar. Bring it to the boil. Remove from the heat and for each original 1 pint / 600 ml of liquid, add 1 oz / 25 g citric acid.

Bottle the syrup in sterilised bottles. Serve the drink diluted to taste, with plain or sparkling water.

HOT APPLE PUNCH

My mother would make this every Christmas.

1 cinnamon stick
6 cloves
1 orange, sliced
2 bottles / 1½ litres Schloer
2 bottles / 1½ litres Cydrax or cider

Tie the spices in a muslin bag. Put it with the other ingredients into a wide saucepan and simmer for 30 to 45 minutes.

Remove the spices and serve hot in warmed, frosted glasses – made by dipping the rims in a little lightly whipped egg white, and then dip these in granulated white sugar. Leave the glasses aside for an hour for this to dry.

GINGER BEER

This recipe was taught me by Johanna who cooked at Gordonville, the Kingwill family farm in the high Karoo in South Africa.

4 oz / 125 g chopped ginger root
a handful of raisins
1 gallon / 4 litres water
juice and peel of 2 lemons
2 lb / 900 g granulated white sugar
½ oz / 15 g fresh yeast or 1 tblsp / 15 ml dried yeast
1 tblsp / 15 ml tartaric acid

Boil the ginger and raisins with 1 pint / 600 ml of the water for at least 10 minutes. Add the lemon peel and juice. Set this aside to cool so that the ginger should be well steeped.

Add the remaining water and the sugar, making sure it is dissolved. Heat again to a lukewarm temperature. Add the yeast and tartaric acid. Put it all into a plastic bucket, cover and leave for 24 hours before using or bottling in strong (Coca-Cola-type) bottles.

FRUIT PUNCH

For my 21st birthday, my mother gave me a marvellous party at Buchanan Castle Golf Club – where many family portraits hang. We had lots of Scottish dancing and saw in the New Year in traditional Scottish style – my birthday is 1st January. We had speeches, a cake and a performance by Ray Dudley, a young Canadian concert pianist.

It was a memorable send-off as I was to be away from home for many years.

This punch was one of the drinks we served.

3 pints / 2 litres pineapple juice
the juice of 6 oranges and
    4 lemons
¼ pint / 150 ml plum juice
    (from a tin of plums)
soft, light brown sugar
1 pint / 600 ml strong tea
a handful of mint leaves
2¼ pints / 1¼ litres ginger ale
1 banana, finely sliced

Mix together the fruit juices and add brown sugar to taste. Cool this in the fridge.

Make the tea and let it draw for 10 minutes before straining. Chill this and add it to the fruit juice. Add the mint and keep cold until ready to serve. Then add the ginger ale and the sliced banana.

TOMATO AND BUTTERMILK COCKTAIL

1 pint / 600 ml tomato juice
4 drops tabasco sauce
2 tblsp / 30 ml cucumber,
    peeled and grated
2 tblsp / 30 ml celery, finely
    chopped
¼ tsp / 1 ml freshly ground
    black pepper
1 pint / 600 ml buttermilk
1 tsp / 5 ml salt
1 lemon, sliced

Mix together all the ingredients, seasoning to taste. Serve with a slice of cucumber and a slice of lemon in each glass.

For 4

2 pints / 1 litre water
1 stick of cinnamon
1 tsp / 5 ml whole cloves
6 oz / 175 g granulated white
    sugar
3 tsp / 15 ml good tea leaves
juice of 1 orange
4 sprigs of mint

SPICED TEA

Boil the water for 5 minutes with the cinnamon, cloves and sugar. Pour it over the tea and leave aside until cold.

Strain the cold tea. Add the orange juice and serve in tall glasses with the sprigs of mint and lots of ice. This is a great favourite in the United States.

JAMS, JELLIES AND CHUTNEYS

These are mostly made from fruit grown in our garden or picked in the fields and hedgerows.

There are several tips which I have found useful:

(1.) Use dry fruit when possible. It is better not to wash it.

(2.) It is preferable not to use overripe fruit as the jam sets more readily.

(3.) Warm in the oven the dry sugar which you use for the jam before adding it to the fruit. This helps it dissolve more quickly and keeps the jam a better colour.

(4.) You can use special jam or preserving sugar, available in supermarkets. This contains added pectin so the jam sets more quickly, thus needing shorter boiling. But I do not think that the colour of strawberry or raspberry jam is as good when this is used.

(5.) The pan in which the jam is cooked should not be more than half full as it boils up when the sugar is added.

(6.) Skim the froth off the jam before potting to give a good clear colour.

(7.) Store chutneys for 6 weeks before use.

To sterilise jam jars before using them:

(1.) Wash them out in hot soapy water.

(2.) Rinse them thoroughly. Do not dry.

(3.) Sit the jars on their sides in the oven heated to 250°F / 130°C / gas ½ for about 20 minutes.

You can buy packs of paper, labels, and elastic etc. for covering the jars and marking. It is helpful to keep the lids as once you have opened the jar they are useful in place of the paper.

Granma's infallible test for jellies:
Put 1 tblsp / 15 ml methylated spirits in an egg cup and 1 tsp / 5 ml of the juice of the fruit before sugar is added. If it forms into a lump, add 1 lb / 450 g sugar to each 1 pint / 600 ml of the juice. If it separates, boil the juice to reduce the water content before adding the sugar.

APPLE CHUTNEY

3 lb / 1.4 kg apples
3 pints / 1.7 litres vinegar
2 onions
4 to 6 dried chilli peppers
1½ cloves of garlic
1 lb / 450 g seedless raisins or
    dried fruit
1 tblsp / 15 ml ground ginger
12 oz / 350 g soft brown sugar
2 tblsp / 30 ml salt

Peel and core the apples and boil them in the vinegar until soft. Peel and chop the onions, peppers and garlic and add them with the raisins, ginger, salt and sugar. Boil for at least a further 30 minutes.

If you do not want the chutney too hot, but more spicy, add 1 oz / 25 g pickling spice instead of the chilli peppers.

I find it worth cooking a good quantity of chutney at the one time as the cooking smell is very strong and it is better to get it over and done with.

RHUBARB CHUTNEY

4 lb / 1.8 kg rhubarb
2 lb / 900 g onions
2 lb / 900 g apples
1 lb / 450 g sultanas
2 pints / 1.2 litres brown vinegar
2 tblsp / 30 ml mustard seeds
2 tblsp / 30 ml ground ginger
2 tblsp / 30 ml black
    peppercorns
1 lb / 450 g raisins
2 lb / 900 g soft brown sugar
8 dried chillis

Chop the rhubarb and onions finely. Peel and core the apples and cut them up.

Put all the ingredients in a large pot and bring slowly to the boil. Simmer for about 40 minutes, stirring from time to time so that the chutney does not stick.

When it is thick and a deep brown colour, pot as for jam.

GREEN TOMATO CHUTNEY

2 lb / 900 g green tomatoes
2 lb / 900 g apples
1 lb / 450 g soft brown sugar
½ oz / 12 g curry powder
1 lb / 450 g onions
1 pint / 600 ml vinegar
½ oz / 12 g ground ginger
1 oz / 25 g salt

Cut up the tomatoes. Peel, core and cut up the apples. Put all the ingredients in a large, heavy pan and simmer gently until thick and tender, being careful that it does not stick and burn on the bottom. Stir from time to time.

Pot up, cover and store for 6 weeks before use.

BAR-LE-DUC (Gooseberry Chutney)

I used to come across this name 'Bar-le-Duc' without knowing what it was. Obviously French in origin, I presume it may have come to Scotland with Mary Queen of Scots.

One day I was talking with our postmistress in Balmaha, Miss Stewart, and she told me of the recipe. It can be served with meat or poultry. Peach halves filled with Bar-le-Duc are particularly good with a chicken fricassee or fried chicken.

3 lb / 1.35 kg gooseberries, nearly ripe
½ pint / 300 ml brown vinegar
4 lb / 1.8 kg granulated white sugar

Top and tail the gooseberries and bring to the boil in a deep saucepan with the vinegar and half the sugar. Cook for 20 minutes, stirring frequently.

Add the rest of the sugar and cook for 30 minutes until the jam is of a syrupy consistency. Then pot as for jam.

CRANBERRY RELISH

8 oz / 225 g cranberries
1 orange, cut open and the pips removed
4 oz / 125 g icing-sugar (or to taste)

Mince the orange and cranberries. Mix them with the icing-sugar and serve.

GRANMA'S MARMALADE

Made over 3 days.

4 lb / 1.8 kg Seville oranges – special marmalade oranges available January/February
granulated white cane sugar

Day 1: Wash the oranges and cut them in half. Squeeze out the juice, removing the pips. Slice the oranges and put them in a bowl with 10 pints / 6 litres of water and the squeezed juice. Set aside for 24 hours.

Tie the pips in a muslin bag, put them in a china bowl and pour 2 pints / 1.2 litres boiling water over them. Set them aside for 24 hours.

Day 2: Combine the contents of the 2 bowls and boil gently for about 1½ hours. Remove from the heat and leave to stand for a further 24 hours.

Day 3: Take out the bag of pips, squeezing it. Measure the orange mixture. For each 1 pint / 600 ml add 1 lb / 450 g sugar.

291

Half fill a large saucepan and heat everything gently until the sugar dissolves. Then raise the heat and boil as fast as possible watching that it does not boil over – until the marmalade is ready to set. It will take at least 15 minutes fast boiling.

Test for readiness by spooning out some juice onto a cold plate. Leave it to cool and then push it with your finger. When a good skin wrinkles as you push, it is ready.

Pot in sterilised jars, put a wax paper over the surface and cover when cold.

MARMALADE (With 3 different fruits)

This recipe was given me by Mrs Shine, an elderly Scots lady who often had me to stay during the big conferences on Mackinac Island. At that time I was making marmalade for the whole conference so the quantities were enormous. I have put them in brackets, just for interest's sake.

Again this recipe is prepared over 3 days.

7 oranges (70)
2 lemons (20)
1 grapefruit (10)
4½ pints / 2.7 litres water (5½ gallons)
2¼ lb / 1 kg granulated white sugar (2¾ gallons)

Day 1: Soak the oranges, lemons and grapefruit in water for 24 hours.

Day 2: Throw away the first water if you prefer a sweet marmalade. Otherwise use it to make up your measure of water. Measure the amount stated in the recipe into a large pan. Add the fruit which has been soaked. Boil for 1 hour. Leave to stand in a china bowl for another 24 hours.

Day 3: Take out the fruit and cut it up, saving the seeds which you tie in a muslin bag. Put this in a large pan together with the fruit pulp and liquid. Add the sugar. Bring slowly to the boil stirring until the sugar is dissolved. Then boil it rapidly for about 30 minutes or until ready when tested as in the previous recipe. Remove the bag of pips. Pot the marmalade as before.

LEMON OR PAMPLEMOES MARMALADE

This recipe was given me by Moira Kingwill when we spent one very cold winter with her and her husband Roly on their farm in the Sneeuberg in the South African Karoo. The farm is at the peak of the pass, 6,000 feet up, taken by the trekkers in the days of the Great Trek. You can still find the tracks of their wagons.

Roly's grandfather was the first white man to settle there. As he came up over the pass on his ox wagon, his driver turned to him to ask why anyone would want to live where not even the baboons would come!

I have only found pamplemoes oranges in South Africa, but lemons are equally good.

Finely slice 2½ lb / 1 kg fruit. Add 8 pints / 4.8 litres water and soak overnight with the pips tied in a muslin bag. Next day boil the fruit until quite soft – when the peel will squash between your fingers. Remove the pips. Add 4½ lb / 2 kg granulated white sugar and boil it until it sets when tested as described above.

Roly and Moira have striven all their lives to serve their community. In the 1930s, at considerable sacrifice, Roly led the way in stock reduction to preserve the land for future generations. Now this has become established government policy.

They were again away ahead of established practice in creating and financing a farm school for the children of workers on their land. And in their late 70s they started up a home spinning and weaving industry for the unemployed in their main town of Graaff Reinet, 50 miles from the farm. They and many others of all races whom we got to know in South Africa give us great hope for the future of that lovely land.

BLACKCURRANT JAM

3 lb / 1.35 kg blackcurrants
2 pints / 1.2 litres water
3 lb / 1.35 kg granulated white
  sugar

String the blackcurrants. Boil the fruit in the water until pulpy. Then add the sugar, stirring until dissolved. Boil rapidly until setting point is reached – about 15 minutes.

Pot up and cover when cold.

RASPBERRY OR STRAWBERRY JAM

An equal weight of fruit and
castor sugar.
For every 2 lb / 900 g of fruit
take the juice of 1 lemon.

Warm the sugar in a moderate oven. Put the fruit and lemon juice in a large saucepan and heat gently until the juice runs. Mash the fruit and add the sugar, stirring until dissolved.

Bring quickly to the boil and boil hard for 3 minutes. This will be runny but taste very fresh. Or boil longer if you prefer it set. Pot up and cover when cold.

Note: The colour may keep better if redcurrants make up one third of the weight of fruit. This will also improve the setting quality.

CRAB APPLE JELLY

3 lb / 1.35 kg apples, including
2 or 3 green ones
1 lemon, quartered and
squeezed
4 cloves
sugar

Quarter the apples, removing any bad bits but leaving the core and peel. Put them in a saucepan, adding enough water just to cover them. Add all the lemon and the cloves. Cook until the apples are reduced to a good pulp, stirring from time to time.

Turn them into a scalded cloth or jelly bag and hang from a hook over a bowl to drip overnight. Do not press the pulp through the cloth as then your jelly will be cloudy.

Take 1 lb / 450 g granulated white sugar to every 1 pint / 600 ml of the juice. Heat the sugar and juice together slowly until the sugar is dissolved, stirring constantly. Then boil as fast as possible for about 10 minutes. Test for setting.

Pot up and wait until completely cold before covering the jam jars.

Note: When making big apple pies or using apples in other ways, I often boil up the skins and cores in enough water just to cover, strain and measure the juice, and use this for making apple jelly, as above, or mint jelly.

MINT JELLY

Use the Crab Apple Jelly recipe,
leaving out the cloves
2 oz / 50 g fresh mint leaves,
very finely chopped
granulated white sugar and cider
vinegar to measure

Boil the chopped mint in a little of the vinegar for 3 minutes. Strain the mint off and put it aside.

To each 1 pint / 600 ml of juice add 1 lb / 450 g granulated white sugar and ½ pint / 300 ml vinegar (including that from boiling the mint). Bring slowly to the boil until the sugar is dissolved and then boil fast until setting point is reached. Just before taking off the boil add the chopped mint.

Pot up.

BLACKBERRY JELLY

Put the blackberries in a large pan with a very little water over a low heat until the juice starts to run. Then bring to the boil and simmer until the fruit is pulpy. Strain the fruit through a cloth hung from a hook overnight.

Next day, for every 1 pint / 600 ml of juice add 1 lb / 450 g granulated white sugar. Heat these together slowly until the sugar is dissolved and then boil rapidly until setting point.

Pot up as directed. I have used the left over pulp to make ice-cream.

BLACKCURRANT OR REDCURRANT JELLY

Put clean currants in a large pan. There is no need to top and tail them. Barely cover them with cold water, bring them to the boil and simmer until pulpy.

Strain the fruit overnight through a cloth. Next day discard the fruit. To each 1 pint / 600 ml of juice add 1 lb / 450 g granulated white sugar. Heat slowly until the sugar dissolves, then boil rapidly until setting point. Pot up.

ROWANBERRY JELLY

A recipe from Georgina Allen, housekeeper at Brodick Castle.

Remove the stalks from the rowans, wash them and just cover with water in a large pan. Bring them to the boil and simmer until pulpy. Strain them overnight as for the previous fruit.

Measure the juice back into the cleaned saucepan and for each 1 pint / 600 ml add 1 lb / 450 g sugar.

Then for every 1 pint / 600 ml of juice add *either* the juice and rind of half a lemon, tied in a bag, *or* 4 fl oz / 125 ml blackberry juice made by squeezing uncooked ripe blackberries through a cloth.

Heat gently until the sugar is dissolved. Then boil rapidly until setting point. Pot up.

CHEESES

CROWDIE (Cottage Cheese)

One used to be able to make this with fresh, unpasteurised milk by leaving it to sour overnight. Nowadays the pasteurising destroys the natural souring bacteria, so a starter is needed for the process. This may either be lemon juice or yoghurt. From 1 pint / 600 ml milk you should get 3 to 4 oz / 100 ml crowdie.

1 pint / 600 ml milk
4 tblsp / 60 ml lemon juice *or*
   4 fl oz / 125 ml yoghurt
salt and pepper to taste
1 tblsp / 15 ml cream may be
   added

Warm the milk until just over lukewarm heat: 100°F / 38°C. Add the lemon juice to the warm milk and leave in a warm place for some hours or overnight until you see the curds forming and the whey separating.

Scald some butter muslin or a linen tea-towel with boiling water. Lay it in a bowl and pour the sour milk into it. Gather up the ends evenly and tie the cloth, hanging it on a hook or cupboard handle so that the cheese may drain into a bowl. Leave overnight.

Next day take down the cloth and scrape the cheese into another bowl. It may now be seasoned with salt and freshly ground black pepper, or flavoured with garlic, chives or other herbs. Cream may be added at this stage, together with pineapple etc.

FROMAGE BLANC À LA CRÈME

6 oz / 175 g home-made
   crowdie or cottage cheese
4 oz / 125 ml double cream
2 tblsp / 30 ml castor sugar
2 egg whites

If using bought cottage cheese, push it through a sieve to get a fine smooth texture. Blend the cheese and cream together with the sugar. Beat the egg whites stiffly and fold them in.

Turn the mixture into a scalded butter muslin or cloth and hang up to drain overnight. The cheese may be shaped as you like.

This can be used instead of cream with fruit, or in other ways.

Below are a couple of historic recipes which I have inherited. They, of course, refer to unpasteurised milk.

SKIM MILK CHEESE

From my grandmother, Evelyne Sellar, as written for her by the cook.

Let the skimmed milk stand in a warm place till it is as thick as junket.

Wring out a linen cloth and lay it in a bowl with the ends hanging over. Ladle the thick milk into the cloth. Tie the corners together and hang the cloth up to drip. It is well to remember that while cream cheese should be hung in a draught, skim milk cheese should not.

Every 4 hours or so take down the cloth and, with a spoon or blunt knife, scrape down the milk that has caked on the sides and mix it through the rest. When the contents of the cloth are of the consistency of double cream, it can be turned out, whipped, sweetened and used as if it were cream. It is lighter but generally well liked.

If the curd is allowed to hang rather longer, it can be turned out into a bowl and with the addition of a little butter or cream, and some pepper and salt, it can be eaten fresh with or without bread.

If it is allowed to hang still longer till it is of the consistency of fresh-made putty, it should be mixed with a little salt, shaped with butterhands into a ball or square, folded in butter-muslin and allowed to ripen. It should be turned every day.

The time of ripening varies according to taste: but the cheese should be quite good to eat in about a week. In Belgium it is supposed to be at its best when the smell is so strong that it can hardly be approached.

From my Irish Great-Grandmother.
My mother's grandmother was of Irish/French extraction and the Irish cheese below comes from her. The family name was Byrne or O'Byrne. Back in the late 18th century, they were wealthy, with estates in Ireland recorded as bringing in an income of £2000 a year, a lot in those days.

O'Byrne was entertaining an English visitor one day, who, in the manner of the times, complimented him on the quality of all he owned. 'That is true,' replied O'Byrne, 'but

I could lose it all tomorrow for I have never taken the Dispensation.' This referred to the law forbidding any Catholic from owning property unless he converted to the Anglican persuasion. His 'friend' informed on him and his estates were all sequestered, to the fury of his family.

He could not then make a go of it in Ireland for, as history relates, 'he had expensive tastes'. So he shipped out to New Orleans, at that time French.

A few years later, a younger brother's son asked his father about his uncle, but his father would tell him nothing. So the nephew set out for New Orleans to search for his uncle. He never did discover him, but instead found a French girl who became his wife. They had five daughters. As they grew up, O'Byrne saw the Civil War approaching in the United States. Fearing for his girls, he took them all to Europe and married them off in different countries – Denmark, Italy, France – and my great-grandmother married Thomas Sellar, the banker, in Scotland. I wear her engagement ring.

One of the last things I did with my mother before she died was to visit the little church at Killaney where the Byrne family graves are. It is now a ruin with badgers making their holts in some of the old tombs. My brother-in-law is bishop of that diocese and he was able to show us the records with all the O'Byrne names. Now that I have married an Irishman, I find myself back in the O'Byrnes' country.

This recipe takes us back four generations.

ARDAGH CHEESE

Utensils

1 milk pail with 3½ gallons capacity

1 milk pail large enough to hold the first pail and leave a margin (for hot water) of 1½-2 inches.

1 dairy thermometer

1 cream skimmer

1 long knife

One Caerphilly cheese mould 2H lb capacity – any dairy supply company should keep Caerphilly moulds, but a substitute can be made by using a cake tin 2½" deep and about 6" in diameter. About 4 or 5 holes should be knocked in the bottom with a large nail, for drainage, and it should be fitted with a strip of tin the same height as the mould and long enough to fit inside it and overlap 2 or 3 inches.

Use 2½ to 3 gallons of milk according to the proportion of butter-fat – 3.5 is correct and yields 1 lb cheese to a gallon of milk – if the butter-fat is less than 3.5, more milk will be required; if it is up to 4, some of the cream should be skimmed off the evening's milk.

Rennet varies in strength. It is well to experiment with a small quantity and use what will bring about coagulation in 40 minutes, that is to say a curd that will show a clean split when tested. To test put one finger obliquely into the curd near the edge of the pail, draw it to the surface; if the curd opens showing a clean split it is sufficiently set.

Take 1 gallon evening's milk. Next morning, stir the cream well in and add 1½ gallons morning's milk – pouring the fresh hot milk from the cow into the cold helps start acidity.

Stand the smaller milk-pail in the larger one and pour enough hot water into the space between the pails to bring the temperature of the milk to 84°F. It will need very little or none at all. Stir well and add enough rennet to bring about coagulation in 40 minutes.

If concentrated rennet is used it should be mixed with 4 or 5 times its bulk in clean cold water. For making small quantities of cheese it is hardly worth while to use concentrated rennet.

Stir for 3 minutes after adding the rennet. Stir to the bottom of the pail at first, then over the surface to keep down the cream. Stop stirring as soon as streaks show on the back of the spoon.

When the curd shows a clean split, cut it across with a long knife leaving a width of about 1 inch between the cuts. Wait for 3 minutes – this is important – and cut again crossways.

Wait another three minutes, take the inner pail out of the outer, pour away what water is in the outer one, and with a skimmer lift the curd gently from the first pail into the second.

It should now be in cubes and these must not be bruised. If the knife has not reached the bottom of the pail, cut again as before, waiting 3 minutes between each cutting. When the first pail has been emptied, return the curd to it very gently. Replace it in the larger pail and pour hot water into the space between the two, to raise the temperature slowly to 98°F. This is called 'top scald'. The curd should be gently stirred or lifted with the hands to keep lumps from sticking together. The scald should take about 40 minutes.

When the curd feels 'rubbery' when squeezed in the hand, it is time to pour off the whey. Let the curd settle in the bottom of the pail, pour off the whey, cut the curd across and pile the pieces on each other. Pour away what extra whey has come out and break up the curd in small pieces about the size of a bean. Toss these in the pail for about 10 minutes.

Wring out a square of butter-muslin in hot water, pull up the strip of tin till it is well above the rim of the mould, line it with the butter muslin and pile in the curd. Cover it with the muslin keeping it as flat as possible.

Put a piece of wood over the mould, place a 14 lb weight on the wood and leave for 10 minutes. Turn out the cheese. Have ready another piece of muslin to line the mould. Return the cheese, reversed, to the mould and leave under 21 lb pressure for 1 hour.

Repeat the process, this time leaving under 28 lb pressure for 4 hours. The cheese should now be quite firm and smooth. Turn out on a table or shelf, not in a draught or sunshine, and let it stand all night. With a sharp knife take a very small bevel off the edge.

Next morning rub salt well all over the cheese, reverse it and leave it till the evening. Repeat the process and leave till next morning. Then dip it in brine – 1 lb salt to 1 gallon of water (the brine can be used for any number of cheeses).

Stand it in an airy place but not in a draught or in sunshine. Turn it every day for 3 weeks when it should be ripe enough to eat. If carefully made, it should keep uncut for 8 months.

Note: You will, of course, need your own cow. This is not mentioned in the list of utensils!

USEFUL TIPS AND MEASURES

Breadcrumbs: Put any leftover toast or crusts of bread in a flat pan in the warming drawer of the stove, or in an oven after it has been switched off. When completely dry, grind into crumbs in a processor. Store in an airtight jar.

Soft breadcrumbs: Put slices of bread, with or without crusts, in the processor with a steel blade for 30 seconds.

Croutons: Cubes of bread fried gently in a mixture of butter and oil until crisp.

Hard-boiled eggs: Put them on in cold water with salt – to stop the white running should they crack. This method seems to prevent the grey rim forming around the yolk. Bring to the boil and boil for 5 minutes. Then put them under running cold water to help them peel easily.

Skinning tomatoes: Pour boiling water over them, leave for a minute and then peel.

Sour milk and cream: Never throw this away. It is ideal for baking or for making crowdie. To make milk sour, add 4 tblsp / 60 ml vinegar to 1 pint / 600 ml milk warmed to lukewarm.

Vanilla sugar: This is useful for cakes and biscuits. Put a vanilla pod in a deep jar with a lid and fill with sugar. It is ready for use in 2 weeks.

Simmering: The pot should barely bubble.

Lukewarm: Blood heat. Your finger should just feel a prick when dipped in the liquid.

Butterhands: Lined wooden paddles for making butter pats etc. Soak them in cold water before using.

Sauté: To fry gently.

Bouquet garni (pot posy): A bunch of herbs tied in a muslin, usually comprising a bay leaf, a large sprig of parsley, a sprig of thyme and rosemary.

Fairy toast: Very finely cut white bread, dried in the oven. With a ready sliced loaf, toast the thin slices lightly. Cut off the crusts and split the slices horizontally. Dip each split slice in milk and dry them out on a tray in a low oven.

Beurre-manié: Flour and butter mashed together and then whisked into the boiling liquid. Quantities in the specific recipe.

Roux: Melted butter mixed with flour. Quantities in recipes.

Panade: Melted butter mixed with flour and then the liquid added all at once. The whole then stirred together until it forms a ball – as in choux pastry.

Cinnamon sugar: A little ground cinnamon mixed with granulated or castor sugar – about 1 tsp / 5 ml to 4 oz / 125 g, according to taste. Delicious with hot buttered toast, or on a plain biscuit.

Macedoine of vegetables: A colourful mixture of cooked vegetables cut in little cubes – carrots, beans, onions, turnips, peas etc.

Golden syrup: A heavy syrup. If it is unavailable, use corn syrup, though this is lighter.

Cheddar Cheese: You can substitute any well-flavoured cooking cheese.

ROASTING TABLES AND OVEN TEMPERATURES

For all rolled roasts allowing 10 minutes more per lb / 450 g.

Beef

Rare	325°F / 160°C / gas 3	18-20 mins per lb / 450 g plus 20 mins extra
Medium	325°F / 160°C / gas 3	22-25 mins per lb / 450 g plus 20 mins extra
Well done	325°F / 160°C / gas 3	27-30 mins per lb / 450 g plus 25 mins extra

Leg of Lamb 325°F / 160°C / gas 3 35 mins per lb / 450 g plus 30 mins extra

Fresh Loin of Pork 425°F / 210°C / gas 7 for 20 minutes. Then turn the oven down to 325°F / 160°C / gas 3 for further 30-35 minutes per lb / 450 g.
 Note: It is important that pork is well done.

Veal 325°F / 160°C / gas 3 35–40 mins per lb / 450 g

Chicken Up to 3½ lb / 1½ kg weight
325°F / 160°C / gas 3 for 30 mins per lb / 450 g

4 lb / 1.8 kg or over
325°F / 160°C / gas 3 20-25 mins per lb / 450 g
If the chicken is to be stuffed, weigh it after it has been stuffed and roast accordingly.

Duck (Farmyard) 325°F / 160°C / gas 3 20-25 mins per lb / 450 g
(Wild ducks are cooked differently, being smaller. Between 30 minutes and 1 hour each).

Turkey 325°F / 160°C / gas 3 Approx 20 mins per lb / 450 g, but watch it as if it is overcooked it can become very dry.

I recommend slow roasting as it shrinks the meat less, and it certainly keeps the oven cleaner.

When buying meat look for a marbled texture (flecks of fat through the meat) as this will ensure that the meat is tender.

I personally allow 4 oz / 125 g meat without the bone per person. However, in these recipes I have increased this, realising that others' appetites may be greater than mine.

WEIGHTS AND MEASURES

American recipes are often measured in US cups. The following are rough equivalents which I have found a help.

butter		1 tblsp	=	½ oz	=	15 g
		1 cup	=	8 oz	=	225 g
sugar	granulated	1 cup	=	8 oz	=	225 g
	brown	1 cup	=	6 oz	=	175 g
	icing	1 cup	=	4 oz	=	125 g
flour	plain	1 cup	=	4 oz	=	125 g
	sifted cake	1 cup	=	3½ oz	=	100 g
	wholewheat	1 cup	=	4 oz	=	125 g
	cornmeal	1 cup	=	5 oz	=	150 g
rice		1 cup	=	8 oz	=	225 g

1 imperial British pint = 20 fl oz = 600 ml
1 US pint = 16 fl oz = 480 ml
1 US cup of liquid = 8 fl oz = 225 ml
1 gill = ¼ pint = 5 fl oz = 150 ml
1 tblsp = 3 tsp
1 teacup = 8 fl oz
1 breakfast cup = 10 fl oz

Cornflour: 1 tblsp / 15 ml will do the work of 2 tblsp / 30 ml plain flour for thickening.
12 to 14 *egg yolks* = 1 US cup = 8 fl oz = 225 ml
8 to 10 *egg whites* = 1 US cup = 8 fl oz = 225 ml

Dried yeast: 1 tblsp / 15 ml = 1 oz / 25 g fresh yeast

For baking *chocolate cakes:*
3 tblsp / 45 ml cocoa + 1 tblsp / 15 ml butter = 1 oz / 25 g cooking chocolate

P.S. FROM PETER

Having typed out this book for Fiona, perhaps I may be allowed a postscript of my own.

As a husband I have found, to my surprise, that I have much to learn. When we got married, I happily thought that one of my contributions to our home would be to introduce 'time and motion study' in the kitchen. I have always been fascinated in how a job can be done most quickly and efficiently.

So I would make my helpful suggestions: if the vegetables were cut up here by the sink instead of the other side of the room, the mess to clear up would be that much less; if this pot were rinsed immediately and used again, the pile for washing up would be greatly reduced . . . and so on.

At one point we had a Danish friend living with us. She and Fiona were hard at work preparing the meal when I came in and made another of my excellent suggestions. Suddenly the lid blew off. 'Would you please get out of the kitchen. We can't cope with you here. You don't really think of what goes on in anyone else . . .!'

I retired, hurt, thoroughly misunderstood. After all, I only wanted to help.

That evening we happened to have a date to see some friends who lived in the middle of a riot area in Belfast. As we set off in the car after supper the atmosphere was distinctly cool. Halfway there we stopped. This was no good. We would only be a blight on anyone we saw in that mood.

As we reflected for a moment, suddenly the thought struck me, 'Well! You have succeeded in raising in your own kitchen many of the feelings of those who throw the bombs or pull the triggers.' It began to dawn on me how much I still needed to understand other people's feelings. Later that evening we told our friends of what had happened during the day. They immediately felt totally at one with us.

I now gratefully know what I imagine that Fiona knew all along – that much, very much, of the making of a home starts in the kitchen. And I thank God for cooks – and for one cook in particular.

INDEX